THE POLITICAL ECONOMY OF
CONTROL IN SINGAPORE

The Political Economy of Social Control in Singapore

Christopher Tremewan

Foreword by
Peter Carey

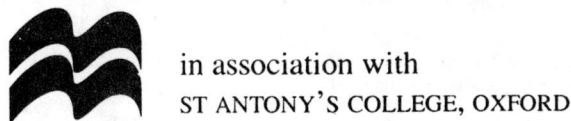

in association with
ST ANTONY'S COLLEGE, OXFORD

First published in Great Britain 1994 by
MACMILLAN PRESS LTD
Houndmills, Basingstoke, Hampshire RG21 6XS
and London
Companies and representatives
throughout the world

This book is published in the *St Antony's Series*
General editor: Alex Pravda

A catalogue record for this book is available
from the British Library.

ISBN 0-333-58823-1 hardcover
ISBN 0-333-65728-4 paperback

 First published in the United States of America 1994 by
ST. MARTIN'S PRESS, INC.,
Scholarly and Reference Division,
175 Fifth Avenue,
New York, N.Y. 10010

ISBN 0-312-15865-3 paper

Library of Congress Cataloging-in-Publication Data
Library of Congress has cataloged the hardcover edition as follows
Tremewan, Chris.
 The political economy of social control in Singapore / Christopher
Tremewan ; foreword by Peter Carey.
 p. cm.
Includes bibliographical references and index.
ISBN 0-312-12138-5 (cloth) — ISBN 0-312-15865-3 (pbk).
 1. Singapore—Social policy—Economic aspects. 2. Singapore-
-Economic conditions. 3. Social control. 4. Singapore—Politics
and government. I. Title.
HN700.67.A8T74 1994
306'. 095957—dc20   93-48288
                                                            CIP

© Christopher Tremewan 1994, 1996
Foreword © Peter Carey 1994

All rights reserved. No reproduction, copy or transmission of
this publication may be made without written permission.

No paragraph of this publication may be reproduced, copied or
transmitted save with written permission or in accordance with
the provisions of the Copyright, Designs and Patents Act 1988,
or under the terms of any licence permitting limited copying
issued by the Copyright Licensing Agency, 90 Tottenham Court
Road, London W1P 9HE.

Any person who does any unauthorised act in relation to this
publication may be liable to criminal prosecution and civil
claims for damages.

10 9 8 7 6 5 4 3 2
04 03 02 01 00 99 98 97 96
Printed and bound in Great Britain by
Antony Rowe Ltd, Chippenham, Wiltshire

Contents

	List of Tables	vii
	Foreword *by Peter Carey*	ix
	Preface to the 1996 Reprint	xi
	Acknowledgements	xiv
	List of Abbreviations	xv
	Introduction	1
1	Historical Origins	6
2	Singapore's Political Economy	30
3	Public Housing: The Working-class Barracks	45
4	Educating for Submission	74
5	The New Education System	109
6	Parliament, Elections and Parties	152
7	The Law, Coercion and Terror	187
	Conclusion	228
	References	235
	Index	248

List of Tables

1.1	Net Surplus of Main Dollar Earners of British Colonies (1948)	12
3.1	Contributions to CPF (percentage of wage)	54
3.2	HDB Racial Limits (maximum percentages)	66
4.1	Comparative Educational Levels (Asian Newly Industrialised Countries)	75
5.1	Educational Levels (percentage total labour force)	120
5.2	Proportion of Population Aged 65 and Over	147
6.1	Legislative Assembly Elections	153
6.2	General Elections, 1968–80	156
6.3	General Elections, 1984 and 1988	160
6.4	Marginal Results in 1988 Election	168
6.5	General Elections since 1955	181
6.6	General Election Results, 1968–88	182
7.1	Comparative Crime Rate, 1987–88	216
7.2	The Elements of Total Defence and Implementing Ministries	224
7.3	Comparative Defence Expenditure, 1990	226
7.4	Singapore Defence Expenditure, 1985–90	226

Foreword
Peter Carey

Much has been written in recent years about the 'miracle' of Lee Kuan Yew's Singapore, an island state with just over three million inhabitants, which has been classed, along with Hong Kong, Taiwan and South Korea, as one of the 'Newly Industrialised Countries' of the Asia-Pacific region. With a per capita income of over US$11,800, a gross national product in excess of most of its Association of South-East Asian Nations (ASEAN) partners, and a share of upwards of eighty per cent of all intra-ASEAN trade, Singapore is indeed one of the economic success stories of the late twentieth century, a 'little dragon' which is often held up as an example for other developing countries.

Hard work, wise leadership, 'Confucian' ethics, discipline – the litany of qualities which are thought to have contributed to the Singapore phenomenon are well rehearsed and endlessly debated. Much less considered, however, are the social costs of this 'success' and the political economy of social control which has underpinned Singapore's relentless rise to developed nation status. In the eighteenth century Voltaire's phrase *'travailler pour le roi de Prusse'* was synonymous with everything that was wrong with a state which sacrificed the spiritual welfare of its citizens to imperious *realpolitik* and the political demands of its rulers. While Lee Kuan Yew's Singapore is far removed in time and place from that Hohenzollern world, the same remorseless quality informs its political system. 'People just get tired of living in the sixth form all their lives', the words of one of the growing number of middle-class fugitives from the island state in the 1980s could stand as an epitaph for a system which has treated people as units of production rather than as human beings. Class, race, gender, religion, all have been used as tools in Singapore's social class experiment which has resulted in the increasing disempowerment of the ethnic minorities (Malays and Indians), the creation of a docile Chinese working-class, the political emasculation of the professional elite, and one of the highest suicide rates in Asia.

It is the achievement of this remarkable book – written by a scholar who has firsthand experience of the repressive realities of contemporary Singapore – to have laid bare the methods by which the state, as represented by Lee's People's Action Party (PAP), in power continuously since 1959, has successfully prevented the development of any meaningful challenge to its authority, and to its crucial relationship with foreign capital which undergirds Singapore's economic strategy, both regional and domestic. By concentrating on four major institutions – public housing (as represented by the Housing and Development Board), state education, parliament and the law – and the interaction between them, Chris Tremewan has been able to present a persuasive picture of the complex system of social control and the way in which the organisation of labour power, apartments, courts, schools and votes in parliamentary elections, translates into the control of people. The thesis presented here will not only change the way in which we understand contemporary Singaporean society and the relationship between the state and its citizens, but will also provoke a debate about the social costs of economic development in other parts of the world, and the future security of the island republic – increasingly a Chinese enclave in a Malay sea – in the twenty-first century.

Ten years ago, when the fateful year of Orwell's novel –*1984* – passed, many in the so-called 'free' world congratulated themselves that his most dire predictions had remained unfulfilled. Reading Chris Tremewan's book one is no longer so sure. One suspects that Winston Smith would find many soulmates in Lee's lion city.

Trinity College **Peter Carey**
Oxford

Preface
to the 1996 Reprint

Since this book was first published in 1994, I have discovered the existence of Singapore's Controller of Undesirable Publications. This government official has recently decided to ban the distribution of this book in Singapore. For readers outside Singapore, this action may lend weight to the analysis proffered in these pages regarding the continuing insecurity of the People's Action Party and the nature of its rigorous, pervasive system of social control. On a deeper level, the Party-state's attempt to prevent this book resourcing a domestic discourse indicates the sensitivity of my primary academic objective: to examine the social conflicts and political partnerships which underlie social regulation in the city-state.

Events since this research was completed in the early 1990s can largely be seen as developments of trends described in the ensuing pages. But three matters need further comment: recent actions against foreigners, Singapore's stance in the international human rights debate and questions surrounding the stability of the system of social control.

The main aspect of Singapore's social control to come into recent international prominence has been its increasing impact on non-Singaporeans. Foreign professionals, their dependents, and temporary workers, who now make up approximately 20 per cent of Singapore's work force, have been increasingly subjected to the more coercive mechanisms of state control.

For example, in 1994, a Singapore court sentenced an American schoolboy, Michael Fay, to a flogging and imprisonment for vandalism. President Clinton objected and the United States' initial negative response to Singapore's bid to host the first ministerial meeting of the World Trade Organisation was seen as a reflection of its displeasure at the administering of the flogging on 5 May.

Also in 1994, Christopher Lingle, an American academic at the National University of Singapore fled the island-state after interrogation by the police and the seizure of his scholarly papers. The Singapore government took exception to an article he wrote for the *International Herald Tribune* (7 October 1994) referring to unnamed Asian governments which relied on 'a compliant judiciary to bankrupt opposition politicians'. The Singapore Government held that the latter observation referred to it. As if to prove the point, it subsequently won damages in the Singapore courts against Lingle and the newspaper.

In February 1995, Nick Leeson, the British general manager of Barings Futures (Singapore), disappeared from Singapore when his gamble on the Nikkei 225 index in Osaka ruined his prestigious parent company, London-based Barings Bank, with billion dollar losses. Singapore is seeking his extradition from Germany to face charges.

On 17 March 1995, a foreign domestic worker, Flor Contemplacion, a Filipina, was hanged for murder in Changi Prison despite appeals from President Ramos for a stay of execution. Her case became a *cause célèbre* in a volatile election period in the Philippines. A massive public reaction against Singapore forced Ramos to sack senior officials and come close to a diplomatic break with his ASEAN neighbour.

The increasing entanglement of foreigners in the Singapore government's comprehensive system of social control needs to be placed within the context of its regionalization drive. Such an explanation would reveal the high degree of cooperation between the Singapore state and Western and Japanese capital in an economic strategy which necessitates the presence of a large number of foreigners in Singapore. It also requires some of them, like Nick Leeson, to be permitted considerable latitude in their international financial dealings.

Yet the dominant debate arising from these events was cast in terms of an alleged clash between Asian and Western values. Generalized notions of Western democracy and individualism versus Asian respect for authority and family values have been explicated in terms of this spurious antithesis. The myopia of the Western media and the involvement of Westerners as 'victims' partially accounts for this superficial treatment and for the loss of focus on what is happening to Singaporeans themselves. In addition, with the disappearance of a credible 'communist threat' to prompt loyalty to the state, the elaboration of an improbable theory of the conflict of civilizations has its uses.

But the PAP-state has had an interest in maintaining the debate at this level for reasons beyond defence of its own domestic authoritarianism. Its attempt at diplomatic leadership in an international human rights discourse configured around the North-South divide has enabled Singapore to appear to stand in solidarity with legitimate Third World demands for economic justice, respect for national sovereignty and democratization of the United Nations as well as to advance more dubious relativist arguments for the circumscription of civil and political rights.

This leadership has paid dividends in consolidating Singapore's regional relationships (especially with China and the SLORC regime in Burma) and in disguising the PAP-state's role as foreign capital's most cooperative partner in penetrating the region. This diversionary diplomacy amounts to the ideological displacement of Singapore's domestic communalist policies on to the international scene: from pitting Singaporeans of differing linguistic and ethnic backgrounds against each other to pitting Asians against Caucasians, thereby using racial politics to cover or pre-empt class politics.

The double-edged complexity of this approach was seen in the Philippine public's reaction to the hanging of Flor Contemplacion. Filipinos issued a decisive challenge to the dismissiveness the Singapore government had often shown towards their country. This was an unexpected reminder that rhetorical solidarity may open Singapore to popular demands for substantive accountability which it cannot control. A regionalization drive which aims to ensure that the governing classes of neighbouring countries have an abiding interest in Singapore's continuing economic growth and in a continuing inflow of foreign investment has thus opened Singapore to new pressures.

The above events and policy developments have unfolded in parallel with Singapore government attempts to resolve questions surrounding the transition of political leadership. In the manner of Deng Xiaoping, Senior Minister Lee Kuan Yew remains the central political personality whose stamp is writ large on political management of the critical issues of recent years. Despite valiant efforts by Prime Minister Goh Chok Tong to prove otherwise, it appears that Lee still regards the only safe pair of hands to be his own. Lee's two sons remain poised to take over their father's paramount role whether formally in the cabinet leadership or informally behind the throne. But the extended melodrama of jostling within the PAP covers up a more important question. How long can the present system of social control persist especially after Lee's final demise?

The conflicts and complexities which this system must mute, suppress or resolve are, if anything, greater now than at the time this research was conducted. Despite strident reassertions of patriarchal leadership, women continue their unorganised opposition to state breeding, childcare and employment policies. There is increasing public unease over the constantly rising cost of housing, health and education. The articulate Dr Chee Soon Juan of the Singapore Democratic Party has provided a new focus for parliamentary dissent. Elections continue to produce an opposition vote of approximately 40 per cent. The government is caught on the horns of several major dilemmas, notably its contradictory desire to become a global information technology centre while preventing its citizens having access to information and, secondly, the narrowing of economic options in the face of intense regional competition. Meanwhile, former Solicitor-General and opposition politician, Francis Seow, publishes unprecedented exposés of the Singapore political system from exile at Harvard University. These factors indicate that the system of social control is being increasingly contested.

Auckland *Chris Tremewan*
July 1995

Acknowledgements

My deepest gratitude is due to Rob Steven, University of New South Wales, whose theoretical insights and friendship made this book an exciting and worthwhile venture. I also wish to thank Bill Willmott and David Small from the University of Canterbury and Jomo Sundaram from the University of Malaya for their comments and encouragement.

Clement John, General Secretary, Asian Legal Resource Centre, Hong Kong, together with friends from Australia, Canada, Switzerland, Sweden and the US provided much of the support which enabled this research to be written up for publication. My heartfelt thanks to all of them.

In Oxford I wish to thank Bob Barnes, Peter Carey and Rosemary Foot for their interest, friendship and assistance. I am grateful for the stimulation of other colleagues at the Asian Studies Centre and the inspiration provided by my fellow writers in the loft at St Antony's: Diana Cammack, Hitoshi Ohnishi and Ryo Oshiba.

I owe a tremendous debt of gratitude to many Singaporean friends who provided material, commented on parts of the manuscript and assured me of the value of the research. For reasons that are obvious from the contents of this book, I cannot thank them by name. I earnestly hope that the book repays their trust and friendship in some measure.

Finally my thanks to my partner Maylene for her unsparing support, to Edna for her lunches and child care, to Yi-Zhen for her lively, intelligent company and to Yi-Wen for arriving in the midst of everything, full of promise.

St Antony's
Oxford

CHRIS TREMEWAN

List of Abbreviations

AWARE	Association of Women for Action and Research
Barisan	*Barisan Sosialis*
BMA	British Military Administration
CCC	Citizens' Consultative Committee
CEC	Central Executive Committee (PAP)
CPF	Central Provident Fund
EIC	East India Company
EOI	Export-oriented Industrialisation
FEER	*Far Eastern Economic Review*
GDP	Gross Domestic Product
GOS	Government of Singapore
GPC	Government Parliamentary Committee
GRC	Group Representation Constituency
HDB	Housing and Development Board
ISA	Internal Security Act
ISD	Internal Security Department
ISI	Import-substitution Industrialisation
JBJ	Joshua Benjamin Jeyaretnam
MCA	Malayan or Malaysian Chinese Association
MCP	Malayan Communist Party
MHA	Ministry of Home Affairs
MPAJA	Malayan Peoples' Anti-Japanese Army
NCMP	Non-constituency Member of Parliament
NICs	Newly Industrialised Countries
NMP	Non-elected Member of Parliament
NTUC	National Trades Union Congress
PA	People's Association
PAP	People's Action Party
SATU	Singapore Association of Trade Unions
SAWL	Singapore Association of Women Lawyers
SCMP	*South China Morning Post*
SDP	Singapore Democratic Party
SMC	Single Member Constituency
ST	*Straits Times*
STW	*Straits Times Weekly*
UMNO	United Malay National Organisation
WP	Workers' Party

Introduction

The task of investigating the nature of social control and its role in Singapore's political economy has not previously been attempted in any comprehensive way. This is partly because the dominant view of Singapore's political economy has given little indication that social control is an important aspect of social relations in the city-state. Singapore has been widely seen as an economic miracle, a veritable haven of prosperity and contentment. More than two decades of almost unbroken economic growth have generally been credited to the efficacy of People's Action Party (PAP) rule and often to the personal wisdom of long-serving prime minister Lee Kuan Yew. If noted at all, the authoritarianism of the government has been recorded as no more than the necessary imposition of discipline on a fractious electorate for its own economic good.

The minority of writers who have recognised the repression accompanying Singapore's economic development have generally been classified along with human rights advocates and opposition politicians as having a particular ideological axe to grind or a personal interest to advance. Often this has been true, but no more so than for many of those who subscribe to the view popular in academic circles that the price of economic growth was well worth the sacrifice.

This study seeks to avoid both standpoints. It is critical of the dominant view of Singapore which abstracts the economy from the reality of concrete social relations. But it focuses on the way Singapore society has been shaped and regulated in accordance with the government's economic strategy. It is intended to add to the literature which is only now beginning to look more carefully and dispassionately at the 'miracle' which has, on balance, been rather uncritically acclaimed. Ten years ago, Japan was lauded in similar fashion, but now there are many studies which reveal the complex social outcomes of its economic strategy. Perhaps Singapore and the other Asian Newly Industrialised Countries (NICs) must now face similar scrutiny.

THE NOTION OF SOCIAL CONTROL

The term 'social control' may seem problematic if it is understood to carry pejorative overtones. Social scientists more commonly refer to social 'regulation' when scrutinising the way institutions interact to produce required patterns of behaviour. 'Social control' has been limited in usage mostly to the more obviously coercive functions of the state exercised, for example, through the judicial system and the law (Cohen and Scull, 1986).

However, the character of regulation in Singapore warrants the extension of the notion of social control to the whole system. The reasons for this include the all-encompassing role of the state, the intentional and explicit nature of its regulatory practices, the perceptions of Singaporeans themselves and the constant threat of state violence.

The Singapore state is the exclusive or major provider of infrastructure (utilities, communications, media, industrial estates, port and airport services) and of social services (housing, health and education). It is the country's largest employer, it sets wage levels, regulates labour supply and controls all unions. It holds approximately 75 per cent of the land and has the power to take the rest. It is the major actor in the domestic capital market, runs giant state enterprises, a trading company and joint ventures with foreign capital. It also directs the apparatus of state coercion: the police and the internal security organisations, the courts and the prisons and a large military force.

While the capitalist state in industrialised countries has lost many of its tasks during the past ten years, the state in Singapore has retained an extensive role. In both instances the state continues to be the main institution through which social relations are expressed and regulated institutionally. But the Singapore state maintains a regime of explicit regulatory intervention reaching into so many aspects of a citizen's daily life as to require a distinctive term.

The political leadership has not been reticent about the way it uses state institutions to regulate the behaviour of citizens:

> I am often accused of interfering in the private lives of citizens. Yet, if I did not, had I not done that, we wouldn't be here today. And I say without the slightest remorse, that we wouldn't be here, we would not have made economic progress, if we had not intervened on very personal matters – who your neighbour is, how you live, the noise you make, how you spit, or what language you use. We decide what is right. Never mind what the people think. That's another problem. (Lee Kuan Yew's speech at National Day Rally 1986, *ST*, 20 April 1987)

One does not need to stay in Singapore long to realise that many people are constantly aware of the political limits on personal behaviour imposed by the state. Almost every action of each government organ, no matter how superficially insignificant, is analysed for its political implications for the individual. When the full weight of state violence is brought to bear on errant individuals through detention without trial, flogging or hanging, this collective anxiety is intentionally reinforced. In the circumstances, it would seem reasonable to speak of a system of social control in Singapore.

At the same time, this system should not be primarily conceived in simplistic terms of state repression. In fact the singular characteristic of social control in Singapore is its success in producing political loyalty and cooperation among the majority of the population. It is not merely or even mainly a matter of direct imposition of the government's will by means of force. Rather the threat of coercion underlies institutional practices which really do produce consent or at least acquiescence. The complex relationship between institutional practices, political loyalty, consent and cooperation lies at the heart of this research.

This notion of social control is not widely understood either within or outside the island-state. Analysing the systemic processes comprising it is therefore an important task in itself. Additionally, this research can assist an understanding of the historical development of political resistance or social conflict. The evolution of regulatory institutions often reveals the way people are resisting the pressure to behave in certain prescribed ways. The PAP-state's present hold on social organisation and information makes it almost impossible for anyone, Singaporean or foreigner, to study disinterestedly the emergence of political opposition, particularly working-class dissent. This indirect method of doing so may make an important contribution.

THE POLITICAL ECONOMY OF SOCIAL CONTROL

The wealthiest ten per cent of Singapore households take approximately 30 per cent of total income, while the poorest ten per cent are left with two or three per cent of total income (Pugh, 1989, p. 842). This inequitable distribution of household income has been worsened by the PAP-state's economic development policies. Although official secrecy and the incompleteness of publicly available statistics make reliable measurements very difficult, it has been estimated that 'the population in poverty increased from some 25 per cent in the mid-1950s to some 35 per cent in the mid-1970s' (Pugh, 1989, p. 850). This trend was exacerbated by the so-called Second Industrial Revolution from 1978 onwards, a government-initiated plan to phase out low-wage, labour-intensive manufacturing in favour of high-technology industries (Salaff, 1988, p. 261). Only a minority of skilled workers improved their incomes, thus increasing the disparity between themselves and unskilled workers.

> Between 1979 and 1983, income inequality widened between workers in different occupations and between workers with different educational qualifications. By 1983 the average earnings of administrative and managerial personnel were five times more than those of production and service personnel. (Bello and Rosenfeld, 1990, p. 331)

The island-state's complex ethnic social composition thus has become further divided along class lines through increasing inequality.

The inequities of income distribution within Singapore are mirrored by the disparity between the lower classes of Singapore and those in Malaysia and Indonesia. Since colonial times, Singapore's economy has developed by means of raking off not only the surplus from its own productive sector, but also that of neighbouring countries. The country's strategic geographical location, both militarily and for the commodity trade and the building of a highly developed infrastructure, established the pattern of an entrepot using Malaya and other Southeast Asian countries as its hinterland. This pattern has been perpetuated by post-independence strategies of foreign investment which have continued Singapore's role as a regional node for the entry of foreign capital to Southeast Asia and as a centre for servicing this investment.

In brief, this is the political economy of social control in Singapore. In the face of the inequality produced, this process of capital accumulation requires guarantees, both within Singapore and regionally. While focusing on the domestic system of social control, this study places it in the context of the broader interest of both the PAP-state and of foreign capital in sustaining Singapore's regional economic role.

But to comprehend Singapore's political economy in any depth it is necessary to identify the political relationships of which economic forms and strategies are the concrete expression. It will be argued that the relationship between the Singapore capitalist class, represented by the PAP-state, and foreign capital constitutes the central political alliance which maintains the economic strategy and which thus underlies the system of social control. Neither the inequality nor the comprehensive system of social control in Singapore are obvious to the casual observer. The task of determining the nature of social control, understanding how it works as a complete system and accounting for the effective camouflage of state violence, requires an investigation of this social relation between the Singapore state and foreign capital which is its political root. From the time of the anti-colonial struggle until the present, social conflict frequently has manifested itself in various forms of opposition to this alliance. This conflict explains why some of the most severe regulatory actions by the government have been directed at those groups and individuals who challenge or have the potential to challenge the alliance.

SCOPE OF THE STUDY

This study focuses on four major institutions and their mediation of social control. Public housing, state education, parliament and the law have been chosen, partly to highlight different aspects of regulation but also to show how they interact among themselves and with other institutions to form a complex system of social control.

Institutions are seen as organising particular practices which themselves have specific ideological effects. One of the tasks of this analysis has been to uncover the effects of practices which appear to organise things or commodities (labour power, apartments, schools, votes) but which actually control people.

The emphasis on state institutions has been largely explained in terms of the state's dominance. Non-state institutions such as transnational corporations do play a role in social control. But control over workers in the factory has become so complete that social conflicts have been mainly regulated by the state outside the workplace. Other state institutions such as health and the media are important but it would take a study of unwieldy length to deal with them without, perhaps, adding very much to the overall conclusions of this study.

To set the scene, the initial chapter deals with Singapore's colonial history, the rise of the Lee Kuan Yew faction of the People's Action Party and the transition to independence. The second chapter gives an overview of Singapore's political economy, providing a periodisation which is carried through into the subsequent detailed analysis of social control.

1 Historical Origins

The political alliance between the local capitalist class and foreign capital which is central to Singapore's political economy has its roots in colonial history. This history can be divided into two broad phases: the colonial period, 1819–1941, and the transition to political independence, 1942–65.

THE COLONIAL PERIOD, 1819–1941

On 30 January 1819 Stamford Raffles of the East India Company signed an agreement with the Temenggong and the Sultan of Johor permitting a British 'factory' on Singapore island. The East India Company (EIC) saw Singapore as additional security for its India–China trading route and as a counter to the Dutch monopoly on trade in the Malay archipelago (Wong Lin Ken, 1991, pp. 29–31). Raffles established Singapore as a free port to enable the British to conduct regional trade without having to pay the high differential duties imposed by the Dutch on trade through Batavia. Very quickly Singapore drew the highly developed regional trade of Riau and South Sumatra, took a large part of Penang's commerce and attracted shipping from Siam, Cambodia and Cochin-China as well as European shipping from India.

This success led to Singapore being acknowledged as a permanent British possession through the Anglo-Dutch Treaty of London signed in March 1824 and the Treaty of Friendship and Alliance between the East India Company, Sultan Hussein of Johor and the Temenggong in 1824 (Chew, 1991, p. 39). The latter treaty was not so much the beginning of an alliance as the end of one. It ceded title to the tiny island and its environs in perpetuity thereby extinguishing Malay sovereignty in favour of the British at a crossroads of the Malay archipelago.

By 1821 the population had risen from little over a hundred to approximately 5000 (3000 Malays, 1000 Chinese, 500 or more Bugis) (Turnbull, 1989, p. 13). Nanyang Chinese, many of them already wealthy merchants with developed regional networks, found Singapore highly attractive and came from Malacca, Riau and Penang. Ethnic communities were settled in geographical quarters by Raffles and his subordinates. Under a *kapitan* system, each community was to regulate its own affairs. There was only a token garrison for external defence.

In 1826 the EIC united Penang, Malacca and Singapore to form the Straits Settlements and ruled them from India. During this period, despite fluctuations in trade, Singapore gained from the general expansion of trade arising from such developments as the liberalisation of Dutch trade policy, the founding of Hong Kong, the opening of Chinese Treaty ports and the opening of Siam to the British. It soon supplanted Batavia as the entrepot for Siamese trade with the archipelago.

The pattern of entrepot trade which was consolidated involved European traders receiving goods on consignment which they sold on commission relying on Chinese traders as middlemen. This was the mutually beneficial relationship between British capital and Chinese traders which underpinned Singapore's economic growth throughout the colonial period.

By 1827 the population of Singapore was 16,634 and the Chinese were now in the majority. The population more than doubled to 35,389 by 1840, rose to 81,734 by 1860 and then to 96,087 by 1871 (Saw, 1980, p. 12). By the 1860s, 65 per cent were Chinese. Malays had slipped to third place and were increasingly marginal to commercial activity (Turnbull, 1989, pp. 36–7). Thus, in addition to free port status, the other fundamental basis of Singapore's economic growth was free immigration. Not only could merchants freely relocate to the newly opened most favourable trading site in the region but there was also access for the cheap labour needed by British capital to extract raw materials from the Malay hinterland later in the century.

The Chinese community was differentiated in a number of ways. First, between those who were Straits-born and intended to remain in the region and those who were China-born and intended to return after making enough money. Secondly, the Chinese were divided according to four main dialect groups from south-east China: Hokkien, Teochew, Cantonese and Hakka. The Hokkien and, to a lesser extent, the Teochew, dominated commercial life.

During this period the EIC administration in Singapore remained minimal and weak. Each ethnic community was largely left to regulate itself which the Chinese community did through guilds and secret societies. The latter were not outlawed until 1889 because of their value in maintaining social control within the Chinese community even if they did so with considerable violence. These organisations also acted in concert with Chinese merchants in running the coolie trade and prostitution. In 1853–4 the annual total of male labourers arriving from China reached 13,000 (Turnbull, 1989, p. 53).

Although the secret societies and the majority of the Chinese population were highly politicised in such causes as overthrowing the Manchu dynasty, their political struggles were confined largely to their own community. Even when Britain was at war with China in the 1850s there was no threat to the British administration in Singapore. The Straits Chinese merchants in fact expressed loyalty to British rule. Many of them cultivated British officials and adopted English social habits in the interests of commercial success, leading one historian to note that 'to some extent, the Chinese merchants leagued themselves with the [British] ruling class against the rank and file of their own countrymen' (Turnbull, 1989, p. 55). This social pattern persisted into the next century and reflected the emergence of a class from which the People's Action Party was to draw its main leadership (Regnier, 1991, p. 270).

In 1858 the EIC was abolished but the Straits Settlements were still administered from India. The 1863 Indian Stamp Act had the result that Singapore's administration became self-supporting through minimal port document fees which were added to the existing revenue from opium, gambling and alcohol. In 1867 the administration of the Straits Settlements was transferred to the Colonial Office in London and Singapore became a crown colony. Although Singapore also existed as a garrison this remained token and it was Britain's general maritime supremacy which guaranteed its security from invasion by rival Western powers.

British traders hoped that direct rule by the British state would give them a greater say in Singapore's development through 'unofficial' representatives who were able to advise the governor. They were able to press more directly for forms of social regulation which assisted their trade (suppression of piracy, an upgraded judicial system, suppression of the excesses of secret societies) or for the extension of British power to open up the Malay states. They opposed measures which threatened their profitability such as port charges and restrictions on the immigration of labour. But they had mixed success because the colonial state, while governing in their general interest, did not do so in every case. The Chinese mercantile community had little difficulty in accommodating itself to the new administrative arrangement.

The opening of the Suez railway in 1858 and then the canal in 1869 confirmed the Straits of Malacca's supremacy over the Sunda Straits as the major sea route to East Asia (Wong Lin Ken, 1991, p. 51). The extension of British protection to the Malay states from 1874 saw a sharp increase in the penetration of British investment in the peninsula. Singapore's trade expanded eight-fold between 1873 and 1913 mainly involving the bulk movement of copra, tin, rubber and sugar. Between 1895 and 1900, the first five years of the Federated Malay States, Malayan trade doubled. Thus, Singapore's influence over Malaya grew apace.

Singapore's entrepot relationship with Malaya developed through the export of primary products and the import of manufactured goods, capital and labour. Singapore became ever more prosperous as the commercial base of an alliance between British capital and a Chinese intermediary merchant class for the economic penetration of Malaya. European investment controlled primary production as well as the trade associated with it (through the large agency houses) and funded infrastructural development. Chinese merchants operated a network of domestic commerce of small-scale collection, distribution and retailing and became increasingly dependent on their links with foreign-owned estates and mines in Malaya.

There was a sharp increase in Chinese immigration from the 1870s with the development of tin mining to a new level on the peninsula. There were 34,000 immigrants in 1878 and 103,000 in 1888. Although most went on to Malaya or Indonesia, between 1870 and 1900 the Chinese population of Singapore tripled (Turnbull, 1989, p. 85). By 1914 Chinese comprised more than 75 per cent of the population, a proportion which has roughly held since.

The intermediary class of Chinese merchants which managed this labour supply and much of the entrepot trade understandably welcomed the stability of the colonial rule from which they benefited so much. This structure of entrepot trade not only with Malaya but with Indonesia and elsewhere largely remained until the Second World War.

Regulation of the crown colony developed as the apparatus of a modern colonial state was extended to include all ethnic communities. The growth of a professional British civil service and initiatives in such areas as the judicial system, health, education and welfare had many implications for social regulation of the various ethnic communities and social classes. Of particular note is the establishment of a Chinese Protectorate in 1877 which began to control the labour trade, prostitution and the secret societies. The Societies Ordinance of 1890 was enacted to suppress secret societies. This marked the beginning of the process of extending state control comprehensively over the Chinese community.

Another step in this process was the Immigration Restriction Ordinance which came into force in 1930 to restrict the inflow of unskilled male labourers at a time of rising unemployment. Chinese immigration dropped from 242,000 in 1930 to less than 28,000 in 1933. Adult male immigration dropped from 158,000 to 14,000 (Turnbull, 1989, p. 134). This marked the end of the unrestricted flow of Chinese labour which had supported British capital's penetration of Singapore's hinterland. This legislation ensured that Singapore's Chinese population would increasingly be locally born and be more settled because it pressured immigrants to choose a permanent domicile. The freedom to come and go between Singapore and China was restricted. The new law therefore also ensured that the question of citizenship and ethnicity would become a central issue in the process of decolonisation especially in relation to the possible union of Malaya and Singapore. Already by 1931, 36 per cent of Singapore's Chinese population were locally born (Turnbull, 1989, p. 145).

By the inter-War period, the split between the Straits Chinese, English-educated merchants and professionals who worked closely with the British administration and the Chinese-born and Chinese-educated merchants had been institutionalised in the form of two organisations: the Straits Chinese British Association and the Singapore Chinese Chamber of Commerce (Chui, 1991, pp. 72, 76). Members of the former, a small minority, derived their influence from their cooperation with the British administration and their willingness to hold official positions. They generally had little interest in Chinese politics preferring to see themselves as British subjects and to assist their colonial masters in ruling the colony.

However, members of the latter looked towards China, kept their distance from the colonial administration and concentrated on philanthropy and politics within the Chinese community where they had considerable sway. Political divisions within the Chinese community continued to reflect developments in China with reformist and revolutionary movements arguing the merits of the Ch'ing dynasty early this century (Chui, 1991, pp. 66–91). This gave way to nationalist and communist streams. By the Second World War the Malayan Communist Party had sufficient popular support to influence the transition from colonialism to political independence.

During the crown colony period the colonial state functioned through the governor who worked closely with the upper strata of British business and a tiny section of wealthy and professional English-speaking Asians, mainly Chinese. But the underlying relationship which ensured Singapore's success was that between British capital and the Chinese merchant class as a whole even though the Chinese-educated section of it appeared politically apathetic to colonial rule. Local capital continued to play a dependent and complementary role to British-controlled primary production and trade. Singapore's entrepot economy maintained this structure during the first half of this century.

This pattern of accumulation was secured by British military dominance and by increasingly effective state control of domestic opposition, notably the suppression of the emerging Malayan Communist Party and the trade union movement in the 1930s. This regulatory guarantee also operated regionally in the sense that the security of the Malay states and Singapore was seen to be intertwined.

In summary, Singapore's colonial history began in the context of Anglo-Dutch rivalry. The British built up a trading centre populated largely by immigrants. The colonial administration exercised only such control over the local population as was necessary for the realisation of its commercial and strategic objectives. The power base of the British state lay in the British ruling class and a political base in the local community was not essential to its grip on state power in the colony. But, while British rule in the Malayan states required political alliances with the Malay aristocracy, the formal termination of indigenous Malay sovereignty in 1824, the influx of Chinese migrants and the regional importance of Singapore's Chinese merchant class did place the Chinese community at the centre of Singapore's politics.

THE TRANSITION TO INDEPENDENCE, 1942–65

The end of colonial rule and the era of classical imperialism was precipitated by the intervention of a rival imperialist power, Japan. It sought simply to replace British rule with its own but unleashed nationalist forces all over Asia in the attempt.

The Japanese Occupation of Singapore from 1942 to 1945 marked the end of British imperial legitimacy. The pillar of the British right to rule was the protection of the colonial system of capital accumulation. The British failure meant an enormous loss of prestige and trust in the eyes of those under colonial rule. Paramount among these were the Chinese who suffered greatly during the Occupation with up to 80,000 being massacred in Malaya and Singapore.

The Japanese wartime methods of domestic social control have a note of familiarity in modern-day Singapore: a pervasive internal security apparatus, a system of collective security of households, wards and districts, constant surveillance of religious organisations and the banning of all others except those officially approved. The Occupation succeeded in undermining the previous pattern of accumulation but not in simply replacing one imperial power with another. Rather it advanced the development of powerful nationalist, anti-colonial forces which were to shape the economic strategies of newly independent states in the region and limit the political options of foreign capital.

The Attempt to Restore Colonial Rule, 1945–55

Despite pressure from the Americans, the British planned to reimpose colonial rule and to strengthen Singapore as the base of British military power in Southeast Asia. The wartime planners in the Colonial Office miscalculated both the strength of Malay nationalism and the commitment of the Chinese both in Singapore and Malaya to a Malayan nation and to socialism.

Immediately after the 1942 defeat the Colonial Office began planning for a 'radical post-war reorganisation' of the territories to overcome the administrative disadvantages of the previous arrangement and to forestall demands by the US for the dismantling of its colonial rule in the area (Turnbull, 1989, p. 216). By 1943 it had drawn up the Malayan Union proposals under which the Malay states and Straits Settlements, with the exception of Singapore, were to be united under one colonial administration (Lau, 1991). The Colonial Office decided Singapore should be kept separate 'as a free port, an imperial defence base, and also because of the Malay states' long-standing fear of Singapore's domination' (Turnbull, 1989, p. 216).

In the short term it was thought Singapore would act as the main base for 10 army divisions retaking East Asia from the Japanese, remaining under military rule while Malaya reverted to civilian control. In the longer term, it was envisaged that Singapore would be 'a sort of District of Columbia', an enlarged municipality if not a full colony, from where the British Governor-General for Southeast Asia would coordinate policy in British colonies throughout the region (Turnbull, 1989, p. 219). These colonial territories (the Malay states, the Straits Settlements and Borneo territories) were considered as a package not only in settling on a new configuration of British colonial power but also as a strategic bloc for Western interests in the region.

However, the US saw the continuance of direct colonial rule in the face of nationalist aspirations as a possible complication in the securing of Western interests. It was no longer necessary and, because of nationalist struggles, often no longer possible to hold state power in order to take advantage of a country's productive capacities. The US had discovered this much earlier than other advanced industrialised countries and had long championed an 'open door' policy as in China. Opening a country to the economic interests of all major powers also meant they could be economic rivals without becoming military adversaries. From its post-War position of dominating the world economy the US was pressing access to the markets and resources of the crumbling British Empire. But the prospect of sharing its hard currency surplus was not immediately attractive to a cash-strapped Whitehall. Malaya was by far its main dollar-earning colony (Table 1.1).

Table 1.1 Net Surplus of Main Dollar Earners of British Colonies (1948)

Colony	Net surplus ($ million)
Malaya	172.0
Gold Coast	47.5
Gambia	24.5
Ceylon	23.0

Source: Hua (1983) p. 91.

In 1951 Malaya's rubber exports to the US were valued at approximately US$405 million, while total exports from the UK itself to the US were less than US$400 million. Malaya was termed Britain's 'dollar arsenal' (Li, 1982, p. 169). As an entrepot service centre for Malaya's exports and a strategic military base, Singapore's role was crucial. Therefore, initially and in the face of growing anti-colonial sentiment, Britain tried to retain the old imperialist model of holding state power in a colony in order to secure exclusive control of the surplus from natural resources.

The Malayan Communist Party (MCP) and its armed wing, the Malayan Peoples' Anti-Japanese Army (MPAJA), had cooperated with the British Military Command during the Japanese Occupation. Immediately after the War, the newly legalised MCP made proposals to the British Military Administration (BMA), whose return it did not resist, for steps towards democratic self-government for a unified Singapore–Malaya.

> However, it was obvious that after having made use of the guerilla forces during the Japanese Occupation, the British did not trust them once the Japanese were defeated. The British returned to reimpose their rule. They had no intention of handing power over to the communists, sharing power with them or even allowing them to play a complementary role. But they had to be treated cautiously.... After all, the MCP controlled an armed force of about 10 000 and its prestige and that of the MPAJA were high among the people. Faced with the problem of reestablishing the economy, the British could not very well afford to be confronted with an armed revolution.   (Khong, 1984, p. 50)

By October 1945 the MCP understood the British position. By this time the British had closed down two Chinese newspapers and jailed their editors. They had also responded with troops and police to MCP-sponsored hunger marches and demonstrations for jobs, food and democratic rights, resulting in several deaths (Khong, 1984, p. 52). One estimate puts the number of MCP supporters in Singapore in the immediate post-war months at 70,000 (Turnbull, 1989, p. 223). The MCP-backed Singapore General Labour Union was established on 25 October 1945 and it quickly grew as it led major strikes beginning with a dockers' strike in November. The BMA's incompetence and corruption (it was popularly called the Black Market Administration) along with its repressive measures led to a general strike on 29 January 1946. It was estimated that between 150,000 and 173,000 took part in Singapore alone (Khong, 1984, p. 56). Twenty-seven union leaders were later arrested, ten of whom were banished without trial (Turnbull, 1989, p. 224).

The BMA exacerbated the situation by its political programme. First it brought forward the Malayan Union proposals which reasserted and strengthened colonial rule while keeping Singapore separate from Malaya. In formulating its plan the Colonial Office had faced the problem of the pre-war principles governing Anglo-Malay relations on the peninsula. These were the sovereignty of the Malay rulers, the autonomy of the Malay states and the notion of Malaya as a Malay country. Although Malay sovereignty was in practice largely a legal fiction, these principles of the treaties with the Malay states were an obstacle to the full exercise of British power. The Colonial Office, through the Malayan Union scheme, attempted to overcome this block by a constitutional union of the Malay peninsula and by the creation of common citizenship. These initiatives would override the power of the Malay royal houses and give equal citizenship rights to an increasingly settled Chinese population (partly to counteract the extension of nationality by China to overseas Chinese). By 1941 Malays were only 41 per cent of the peninsula population and the Chinese 43 per cent. The Malay rulers and the nationalist movement represented by UMNO opposed what they saw as a Chinese takeover under the wing of British power. The addition of Chinese-dominated Singapore would have worsened the imbalance and have made the scheme even less acceptable to Malay nationalism (Lau, 1991, pp. 44, 56–8, 282–4).

Despite vehement opposition from all quarters, the Malayan Union was created in April 1946 and Singapore reverted to civil administration as a crown colony. The MCP saw the separation of Singapore as 'an attempt by the British to use Singapore's economic hold over the mainland to control the politics of the Malayan Union without having to bear the responsibility' (Hua, 1983, p. 79). The continuing storm of protest in Malaya from all races and classes, including the Malay rulers, led to the British making a deal with the latter. The Federation of Malaya, which guaranteed the rulers' interests while maintaining British control, replaced the Malayan Union in February 1948. But no other sectors of society were consulted. Anti-colonial protests built up. A nationwide shutdown and general strike on 20 October 1947 attracted widespread support in Singapore and Malaya.

Secondly, the British administration cooperated with employers, planters and agency houses to ensure that commodity production resumed its former levels and that workers were denied even modest improvements in wages and conditions. In response to both the constitutional proposals and the labour situation, the growth of unions was phenomenal, with massive strikes and demonstrations in Malaya and Singapore from late 1945 (Hua, 1983, pp. 69–75). From 1 April 1946 to 31 March 1947, 1,173,000 working days were lost in Singapore due to strikes (Khong, 1984, p. 125). The British reacted by applying the Societies Ordinance which required all unions to register and operate under highly restrictive conditions.

The labour movement was much stronger in Singapore than Malaya and kept up pressure on the administration until the Singapore Federation of Trade Unions (along with the Pan-Malayan FTU) was banned under the Trade Union Ordinance on 31 May 1948. Throughout 1947 and into 1948 police repression of trade union activity was relentless. Workers were killed in several places in Malaya (Hua, 1983, pp. 85–8). With the heavy restrictions on political activity and union organising, the British left the anti-colonial forces with little choice but open revolt.

> Before outlining what I can only describe as the aggressively restrictive measures taken by the British to curb the MCP and its front organisations in 1947 and early 1948, I should emphasise the fact that MCP policy between August 1945 and early 1948 was that of a Peaceful United Front with the object of achieving a more or less constitutional takeover of power. The policy was predicated upon British acceptance of open political, trade union and similar activities which would be considered legal in Britain itself. It was no doubt partly predicated upon the MCP's retention of a significant administrative-cum-intimidatory power. I would argue that it was only when it became apparent that both major avenues of expression, political and trade union, administrative-cum-intimidatory, were almost completely to be denied to militant left-wing groups that the MCP decided to reverse its previous policy. (Stenson, 1971, p. 8)

The colonial state pre-empted any final showdown on the streets when it dispatched Gurkha troops to Johor in early June 1948 and in mid-June the Governor-General declared states of emergency progressively throughout Malaya and Singapore (Chin, 1983, p. 9; Hua, 1983, p. 88). The Emergency Regulations empowered the government to detain without trial, ban publications, take possession of any building or vehicle, control all movements on the road, disperse any meeting, impose curfews, arrest anybody without warrant, impose the death penalty for possession of arms, punish anyone the police considered to be disseminating false information, confiscate businesses suspected of aiding the MCP, detain any villagers suspected of aiding or consorting with the MCP, use all force necessary to arrest persons carrying firearms or suspected of consorting with people who do and, finally, evict persons occupying state land (Khong, 1984, pp. 151–2).

The MCP was proscribed along with other nationalist parties and organisations. Newspapers were closed and editors imprisoned. Thousands of political activists and trade unionists were imprisoned or deported. Banishment was legally possible because the citizenship status of many non-Malay residents was not finally determined. Chinese and Indian activists were thus deported to their respective countries of origin. Initially, this meant sending thousands of left-wing Chinese back to Kuomintang-ruled China. There had been more than 13,000 arrests and deportations by the end of 1948 and there was a net loss from Malaya to China of almost 29,000 persons between January and July 1949 (Hua, 1983, p. 95). For the 12 years of the Emergency, one British observer estimated the colonial government 'deported 90,000 communists and their supporters, and at one time detained 20,000 communists' in Malaya and Singapore (Josey, 1980, p. 189). At a conservative estimate approximately 1200 Singaporeans were arrested and detained without trial between 1948 and 1953 (Turnbull, 1989, p. 242). Most were Chinese-educated activists. But English-educated 'radicals' from such organisations as the Teachers' Union and the University Socialist Club were also taken in.

Six months after the declaration of the Emergency, in December 1948, the MCP responded by launching a military offensive. It had made the ideological commitment to armed struggle in March but planned a longer preparatory period of industrial disruption than was possible once the British took the initiative in June (Khong, 1984, pp. 145, 148). Its armed wing, renamed the Malayan National Liberation Army (MNLA),

> comprised no more than 10,000 active regulars, against which, British imperialism ranged 40,000 regular British and Commonwealth troops; 70,000 armed police personnel; 300,000 Malay Homeguards; including aircraft, artillery and naval support.... The US gave full support to the British, and among other things supplied arms and helicopters. The [US] Griffin Mission of 1950 also recommended that immediate aid should be given for: radio and similar communication technology for the police; road building and earthmoving equipment; teacher training for Chinese primary schools and the revision of Chinese textbooks. (Hua, 1983, p. 97)

According to another source 'that Britain was hard pressed in Malaya was evinced by the fact that by March 1950 there were nearly 100,000 troops and police (both British and local) who were having only limited success checking the three thousand or so guerillas' (Chin, 1983, p. 11). In addition to anti-guerilla warfare, the methods used by the British included the extraction of information through torture, strafing villages and resettling thousands of Chinese squatters in guarded camps to prevent contact with the MNLA.

The ferocity of the British military response indicates the geopolitical importance Malaya and Singapore had for Western interests in the face of anti-colonial struggles throughout Asia. Commonwealth military cooperation in support of the British was formalised under the ANZAM (Australia, New Zealand and the

Malayan Area) consultative framework established in 1948. Although the MNLA was largely defeated by 1955, the permanent stationing of Commonwealth troops in Malaya as part of a Commonwealth Strategic Reserve began in that year (Chin, 1983, pp. 8–22). This deployment was partly due to regional security concerns after the French defeat in Vietnam as well as continuing operations against the MNLA.

Armed revolt was impossible in Singapore with its small land area and its large British military bases. The Emergency therefore affected the anti-colonial movement in Singapore by confining it to the narrow limits of permissible trade union activity and of legal political parties which were cut off from the main weight of the Malayan anti-colonial movement. In mid-1948 the majority of the Singapore communist leadership went to Malaya where various levels of opposition could be continued. Activists who remained in Singapore faced police harassment, detention without trial and deportation.

> The first side-effect of the Malayan emergency in Singapore was to cripple leftwing political movements and leave the stage to conservative politicians, who were willing to cooperate amicably with the colonial authorities in working for constitutional reform, modest social change and the retention of the colonial economy. (Turnbull, 1989, p. 233)

But British strategy in Singapore was also circumscribed. In a cosmopolitan city-state the colonial state could not use the same degree of violence as in Malaya without undermining the economic interests it was preserving. It could not use the full capability of the massive military power present on the island and had to rely mainly on police action. However, aggressive police tactics also had counter-productive results by tending to feed popular opposition.

These limits on British rule provided some political space for the left. Hence, the political irony of a resurgence of labour activism in Singapore at the same time as British forces were gaining a military victory over the MCP in Malaya.

These tactical limitations also infused with urgency the British attempts to promote the upper-class Progressive Party with its wealthy English-educated leadership. This marked a decisive shift in the British policy of social control towards handing over state power to an acceptable local partner. The Progressive Party was encouraged to bring forward proposals for constitutional change. This came in the form of the Rendel Commission, which proposed a partly elected legislative council without sovereign powers. It quickly became clear to the British, however, that the Progressive Party was not a credible vehicle for its political objectives and that the Rendel Commission's reformist proposals would not be tolerated for long.

> The Chinese masses regarded them [the Progressive Party] as collaborators, supporting the colonial government's unpopular policies on education, language, immigration, citizenship, and national service.... To the Chinese-educated and a minority of English-educated radicals the activities of the

legislative council were unreal and irrelevant, and the genuine political issues of the time took place outside of the council chamber. (Turnbull, 1989, p. 239)

The British needed an ally with apparently contradictory attributes: mass support in obtaining state power and a commitment to British interests once in power. Unlike Malaya, Singapore did not have a local aristocracy to be transformed into a capitalist class. The continuing dependence on British commerce and the split between the English-educated upper class and the Chinese-educated merchants meant that the existing local capitalist class was weak. Although the British cultivated the Progressive Party and then the Labour Front it was apparent that their English-educated leadership lacked mass support. The Chinese-educated merchants and intellectuals, on the other hand, had been politically marginalised in colonial politics and, if not already avowedly anti-colonial, identified their long-term interests as lying with the Chinese community and were susceptible to political pressure from within it.

At the same time, the left realised it could get state power in the short term only by means of an alliance with political forces that would lend it a legal cover but have insufficient mass base to entrench themselves. Lee Kuan Yew, a Straits Chinese and his small coterie of English-educated upper-class nationalists saw the British conundrum and the left's need for legitimacy as a political opportunity.

The Route to Power

While studying in England in the late 1940s Lee Kuan Yew realised that the mass-based, left-wing, anti-colonial movement continued to have popular support in Singapore despite the intensifying war against the MCP in Malaya. In January 1950, shortly before his return to Singapore, he addressed a student discussion group, the Malayan Forum. His speech revealed his assessment that the British would ultimately need to identify a reliable ally to protect their interests after they relinquished state power. He also revealed a clear understanding of his class interest: making a deal with the colonial power would be the most likely way to ensure that the colonial rulers were replaced by the English-educated upper class or, in the language of the day, by the bourgeois nationalists.

> We, the returned students, would be the type of leaders that the British would find relatively the more acceptable. For if the choice lies, as in fact it does, between a communist republic of Malaya and a Malaya within the British Commonwealth led by the people who, despite their opposition to imperialism, still share certain ideals in common with the Commonwealth, there is little doubt which alternative the British will find the lesser evil.... But if we do not give leadership, it will come from the other ranks of society, and if these leaders attain power, as they will with the support of the masses, we shall find that we, as a class, have merely changed masters....

> But our trump card is that responsible British leaders realise that independence must and will come to Malaya and that therefore it will be better to hand Malaya to leaders sympathetic to the British mode of life, willing for Malaya to be a member of the British Commonwealth and, what is most important, willing to remain in the sterling area. For the alternative is military suppression, a policy which another imperialist power has found impossible in Indonesia....
>
> If we fail to fulfil our duty, the change that still will come must be a violent one, for, whatever the rights and wrongs of communism, no one can deny its tremendous appeal to the masses.... But if the majority of us choose to believe that Malaya can be insulated from the nationalist revolts that have swept the European powers from Asia, then we may find that there is no place for us in the Malaya that is to be after the British have departed. (Minchin, 1986, pp. 46–8)

Reference to Malaya in this way so as to include Singapore was part of the creed of the nationalist struggle. Hence, Lee was addressing Malayan as well as Singaporean colleagues. His advocacy of a class strategy to build an alliance with British imperialism was not new. The British deal with the Malay sultans two years earlier had shown their willingness to work through the local traditional ruling class in the face of popular revolt. The aristocracy's interest in maintaining its class position by becoming a capitalist class had also been widely understood.

What was significant in Lee's speech was his advocacy of the case for bourgeois Chinese nationalists to share state power with the Malay capitalist class in an independent Malaya. He was explicitly linking his own destiny as an English-educated Chinese to that of the Malay upper class and not to the anti-imperialist movement which had engaged the sympathies of most Chinese in Malaya. He was establishing a mutual interest in defeating the anti-imperialist movement and in consolidating a relationship with the British.

After returning to Singapore in the early fifties, Lee and his former student friends continued to meet. Regular discussions with Goh Keng Swee, Toh Chin Chye, S. Rajaratnam and others were held in Lee's basement dining room at 38 Oxley Road. Their main topic was how to obtain popular support in their bid for state power. In 1979 Lee recalled:

> Our primary concern was how to muster a mass following. How did a group of English-educated nationalists – graduates of British universities – with no experience of either the hurly-burly of politics or the conspiracies of revolution, move people whose many languages they did not speak and whose problems and hardships they shared only intellectually? (Minchin, 1986, p. 66)

Lee and his group of returned students did their political reconnaissance thoroughly. They knew the existing legal parties were proving weak and incompetent and lacked wide political appeal. They also knew that the Malayan Communist Party and its open mass organisations were the most popular and highly organised political force in Singapore. A wide range of unions, educational institutions, vocational and cultural associations were sympathetic to the left and, being predominantly Chinese, to political developments in China. The political aspirations of the majority of Singaporeans were, they knew, represented by the left.

> The Communists, although they had only a few hundred active cadres, could muster and rally thousands of people in the unions, cultural organisations and student societies. By working and manifestly appearing to work selflessly and ceaselessly, they won the confidence and regard of the people in the organisations. Having won the confidence and regard, they then got the people to support their stand. (Lee Kuan Yew, 1961, p. 21)

The Lee group concluded that it had to co-opt the popular legitimacy of the left in order to impress upon the British that it was capable of delivering mass support for a non-communist, pro-British post-independence regime. Without the left, they could never come to power (Bellows, 1970, p. 20). This conclusion coincided with the left's need for a non-communist, legal, electoral front to give it a role in the transition to independence. It saw the impossibility of an extra-legal bid for power in an island garrison and, thus, the necessity of being represented in the political formalities of transition.

A political alliance between the left and a group of English-educated nationalists had, as the Lee faction knew, been tried before with inconclusive results (Regnier, 1991, p. 270). The Malayan Democratic Union, formed in 1945, had been unexpectedly successful in mobilising popular support against the colonial government. It collapsed in 1948 with the beginning of the Emergency. 'Within a few years, however, as aspiring politicians reviewed the MDU period, many perceived what they considered to be a winning strategy.... Four ministers in the present PAP government were MDU members' (Bellows, 1970, p. 70).

From the moment of his return, Lee had begun the process of showing how he could be useful to the left and thereby that he was a political leader to be taken account of by the British. He made contact with a variety of political movements and began to develop a public profile as a clever, aggressive young lawyer defending political cases in the colonial courts. His legal assistance to the Postal Workers' Union during their strike in May 1952 won him public recognition as an activist lawyer. He was eventually retained by over 100 unions and associations (George 1984, p. 33; Minchin, 1986, p. 72).

But Lee undoubtedly knew that he was not fully trusted by the left or the community organisations he legally represented (Bellows, 1970, p. 132). When he met with activists, Lee recalled in parliament on 23 February 1977, 'They denigrated me. They said I had an air-conditioned office and I slept in an air-conditioned room. I was bourgeois'. He lived in a large bungalow near the city centre, he owned a Studebaker, bred German shepherd dogs and went on holidays to the Cameron Highlands. His contact with the dynamism of the mass movements unnerved him. As a union adviser he was often 'out of his depth', sometimes begging activists to tone down their protests (Minchin, 1986, p. 77). Not being able to speak Chinese himself, he sought advice from Chinese-speaking expatriates and expressed relief that he could attempt his united front ride to power protected by the presence of the colonial government (Minchin, 1986, p. 71).

The People's Action Party was formally established on 21 November 1954 and included both the left and the Lee group.

> The PAP was organised by fourteen persons meeting over a period of months in the recreation room of Lee Kuan Yew's home. In essence, what the English-educated, middle-class, non-Communist majority of this coterie did was to establish a working agreement with individuals who had proven organisational skills and symbol-wielding abilities and were evidencing these aptitudes in the 1954–56 riots and demonstrations.... There was no way for the non-Communist PAP leadership to detach itself from the Communists if it wished to win the support of a majority of Singapore's electorate. (Bellows, 1970, pp. 19–20)

The PAP's structure consisted of a network of local branches represented at an annual conference. The conference elected the governing body, the Central Executive Committee (CEC). The left had control of the branches of the Party and, by agreement in order to prevent proscription as a communist front, the Lee faction held the majority of seats on the CEC. The Lee faction had the head, the left had the body. From the beginning, it was a coalition of convenience and both elements intended to use the PAP as the electoral vehicle to carry them through to being the first government of an independent Singapore and, eventually, after merger, of an independent Malaya.

Forging a New Alliance

Having achieved the alliance with the left as a stepping stone to state power, the Lee faction had to pursue its main objective of building an alliance with the British. The Lee faction had certain advantages in this task of building their power base. From 1951 or 1952, Lee was in touch with British officers in the Special Branch who had already decided not to arrest him on his return but to see how he developed politically (Minchin, 1986, p. 63). He eventually established a close working relationship with the Director of the Special Branch. In his early days of meeting the left leadership, Lee was receiving briefings on them from these security contacts. Alex Josey, formerly of MI6, became Lee's close friend and eventually his prolific biographer.

Sir William Goode was made Governor of Singapore on 11 December 1957. As Singapore's Chief Secretary, he had controlled the Special Branch since 1953 and was intimately acquainted with Singapore politics. Lee maintained close contact with Goode in the year leading up to the 1959 elections and is said to have obtained information from him. Goode had responsibility for handing over to a non-communist, pro-British leadership and it seems that he eventually favoured the Lee faction over the failing and unpopular Labour Front. Goode's information is said to have given Lee considerable political advantage over the Labour Front as well as over the left in the PAP (Bellows, 1970, p. 35; George, 1984, p. 43).

This information should not be taken to suggest a conspiracy between Lee and the Colonial Office or that the Lee faction's strategy was thought out in detail from the beginning and followed step by step. Rather the alliance-building process was one of identifying mutual interests and not simply a sustained act of political cleverness by either side. The British were actively seeking to support the political force that would serve their interests best. It is unlikely that any faction could have made it successfully to the 1959 election victory if the British had set their face against it.

In establishing its fitness to rule in British eyes, the Lee faction demonstrated its ability to co-opt left-wing mass support and to monopolise the left's agenda in the legislative assembly. It did this while retaining control of the PAP in the face of left-wing challenges and cooperating unflinchingly in the suppression of the left's leadership and grass-roots organisation.

The first task of supporting the left's agenda in the legislature while undermining it was a complex one. One way Lee did this was by denouncing the government's repression of the left while maintaining ideological distance from them. He spoke eloquently and frequently in support of democratic freedoms in the Legislative Assembly to which three PAP candidates were elected in 1955.

> If it is not totalitarian to arrest a man and detain him when you cannot charge him with any offence against any written law – if that is not what we have always cried out against in fascist states – what is it?...If we are to survive as a free democracy, then we must be prepared, in principle, to concede to our enemies – even those who do not subscribe to our views – as much constitutional right as you concede yourself.... What he [Chief Minister Marshall] is seeking to do in the name of democracy is to curtail a fundamental liberty, and the most fundamental of them all – freedom from arrest and punishment without having violated a specific provision of the law and being convicted for it. (Lee quoted in *FEER*, 2 June 1988)

This speech was delivered in September 1955 when the Labour Front government was proposing the Preservation of Public Security Bill, a milder version of Singapore's current Internal Security Act. At the same time, the Lee faction was using its executive power in the PAP's Central Executive Committee (CEC) and contacts with the British to undermine the left and have its leaders imprisoned. The pattern of arrests and the way Lee always seemed to have the right information at the right time has been termed 'fortuitous' for the 'moderates' (Chan, 1985, p. 150).

By this means the far more charismatic and popular left leaders of the PAP were progressively prevented from using the officially sanctioned parliamentary arena as a political platform through which to establish national political leadership without the Lee faction's mediation. The Lee faction's eventual monopoly had the important ideological consequence of enabling the rhetoric of bourgeois nationalism to dilute and divert the rhetoric of anti-imperialism.

The Lee faction also performed the valuable function for the British of bringing the politics of the majority of Singaporeans into a parliamentary forum which the British controlled in cooperation with a variety of factions of the English-educated upper class. Before this the legislative assembly was largely irrelevant to the mass political movements as a site for political contest.

The second set of tasks which the Lee faction simultaneously undertook involved publicly supporting the left leadership while attacking the left's organisation behind the scenes and keeping tight control of the central organs of the PAP. This required considerable political agility and a willingness to use the colonial apparatus of state repression.

For example, on 11 June 1955, seven left-wing leaders were detained under security legislation before a general strike. While publicly requesting their release, the Lee faction privately expressed the view that the Labour Front government's actions were 'feeble and lamentable in the extreme' because the Special Branch had recommended 300 detentions (Bellows, 1970, p. 22). The left wing of the PAP quickly became suspicious.

In order to avoid lending substance to the charge that the PAP was a communist front, the left did not put up candidates for the PAP's Central Executive Committee (CEC) elections on 26 June 1955. For the same reason there was an understanding that, when the left did eventually enter the CEC, it should maintain a minority position and not take any offices. But on 8 July 1956 at the second Party Conference the left won four of the twelve CEC seats and proposed redrafting the constitution to enable branches to nominate CEC members. This move indicated an anxiety over the Lee faction's tactics and was aimed at entrenching the constitutional basis for an eventual capture of the CEC. However three left-wing CEC members were soon arrested under the Preservation of Public Security Ordinance (Chan, 1985, p. 149). Lim Chin Siong, the most charismatic opposition leader, CEC member and PAP member of the Legislative Assembly, was arrested on the night of 26 October 1956. He remained incarcerated until after the Lee faction came to power in 1959 (Clutterbuck, 1973, p. 130). In this way the most powerful and popular orator of the left was excluded from the assembly as well as the CEC for the remainder of the decade.

In August 1957 the left made a stronger bid to take over the CEC. This move was precipitated by the All Party Mission to London in April–May 1957 at which Lee, representing the PAP, accepted terms for independence which were against party policy. He agreed to the establishment of an Internal Security Council which would enable a conservative government in Malaya, a Lee-led government in

Singapore and the British to clamp down on the left throughout a merged Malaya and Singapore.

The left needed to win the CEC elections in order to repudiate Lee's stance. They won half the seats. This victory was sufficient. They already controlled the rest of the Party. The Lee faction initially refused to take up their seats. Ten days after the election, five of the left CEC members (and 30 non-CEC members) were detained under the Preservation of Public Security Ordinance (Pang, 1971, p. 4). An embarrassed Lee denied the government statement that the arrests were made to save the PAP from a communist takeover (Clutterbuck, 1973, p. 146; George, 1984, p. 43).

To ensure that Lee faction control of the CEC would never be under threat again and to obviate the need for any future purge, the party rules were amended to establish a cadre system. Cadres were chosen from among the party members by the CEC. Only cadre members could attend the party conference and vote for the CEC. The list of cadres was secret. The CEC could suspend, demote or expel any member. This reorganisation has been termed 'the iron law of oligarchy' (Bellows, 1970, p. 24). Lee himself put it well: 'The Pope chooses the cardinals and the cardinals elect the Pope' (George, 1984, p. 45). There was only one pope in the PAP from 1954 until 1992. Lee Kuan Yew held the post of party secretary-general throughout.

In March 1958 with PAP electoral victory increasingly likely, the CEC decided to conduct a wholesale purge of the lower echelons of the party. It required all party members to re-register. By means of a select committee of six persons from Lee's faction, a process was begun to weed out the left from the membership and to ensure that none rose to the higher levels of the Party. Approximately 500 members were put on probation. While this action could not prevent left-wing control of the intermediate and lower levels of the Party, it did further secure the top level for Lee. In addition, PAP candidates for the 1959 elections had to sign an undertaking that they would resign from the assembly if they quit the PAP.

The Lee faction also cooperated with the British and the Labour Front administration to eliminate any future threat to its position from the incarcerated left leadership. This was revealed by the Chief Minister shortly before the 1959 elections. The Labour Front government (1955–9) under David Marshall and then Lim Yew Hock governed under the Rendel Constitution: severely curtailed powers had to be exercised within the limits of continuing British colonial rule. While the Labour Front tried to negotiate full independence, the PAP, especially Lee himself, castigated it with great flair for being a tool of the British. At the same time, the Labour Front was acting under pressure from the British and from Lee to detain left-wing PAP leaders and, thus, save Lee from imminent political eclipse. That this must have been particularly galling for Chief Minister Lim Yew Hock is clear from his 1959 outburst in the Assembly.

The truth shall now be told. If one side can play dirty and begin to be dirty, I shall play the same game and do it too, and let the country and the world and God decide. The subversive clause was put in as a result of the Honourable Member [Lee Kuan Yew] and I seeing the Secretary of State for Colonies. (*Colony of Singapore, 1955–9*, vol. 3, cols 2164–5)

Lim was fingering Lee as one of the chief architects of the security provisions resulting from the constitutional talks in London, notably the clause that 'persons known to have been engaged in subversive activity should not be eligible for election to the first Legislative Assembly of the new State of Singapore' (Clutterbuck, 1973, p. 144). While the Singapore representatives publicly objected afterwards to the provision for the purpose of maintaining credibility back home, it has been generally claimed that they privately welcomed it. Lim's claim that Lee was one of its main proponents has been accepted by a number of writers (Bellows, 1970, p. 138; George, 1984, p. 44; Minchin, 1986, p. 83–4). Later in his speech, Lim continued, 'I did so many things for the good of the country. I did so many things for the good of the PAP after discussions with the PAP. Such is politics in Singapore today' (*Colony of Singapore, 1955–9*, vol. 3, col. 2167).

Consolidating the Alliance

The PAP's accession to government in 1959 was a crucial milestone for the Lee faction. It had positioned itself well. It inherited the administrative apparatus of the state by virtue of being the legal leadership of an independence movement which swept to power while the movement's most popular leaders languished in detention.

> Critics called it cheating, admirers called it flexibility, neutrals called it opportunism, but the fact is that it was a competent display of sustained dissimulation lasting nearly seven years. And it was successful.   (George, 1984, p. 40)

But the final political battle remained to be fought. The left was implacably opposed to the Lee faction's class strategy of alliance-building with the British. The left's strong organisation still gave it the potential to take the fruits of electoral victory for itself. The mass electoral support the PAP had attracted

> was largely indirect or constituent, being channeled through, and derived from, the multiple, pro-Communist-controlled secondary organisations. For the majority of the PAP electorate, secondary association leaders were political reality. Identification with the second-level leadership was the relevant and decisive affiliation.   (Bellows, 1970, p. 26)

The Lee faction had to consolidate a domestic power base and prove its ability to govern if it was to have a future in Malaya–Singapore politics. This entailed winning over other sections of the local capitalist class and as many of the lower classes as possible.

While British capital constituted the most important power base of the Lee faction, the practice of governance required at least the support of the other sections of the local capitalist class. Winning over the more pro-British sections of its own class was not a serious problem. The comparative weakness of the local capitalist class meant that they could do nothing to prevent Britain supporting the Lee faction. It then became in their interest to live with the result. Prior to 1959 they regarded the faction as radical activist interlopers but Lee began to reassure them before the polls by stating that the real battle would start after the elections: 'The ultimate contestants would be the PAP and the MCP' (Lee Kuan Yew, 1961, p. 30). By the 1963 elections this battle had been joined and much of the local capitalist class, although not the more nationalistic Chinese-educated elements, was right behind the PAP.

The lower classes had to be won over in order to weaken the left's power base. The alacrity with which the Lee administration used police-state tactics must have encouraged many to support it in 1963. But the Lee faction's grip on the state security apparatus was only one of its advantages in pursuing this goal. For several years on the national stage, its members had articulated the ideology of bourgeois nationalism as a left-wing ideology. Even as it moved rapidly to ensure that the Singapore economy remained within the Western orbit, the Lee faction was able to characterise all its policies as truly socialist and in the interest of nation-building.

Linked to this control of the PAP ideology was the Lee administration's control of the PAP's political programme. It quickly began to implement some of the most popular aspects of this programme: educational reform, public housing, better health system, community centres and other facilities. The left's leaders were forced into the position of criticising a government which was carrying out their policies. At the same time increasing numbers of the lower classes were moving to take advantage of the opportunities they saw the Lee administration offering them. They had supported the PAP in 1959 and saw no inconsistency in supporting it again in 1963 when it was delivering on its promises.

The Lee leadership was also assisted by the fact that approximately 20 per cent of the labour force was employed by or dependent on the British military bases or related expenditure downstream (Bellows, 1970, p. 113; Krause, 1989, p. 438). Left-wing rhetoric about expelling the imperialists would not necessarily appeal to this sector of the population.

But it was still by no means certain that the Lee faction could survive a sustained challenge from the left. The Lee government therefore took the initiative in neutralising the left's leaders and organisation. It also went to great lengths to ensure that no alternative political force arose on either the left or the right for the people to support or for the British to deal with.

To keep mass support before the 1959 elections Lee had stated that the release of detained left-wing leaders was a precondition for the PAP taking up the reins of government if it was elected. On taking power he therefore arranged for some of them to be released. But freedom from custody was to prove a prelude to a careful process of political vetting whereby they were co-opted, neutralised or eliminated.

When he was lawyer for the detained left leaders in the years after 1956, Lee had unusually free access to them and was able to gather extensive information for later use.

> I used to see them there [in prison], arguing their appeals, reading their captured documents and the Special Branch precis of the cases against them.... I also saw the official version in reports on them. (Lee Kuan Yew, 1961, p. 17).

This previous legal work for the detainees and full access to security files after assuming the reins of government underpinned a revitalised anti-communist campaign. It was a comparatively simple tactic of state terror to label a political rival on the left as a communist or pro-communist and, thus, as an anti-national servant of another power even though the latter appellation might equally have described members of the Lee faction.

Lee has since stated that there were few actual MCP cadres in Singapore and that he did not know who they were (Lee Kuan Yew, 1961, p. 21). He also said in the assembly while still in opposition:

> Whether a person is a Communist or a Communist agent, only he knows and God knows. Between his conscience and God of course lies the Special Branch and it is up to them to show that these men whom they have arrested are Communists or Communist agents. (*Colony of Singapore 1955–9*, vol. 4, col. 2598)

In histories of Singapore, especially those published in Singapore, the opponents of the Lee faction are often labelled 'extremists' and 'pro-communists' as against Lee's 'moderates' and 'non-communists' (Pang, 1971; Chan, 1985). These labels tacitly recognise that not all or even most of those on the left were MCP members. The left was, in fact, a broad spectrum of groups committed to national independence and some form of socialism.

By 1961, the left was thoroughly disenchanted. All the detainees had not been released, a new amendment to the Citizenship Bill rendered some of the left leaders stateless and restrictive policies were being implemented with regard to Chinese educational institutions and the trade unions which were the main bases of left power. The left began to campaign on these issues. The Lee faction carried the battle to them with proposals for independence through merger with Malaya on grounds unacceptable to the left (Pang, 1971, p. 13). The left retaliated by withdrawing support for a PAP candidate in a by-election resulting in a PAP defeat.

The final split came in 1961 after Lee forced a vote of confidence in the legislature on the merger proposals. The left split from the PAP taking along its mass base. Thirteen PAP Assembly members departed to set up the *Barisan Sosialis* (Socialist Front). With them, according to one writer, went more than 80 per cent of the PAP membership, all but two of the Party branches and 19 of the 23 paid organising secretaries (Pang, 1971, p. 15). According to other analysts, 60–70 per cent of the membership left and 30 of the paid staff (Bellows, 1970, p. 28). Most cadres also left the Party (Chan, 1985, p. 153) but there is disagreement over just how many. All agree, however, that not even the skeleton of the Party remained. The Lee faction was now the PAP.

> One of the most important problems confronting the PAP in mid-1961 was that the party had lost most of its voter appeal.... Once these [left] organisations pulled away from the PAP, the remnants of the party were unable, save in a few instances, to arouse in the electorate those reifying, personally meaningful connotations and associations which a party slowly accrues over time. (Bellows, 1970, p. 46)

Despite appearances the situation was actually more serious for the *Barisan* than for the PAP remnant. Probably neither the *Barisan* nor the Lee faction recognised this. The latter was surprised at the extent of the defections. But, by forcing a split with the left, the Lee faction had finally isolated its opponents so that the full weight of the security apparatus could be brought down upon them. Furthermore, it was now possible to redouble government efforts in education, housing and welfare in the certainty that these policies would win loyalty among the lower classes for the Lee-dominated PAP and not the left.

The *Barisan Sosialis*, for at least the next 18 months, had the majority support of the Singapore electorate (Bellows, 1970, p. 75). But the systematic harassment of its leadership by the government, the deregistration of its grass roots organisations, the PAP's strident anti-communism along with its calls to national loyalty and solidarity in the face of Indonesian confrontation, all took a severe toll. The *Barisan* was put on the defensive and had no capacity to deliver concretely on its political programme from its position in opposition. Furthermore, it could not match the parliamentary performance of the English-educated PAP leadership who had ensured that parliament became a central symbol of national independence and who had outmanoeuvred the left on the constitutional issue of merger with Malaya.

But the PAP, shorn of its popular base, still had to prove to the British and the Malay government in Kuala Lumpur that it could win an election. Only this achievement would give the Lee-led PAP maximum political weight in the new Federation of Malaysia. With the departure of the mass organisations, the PAP had no way of reaching the local level with what remained of the party structure. It faced very strong *Barisan Sosialis* organisation at this level. The PAP government therefore established networks of government community organisations to replace the party organs it had lost. These organisations delivered both welfare services and government propaganda at the local level. The PAP had much of its party-state apparatus in place by the time of the 1962 referendum on merger and the 1963 elections.

To ensure that its electoral chances were further enhanced, on 2 February 1963 the PAP government detained 111 opposition leaders without trial in Operation Coldstore, aptly named since some of them were imprisoned without trial for nearly 20 years. Lim Chin Siong, the left's most popular leader, was arrested again. First arrested in 1956, he had been released after the 1959 elections but not given citizenship papers or PAP cadre status. In solitary confinement he became suicidal from torture and maltreatment, was eventually broken after 7 years, forced to confess and beg for mercy in public and then whisked from Changi Prison directly to England 'reduced to a vegetable' (George, 1984, p. 69). His fate was similar to that of many others (Amnesty International, 1980). More arrests followed later in 1963.

The PAP proceeded to gerrymander the elections and not merely by manipulating the state media:

> Former detainees were physically prevented from nominating in the one hour available for their personal presentation of papers. The election was called with minimum notice and the campaign period of nine days included the holidays and festivities associated with Malaysia's inauguration. Sites and permits for rallies were hard to come by. Printing facilities for opposition parties were almost unobtainable. Notice was given of the deregistration of seven leftist unions and SATU [Singapore Association of Trade Unions] funds were frozen at the eleventh hour to prevent their being spent for electoral purposes.... [At PAP rallies] searchlights were used to show up dissenters in the crowd.   (Minchin, 1986, p. 130)

The PAP won the election with 46.9 per cent of the total valid vote and the headless, persecuted *Barisan Sosialis* gained 33.3 per cent.

The popular leadership of the independence movement was thus formally and finally excluded from state power. They had misjudged, thinking that they could simply take state power from the Lee faction after 1959. By 1963 the left had begun to lose its mass base and had come under direct attack from the combined British, Malayan and Singaporean internal security apparatus. This ensured, as had been prepared for as early as 1958, that the left was unable to regroup and consolidate itself as a credible legal opposition.

The 1963–5 interlude of merger with Malaysia provided the expected opportunity for the PAP to shelter under the federal structure while finally defeating its political opponents. It also saw an aggressive attempt by the Singapore-based and essentially Chinese PAP, which was in opposition in the federal parliament, to replace the Malayan-based Chinese entrepreneurial class (MCA) in its alliance with the Malay ruling class, a coalition which constituted the federal government.

But Singapore was decisively rejected as a potential partner in the ruling coalition when it was expelled from Malaysia in 1965. The PAP had been unable to come to an accommodation with the Malay capitalist class which suspected the PAP's ultimate ambition was to challenge its political supremacy. Consequently, the PAP suddenly found itself as the government of a tiny, independent city-state.

The main feature of the tumultuous post-war period in Malaya and Singapore was the organisational and ideological strength of the independence movement. The realisation of the popular desire for a simultaneously nationalist and socialist revolution was forestalled by large-scale military violence. In Singapore the cooperation of the Lee faction in co-opting the movement's legal parliamentary front and suppressing its leadership brought about its defeat. To the Lee faction's political credit was the transformation of the PAP from an anti-imperialist party of the Chinese lower class to a party of the small, pro-British, English-speaking capitalist class. It also brought Singapore politics into a parliamentary institution it controlled and it had won an election without its mass base. Deregistration, banning, withholding or revocation of citizenship, deportation, smear campaigns, fixed elections, widespread surveillance, police intimidation, detention without trial and torture had become part of the PAP repertoire. The PAP's political success had enabled it to forge an alliance with British capital.

However, the faction's success in taking over the PAP was not repeated in its attempt to realise wider ambitions through joining a coalition with the indigenous ruling class of Malaya. Thus, in 1965, as the leadership of a separate nation, the PAP encountered the ambiguities and difficulties of being an immigrant Chinese government in a Malay region, of having a weak class base from which to govern, of declining entrepot trade and of rising unemployment. The alliance with British capital, which retained a heavy economic and military presence on the island, remained its critical power base but the relationship would need to be shaped to the new global context.

2 Singapore's Political Economy

Singapore's economic success is often explained in terms of its geographical location, an expanding regional or global economy, a hard-working population and, most especially, the honesty, reliability and wisdom of the PAP government (Chen, 1983, pp. 7, 24; Chia, 1989, p. 271; Lim Chong Yah, 1989, pp. 206–7; Sandhu and Wheatley, 1989, pp. 1096–7; Milne and Mauzy, 1990, p. 132). While these factors have contributed to Singapore's economic development, they are insufficient to elucidate the politics of Singapore's economy. Such explanations beg important questions about the role of the state and of foreign capital and about the persistence of political conflict and its influence on economic strategy. These are not matters extraneous to economic analysis. Singapore's economic development needs to be related to its social and political history so that the politics of contemporary economic forms can be fully understood. This implies the necessity of a periodisation of Singapore's political economy.

The previous chapter focused on the colonial origins of Singapore as an entrepot and of the alliance between the PAP and British capital. It traced the emergence of this relationship from a period of war between the major powers and the prolonged resistance to colonial rule which was met by state violence. Singapore's changing social composition and its underlying tensions, the economic strategy of foreign capital and social regulation by the state arose as major aspects of this history and now need to be traced through the phases of Singapore's political economy.

BEFORE 1959

The island's growth as an entrepot while Britain held state power was the first phase of Singapore's political economy. It has already been noted that an intermediary class of Chinese merchants came to play a complementary role to British-controlled primary production and trade and that this economic structure remained largely unchanged until the PAP came to power. Between 70 and 75 per cent of the labour force was involved in the trade and services sectors which generated approximately 80 per cent of Singapore's income for the first six decades of this century. Over the same time manufacturing contributed between five and ten per cent of national income while employing ten to fifteen per cent of the work force (Rodan, 1989, p. 41).

By the 1950s there were domestic and global pressures for industrialisation. The strength of nationalist movements throughout the British Empire limited British capital's attempts to raise its profitability in order to compete with US capital. To have any chance of securing Malaya's wealth via Singapore, Singapore's powerful anti-colonial movement had to be contained. Yet the demand for independence through merger with Malaya could not be resisted. Any development of Singapore's economy would need to accommodate this political aspiration. The relinquishment of state power to a local class ally would impel foreign capital to share the profits of its investment with this partner but it would remove the foreign state from political accountability for domestic social control.

IMPORT-SUBSTITUTION INDUSTRIALISATION, 1959–65

In the mid-fifties plans were drawn up for import-substitution industrialisation (ISI) (Mirza, 1986, p. 29) which was to be the economic strategy marking the second phase of Singapore's political economy. The formation of a common domestic market and political union with Malaya were central to this strategy which eventually became a policy plank of the PAP in the 1959 elections. ISI was to be the economic form of the alliance with foreign capital after independence. Foreign capital could retain its interests, continuing to profit from the acquisition of raw materials and also from the provision of technology and credit. Its local allies, the Malay ruling class with its Chinese entrepreneurial collaborators in Malaya and Singapore's Chinese capitalists, would receive a share of the profits from local production enabling the consolidation of a stronger local capitalist class within a Malaya–Singapore federal polity. The strategy was politically justified in the rhetoric of economic nationalism and nation-building.

Within Singapore the lack of a strong domestic capitalist class had opened a route to power for the Lee faction of the PAP but it also left the Lee administration politically exposed. An ISI policy would require control over a newly constituted industrial working class yet the PAP was without the aid of an entrenched industrial bourgeoisie to command the loyalty of workers.

The PAP government sought the domestic power base to defeat the left and to acquire the social power to regulate the lower classes by entering Malaysia. The PAP leadership initially saw Singapore's expulsion in 1965 as a severe blow because without a sizeable internal market and a hinterland the ISI policy could not work for Singapore. Its economy appeared to be back where it was prior to merger: declining entrepot trade and rising unemployment.

But the PAP had also begun systematically to extend the role of the state and to tie in its parliamentary political organisation to the Singapore state administration. From this period it becomes appropriate to refer to the 'PAP-state' to describe this characteristic of PAP governance.

> Executive power was subsequently employed by the PAP to extend its influence to all spheres of social activity, enabling it to establish control over all political groups. A virtual 'state party' emerged which not only entrenched the PAP, but also conditioned economic and industrial policy. (Rodan, 1989, p. 50)

The hard edge of this policy was revealed in Operation Coldstore in February 1963 (see Chapter 1) which rounded up more than 100 trade union leaders and other opposition leaders. The damage done to opposition organisation by this security police operation and the fear inspired by it led to a 90 per cent decline in work stoppages between 1963 and 1964 (Bello and Rosenfeld, 1990, p. 304). During merger with Malaysia, left-wing trade unions suffered wholesale, arbitrary deregistration and the pro-PAP National Trades Union Congress (NTUC) was made the sole legal trade union confederation (Minchin, 1986, p. 120).

Thus, several important factors combined to enable a rapid and successful shift in economic strategy. By 1965 the PAP-state had largely defeated the parliamentary left and was undermining the power of organised labour. The government was acquiring an increasing capacity to regulate an industrial working class. The transitory nature of ISI in Singapore also meant that there had been little chance to build up a strong local capitalist class as in other Asian newly industrialised countries (NICs). The PAP-state was consequently able to sacrifice not only workers but also local capitalists to the greater competitive power of foreign capital. In other words the PAP-state found it enjoyed not only political supremacy but also a degree of political autonomy which enabled it to move quickly to a new accumulation strategy.

These political attributes of the PAP fitted it for a high level of cooperation with foreign capital during a decade when the advanced industrialised countries, especially the USA, began to increase direct investment in production based in favourable overseas locations in order to avoid domestic limits on profitability and the problems of continuing to hold state power in a colony. It became feasible for former colonies to attract both credit and technical expertise to establish manufacturing sectors and, in Singapore, for the state to take a leading role in this.

> The assumption behind the [PAP-]state's high profile was that it could shape the factors of production, most notably through the enforcement of low wages, to give Singapore a comparative advantage in having labour-intensive production. This was taking place, of course, at a convenient juncture in the development of international capital. The absence of politically powerful vested interests to defend the import-substitution strategy, so characteristic of many other countries in the region, also made for a swift transition. (Robison *et al.*, 1987, pp. 7–8)

There was therefore a conjunction of the political need of the PAP government to retain political ascendancy by finding a new path to industrial development with the need of foreign capital to identify sites for production. The new strategy, export-oriented industrialisation (EOI), became the economic form of the alliance between the PAP-state and foreign capital from 1965 onwards.

EXPORT-ORIENTED INDUSTRIALISATION, 1965-78

The third phase of Singapore's political economy was the implementation of the EOI policy from 1965 to 1978. Having developed the corporatist state to overcome its political rivals, the PAP-state was now able to exercise this executive power to achieve the social and economic goals of its alliance with foreign capital. The formation of a disciplined work force was the highest priority, one which coincided with the PAP's need to maintain its political dominance. The persisting tradition of union militancy had therefore to be dealt a final blow along with other institutional bases for political dissent.

Thus, this period saw the consolidation of the party-state and its ideology, the introduction of repressive labour laws and the final destruction of autonomous unions, further manipulation of the electoral process and the silencing of the press and educational institutions.

> the PAP exploited its considerable relative political autonomy to secure a monopoly over legitimate political action through certain representative bodies, such as the NTUC. In this way, the PAP cultivated corporatist structures as a way of consolidating its relative autonomy rather than as a prerequisite for its political autonomy. It matters little that the NTUC, for example, is politically ineffective in representing a point of view to government; what matters is that the NTUC is the only legitimate channel through which labour is represented and that the objectives of the NTUC are effectively integrated with those of the PAP. (Rodan, 1989, p. 30)

The NTUC acquiesced to the outlawing of strikes in 1967 under the Criminal Law (Temporary Provisions) (Amendment) Act and subsequent legislation ensuring PAP-state control of the union movement (Vasil, 1989, pp. 154-6). The NTUC rapidly became a part of the PAP-state with PAP leaders in its top positions. The position of secretary-general of the NTUC eventually became a cabinet post.

The 1968 Employment Act and Industrial Relations Act removed many worker rights and protections, giving management full discretionary power over most aspects of labour relations including dismissals, promotions and transfers (Bello and Rosenfeld, 1990, p. 304). This legislation heralded a low-wage policy which could no longer be resisted by union activism.

In contrast to other Asian NICs, EOI was undertaken almost exclusively through the inflow of direct foreign investment.

> The expansion of Singapore's industry in the late '60s coincided with a large inflow of foreign direct investment and is almost wholly explained by this....

Foreign capital has so overwhelmed indigenous firms that the latter have played no role in most export industries and a small role in the rest. (Hamilton, 1983, pp. 57, 63)

That is, unlike other NICs where a local capitalist class had emerged with real political power to protect its interests, the PAP could ignore the demands of its local capitalist class as well as the working class.

The PAP-state's new control over workers and its offer of major tax incentives to foreign investors were successful in attracting foreign investment (Chia, 1989, pp. 266–70; Bello and Rosenfeld, 1990, p. 292). 'By 1968, a range of comprehensive economic, social and political measures had been adopted to attract international capital to Singapore...[and] dramatic results had been achieved in industrial growth and employment generation' (Robison *et al.*, 1987, pp. 7–8). By December 1978, foreign investment accounted for 78.5 per cent of total gross fixed assets in manufacturing. For the period 1976–8, wholly owned foreign companies produced over half of all manufactured exports; companies at least 51 per cent foreign-owned produced 87.4 per cent (Rodan, 1989, p. 130).

This inflow of foreign investment reflects several other political developments. First, the British surrender of state power opened Singapore to all major industrialised powers which could now compete to conclude a class alliance with the PAP. Although the Anglophile PAP leadership may have resented it, the global dominance of US capital induced a shift in the weight of the alliance from the UK to the US during this period.

Secondly, the balance of power in the relationship is revealed in the terms on which investment entered Singapore. The generous incentives offered by the PAP-state to foreign capital show that it was desperate for such an alliance in order to ensure its political survival. Without a supportive and strong local industrial capitalist class, the PAP could not extract better terms in the relationship. In its own class interest, the PAP therefore exposed the workers of Singapore to massive exploitation.

Thirdly, Singapore was an attractive proposition for investment because, like other Asian NICs, it offered an unbeatable combination of infrastructure, disciplined labour and technical advancement. As a result of decades of development as an entrepot for the commodity trade, Singapore had a highly developed infrastructure. The defeat of the anti-imperialist movement and the imposition of a system of social control by a strong state produced a disciplined, docile labour force and guaranteed political stability. The combination of infrastructure and disciplined, low-wage labour meant that, by bringing in advanced plant and equipment, foreign capital could achieve an absolute competitive advantage. Low wages and advanced technology create an absolute advantage because of the very high levels of surplus created. Hence, the rapid development of the NICs because of their greater technical progress and higher productive forces.

Fourthly, as a regional node for transnational finance capital (Andreff, 1984), Singapore could be developed as a close-up platform for penetrating surrounding economies, an expansion of its previous role in the commodity trade. Thus, it must have been some compensation for the PAP that, although they could no longer aspire to state power in Malaysia, they could be a junior partner in a political alliance to skim off the surplus from its productive sectors.

Fifthly, during this period the military guarantee of this economic system moved from Britain to the United States in accordance with the pre-eminence of US capital globally and in the region.

In short, after 1965, the PAP was able to reshape Singapore's social structure in accordance with its political and economic goals. It had the power to conclude an alliance on terms unfavourable to the Singapore working class and to the local capitalist class. If it was to maintain its political supremacy domestically and within a Malay region, it had little alternative.

REVOLUTION AND THE LIMITS OF THE ALLIANCE, 1979–86

In the next period the PAP-state began to face the problems of its success with the low-wage EOI strategy. Having solved its unemployment problem, Singapore suffered from a labour shortage by 1978. Facing increasing competition from other Asian NICs, a strong Singapore dollar and a high per capita income, the PAP-state changed strategy. It decided to move out of low-wage, labour-intensive manufacturing to capital-intensive higher value-added manufacturing.

The fourth phase of Singapore's political economy from 1979 to 1985 is thus the PAP-state's attempt to move away from reliance on labour expansion and from competition with other low-wage economies to a higher technological level of production. It recognised the importance of being on a higher level of technological development if its advantages in production were to be maximised.

The PAP called this strategy Singapore's Second Industrial Revolution. It brought in mandatory wage increases, provided incentives for high-technology industrial capital and intensified its control over labour, the media, education and the parliamentary political process. Although productivity improved and there was some shift to higher value-added production, foreign capital, particularly Japanese capital, did not invest in the qualitative upgrading of Singapore's technological base that the PAP had hoped for. The failure of the Second Industrial Revolution became starkly obvious in 1985 with hardly any technological upgrading of the economy taking place, a 40 per cent decline in investment and slackening demand for its manufactured products. What limited success the Second Industrial Revolution achieved (for example, in the manufacture of computer hardware) arose from the Singapore state's capacity to direct domestic resources in support of foreign investment.

For almost two decades Singapore's EOI strategy had produced average annual growth rates of more than 8 per cent (Chia, 1989, p. 253). In 1984 the real GDP growth rate was 8.2 per cent. But in 1985 this plummeted to −1.8 per cent (Lim Chong Yah, 1989, p. 208). Singapore suffered its worst recession in 20 years. The high-wage policy had forced many Singaporean companies out of business and caused foreign investors to seek cheap labour elsewhere.

> Unit labour costs [in Singapore] rose by 40 per cent in 1980–85, four times faster than in Taiwan and the US, while South Korea's costs stayed the same and Hongkong's actually fell. (*Asia Yearbook*, 1987, p. 236)

With the prospect of a highly skilled labour force still decades away despite government educational initiatives (see Chapter 4), Singapore's labour remained less educated and less skilled than its main competitors while its cost was greater (Linda Lim, 1989, p. 179).

The PAP reassessment of economic strategy after the 1985 recession dwelt on the temporary nature of the attraction of cheap labour to foreign industrial capital and on the technological backwardness of Singapore relative to the advanced industrialised countries.

In referring to the diminution of factors which made Singapore labour attractive, then Deputy Prime Minister Goh Chok Tong stated:

> New technology, the microchip revolution and robotic slaves that do not go on strike for better pay and working conditions, have relieved the pressures on American, European and Japanese companies to seek sanctuaries outside their home. (*ST*, 27 February, 1986)

Goh was reflecting what other analysts have concluded regarding the EOI strategy: 'the permanent threat posed by the possibility of re-importation of these labour processes to the centre as a result of technological innovation serves to increase doubts about the viability of this model of accumulation' (Jenkins, 1984, p. 46). This trend was discernible in Singapore already by the mid-1980s with Fairchild returning integrated circuit assembly operations to Portland because new automated processes negated any advantage of cheap labour (Rodan, 1989, p. 197). Thus, the relocation of production to cheap labour sites was limited temporally.

In addition, the type and level of technological transfer was restricted. Foreign capital invested in a very limited range of industries in Singapore and did not transfer the most advanced technology. This is implicit in the report of a Singapore government committee which was charged with finding the reasons for the recession and charting the course ahead. It concluded that

> Singapore is not yet a developed country. A country's development cannot be measured only by its standard of living, or by its per capita GNP. These are only the manifestations of growth, not its driving force. The driving force lies in the factors such as the education level of the population, and the maturity of the

structure of firms in the economy. In terms of both these factors, Singapore has a long way to go. (GOS, 1986, para. 40)

Lee Kuan Yew subsequently noted his country's lack of technological expertise and added that at least two-fifths of Singapore's key decision-making positions were occupied by non-Singaporeans (*STW*, 5 May 1990).

The 1985 recession forced the PAP-state to recognise that the leading edge of technological innovation, which is the primary mechanism for restoring productivity and increasing the rate of profit, derives from the enormous social power of advanced capital (Jenkins, 1984, p. 41). It is a power which is not willingly shared and which cannot be matched by the capitalist classes of any NIC let alone Singapore's enfeebled capitalists even if vicariously represented by a strong PAP-state.

At the same time Singapore confronted its market dependence on the advanced industrialised countries. Approximately a third of its exports went to the US (*FEER*, 26 April 1990, p. 61). Even with technological upgrading and higher productivity there would be no guarantee of overcoming protectionist pressures to gain a greater share of the market. But the sudden recession obviated this problem because the PAP-state discovered that

> there are real limits to this [upgrading]. In the case of US-based capital, which has largely led the upgrading, the most sophisticated processes are still retained in the US or Europe, alongside pools of advanced R & D manpower and the markets for the finished products. In the case of Japan-based capital, there has been considerable reluctance to upgrade operations. The primary concern to ensure access to the markets of Europe and the US has conditioned the evaluation of Singapore's production costs by the Japanese. (Robison *et al.*, 1987, p. 8)

In political terms this state-sponsored revolution foundered because the PAP-state tried unilaterally to alter the terms of its alliance with foreign capital. But divergence from Singapore's low-wage intermediate-technology role was not purely a technical process. It was fundamentally a political move to extract better terms from its alliance partners. In testing the boundaries of this partnership Singapore found that the political pressures exerted by advanced capitalist countries through the withholding of the latest technology, protectionism and the consignment of cheap labour sites to a marginal role in world production had ensured that the period of NICs expanding their share of world industrial output was shortlived and confined to an intermediate technological level (Jenkins, 1984, pp. 47–8; Rodan, 1989, p. 197).

The process was also political in that it put the PAP's domestic hegemony at risk. The electoral challenges to the PAP and other forms of opposition or dissent which emerged during this period showed the critical linkage between the accumulation strategy and social conflict. The lack of cooperation by Singapore's work-force in increasing the pace of industrialisation after two decades of social reconstruction undermined the government's economic objectives and threatened to undermine its political legitimacy.

Even if it did not abandon its long-term objective of becoming a developed industrialised country, the shock of the recession caused the PAP-state to accept a modest, marginal role in global production in the medium term.

POST-1986: MAXIMISING SINGAPORE'S REGIONAL ROLE

After 1985 Singapore had to fall back to low-wage export production. It restored Singapore's international competitiveness through such measures as a wage freeze, reduction in employers' welfare contributions and corporate tax cuts (Rodan, 1989, p. 194). These moves against Singapore workers along with a crackdown on middle class dissent tightened social discipline. Since that initial rescue package to restore profitability and despite subsequent wage increases, Singapore retained its competitiveness as a low-wage economy because it was careful to ensure that unit labour costs remained lower than those of other NICs where wage rises were greater, such as Taiwan and South Korea. It was therefore still able to attract foreign industrial capital (*FEER*, 26 April 1990, p. 61). Facing intense competition from the other Asian NICs, Singapore once again strove to remain at the leading edge of an intermediate level of production.

Within a few years it was obvious that Singapore's crisis was shared by the other NICs.

> By the late 1980s, the NICs' external and internal environments had been radically transformed, and what had been key assets in the period of high-speed growth increasingly became liabilities. Protectionism was preventing export expansionism in the NICs' main markets, while the economic, environmental, and social costs of a strategy of industrialisation imposed from above by an authoritarian elite spawned increasingly powerful opposition movements that directly challenged the NIC model. Moreover, in South Korea, Taiwan and Singapore, the technocrats were forced to confront the same profound structural dilemma that was unravelling the NIC economy: rising wage costs were making the NICs unprofitable as sites for labour-intensive manufacturing at the same time that their continuing technological backwardness severely obstructed plans to create a more capital and skill-intensive, high-tech manufacturing base. (Bello and Rosenfeld, 1990, p. 8)

To deal with this crisis of EOI growth the PAP-state moved to consolidate complementary economic strategies. It prepared to invest in production in the developed capitalist countries and in its emerging competitors. This was reflected in Deputy Prime Minister Goh Chok Tong's admonition that Singapore's next phase of expansion would be outside Singapore with Singapore-based companies 'investing not just in neighbouring countries, but also in developed countries, Eastern Europe and China'. By this means, the PAP aimed to transform 'a mere city state' into 'a great international city state', from 'Singapore Inc.' to 'Singapore International' (*STW*, 21 April 1990).

An accompanying editorial to Goh's statement, reflecting the PAP position, stated that this investment strategy would be led by government-owned companies and would use expatriate Singaporeans now resident in these countries. The strategy would supposedly give access to technology and skilled labour while overcoming protectionism.

This was actually part of a multifaceted strategy. First, by investing in advanced industrialised countries Singapore obtained a share of the surplus where it was distributed. The long-term investment of state pension funds was an example of this. Secondly, by investing in production in these countries, Singapore intended, as stated, to get access to the skills and technology it needed for upgrading its own economy. This trend by NICs to invest in advanced production has been described in terms of the 'interpenetration of capitals' (Jenkins, 1984, p. 46).

Thirdly, investment in other Asian countries was a way to facilitate the penetration of these countries by the advanced industrialised countries thus boosting Singapore's regional role. This quickly became a major objective.

Lee Kuan Yew noted this role in a speech to the French National Employers' Federation in Paris:

> [Prime Minister Lee] said that Singapore was fortunate to have made the right economic choices, and by linking up with Europe, the US and Japan, had played a crucial ancillary role that had ensured its survival. It had made itself a desirable base from which multinationals could extend into other developing countries. The next key role was for Singapore to help accelerate the development of the region, for as its neighbours grew, it would grow too. (*STW*, 26 May 1990)

Singapore was in a position to benefit from a new form of foreign capital investment which was no longer just industrial capital being invested in production through transnational corporations (TNCs). By the mid-1980s, it was the combined force of industrial capital (through TNCs) and banking capital (through transnational banks or TNBs) integrated as transnational finance capital (TFC) that provided the revolutionary thrust of capitalism in Asia (Andreff, 1984, pp. 58, 66). Singapore's expanded and highly sophisticated services sector with its financial and banking infrastructure, transport and communications services facilitated the integration of the operations of transnational banks and transnational corporations.

Singapore's limited industrialisation and the re-emphasis on its regional role was already well understood by a variety of analysts. Yoshihara, citing Singapore as an example of 'ersatz capitalism' or 'technologyless industrialisation', noted that 'if there is anything industrialising about Singapore, it is because it serves as the offshore centre for foreign capital' (Yoshihara, 1988, pp. 115–6). Mirza described Singapore as an 'internationalised' economy which plays the role of 'peripheral intermediation' and exploiter of other ASEAN economies on behalf of Western capital (Mirza, 1986, pp. 1, 73, 192, 272). Singapore's services sector was therefore increasingly seen as collaborating in the penetration of the productive sectors of neighbouring economies and taking a share of the surplus distributed through Singapore to the advanced industrialised countries. This role of acting as a regional centre for finance capital is now a familiar characteristic of the new 'multipolar' global economy.

The degree of Singapore's participation in this process was clear from its position as eleventh in the world for the hosting of both transnational corporations and transnational banks after the UK, USA, West Germany, France, Switzerland, Belgium, Holland, Australia, Brazil and South Africa (Andreff, 1984, p. 62). Singapore became the world's fourth largest foreign exchange market (*STW*, 12 May 1990). Furthermore, over 90 per cent of the overseas activities of TNCs and TNBs were concentrated in the advanced capitalist countries and the NICs and most foreign direct investment took place among these two groups of economies (Andreff, 1984, p. 61). In the advanced capitalist countries most of this mutual investment was in the unproductive sectors to get a share of the surplus as it is distributed. Investment in the NICs has been directed more to securing the surplus in the first place, both within these countries and, in the case of Singapore especially, in the region.

This renewed emphasis on Singapore's regional role naturally involved greater attention to its services sector. Because of its entrepot role in commodity trading, Singapore's services sector held prominence in the economy until the EOI strategy took hold and manufacturing became the engine of growth from the mid-1960s. Some writers have pointed out that services have always had the highest share of national output: 76.1 per cent in 1961, falling to 65.9 per cent in 1972 and then rising to just over 70 percent in 1986. This compares with the secondary sector rising from 19.4 per cent in 1961 to a height of 32.1 per cent in 1981 before declining to approximately 29 per cent in 1986 (Lee Soo Ann, 1989, Table 13.1). The services sector increased by more than six times between 1961 and 1985 (from S$1750 million to S$11,250 million) despite little more than a doubling of the work force.

> In 1985... the tertiary sector accounted for about 64 per cent of the employed labour force, which is lower than its 69 per cent share of the economy. The services sector, far from being diminished by the proposed industrialisation of Singapore, was highly productive despite [sic] employing a lower percentage of men than women.... (Lee Soo Ann, 1989, p. 283)

In 1984, the average value added per worker in the services sector was $23,958 as against $11,165 for the manufacturing sector (Lee Soo Ann, 1989, Table 13.4). In these terms, the productivity of the services sector was twice that of the secondary sector. But this would be to confuse surplus creation with surplus distribution. It was the manufacturing sector which created the surplus and the services sector which distributed it. Without the manufacturing sector, the Singapore economy would have continued its decline of the 1950s and been unable to upgrade its infrastructure to take advantage of the new wave of foreign investment.

Rather, behind the above figures is the restructuring of the services sector in response to the influx of foreign investment. Commerce, both entrepot and domestic trade, was the life-blood of the services sector in 1960 with 44.2 per cent of the sector's output. But this fell to 22.4 per cent by 1986. Transport and communications rose from 18.4 per cent in 1960 to 24 per cent in 1986. The biggest rise was recorded by finance and business services which increased its share from 15.3 per cent to 30.5 per cent over the same period or from S$248 million to S$3778 million at 1968 factor cost (Lee Soo Ann, 1989, Table 13.3). Despite the declining share of entrepot trade, it should be remembered that, in 1983, 85 per cent of intra-ASEAN trade was with Singapore (Mirza, 1986, Table 5.9). Thus, the main point to note is the enormous growth of financial and business services along with transport and communications, a growth which made these activities the backbone of the sector and gave it the capacity to facilitate the regional expansion of finance capital.

Some analysts date the PAP's promotion of Singapore as a centre for offshore banking, finance and other services from the early seventies (Mirza, 1986, pp. 120–89), while others date it from 1968 (Haggard and Cheng, 1989, pp. 121–2). Whatever the exact timing, it is clear that the Singapore government itself was not fully aware of the potential of its alliance with foreign capital to rake off the surplus from surrounding countries through the services sector. This changed with the 1985 recession and the failure of the Second Industrial Revolution.

The PAP's economic committee, headed by the Lee Kuan Yew's son, Brigadier-General Lee Hsien Loong, examined the reasons for the economy's sharp decline and gave particular attention to finance and business services and transport and communications which, together, made up approximately 40 per cent of the entire economy in 1985 (Lee Soo Ann, 1989, p. 287). The Committee recommended that Singapore

> move beyond our being a production base, to being an international total business centre. We cannot depend only on companies coming to Singapore solely to make or assemble products designed elsewhere. We need to attract companies to Singapore to establish operational headquarters, which are responsible for subsidiaries throughout the region. In Singapore such headquarters should do product development work, manage their treasury activities, and provide administrative, technical and management services to their subsidiaries. (GOS, 1986, p. 12)

Therefore, services would be made a primary attraction for TNBs and TNCs to locate in Singapore in order to consolidate even further the relationship with foreign capital. But, more than this, the Committee recommended a shift to becoming an exporter of services:

Services account for an increasing share of our GDP, and our service exports have been growing as quickly as world trade services. Scope for growth is still huge. We need to promote not just Singapore-based activities like tourism and banking, but also offshore-based activities, like construction firms building hotels in China, and salvage firms operating in the Middle East... we have expertise in hotel management, air and sea port management, town and city planning. These skills should be systematically marketed....

Our greatest potential for growth lies in this area: banking and finance, transport and communications, and international services. It has been growing rapidly, and given positive support, should continue to do so. The government must promote services actively, the same way it successfully promoted manufacturing.... (GOS, 1986, Executive Summary, para. 63)

Usually, concentration on services depends on having strong local industrial capital. Singapore's location, however, compensates to a degree for the absence of it. Thus, the PAP-state has been able to alter its economic strategy, not only to compensate for the limitations of its EOI strategy, but also to maximise the benefits it can gain from this new phase of capital export.

Asked what Singapore could do to promote prosperity in the region, [Prime Minister Lee] said the Republic could work towards becoming a training and back-up centre for multinationals operating in countries around it. It could also strive to be a 'spark plug to fire off developments in new areas in the region', thus accelerating the pace of development and change. (*STW*, 26 May 1990)

Brigadier-General Yeo, a PAP minister, described Singapore as 'a major switching node of the world' for people, goods, capital, financial risks and information (*STW*, 9 June 1990).

One of the latest examples of facilitating the operation of TFC based in Singapore or operating through Singapore is the large industrial zones being constructed immediately across Singapore's borders in Indonesia's Batam Island (*FEER*, 30 November 1989, pp. 69–70) and Malaysia's Johor (*FEER*, 26 April 1990, pp. 52–3). The Singapore government has assisted with infrastructural investments and promoted the projects with the respective governments. Its role has been to open up the cheap land and labour of its immediate neighbours to foreign capital. Singapore is to be used for its services ranging from financial services to communications and port facilities, both in the construction of these zones and in the export of their production. Lee Kuan Yew sees the 'triangle' as 'offering a rare mix of a ready supply of labour and land, backed by sophisticated business infrastructure'. He advised that if Singapore employers needed unskilled labour, they might do better to consider relocating to Batam where workers are plentiful and wages low (*STW*, 9 June 1990).

In the case of Johor, Singapore appeared as the second largest investor in approved projects up to 1989 with M$335 billion committed (second to Japan's

M$408 billion). However, much of Singapore's figure is made up of the investments of Singapore-registered subsidiaries of foreign companies, especially US ones (*FEER*, 26 April 1990, p. 52). It is unlikely that these projects will add significantly to the technological base of Singapore's manufacturing sector or result in significant economies of scale. They may, however, lead to considerable growth and healthy profits in Singapore's services sector.

The implication that the Singapore–Batam–Johor triangle is a relationship of mutual growth is called into question by the absence of substantive mutual investment between Batam and Johor. Rather than triangular, the initiative is more likely to develop as two bilateral relationships with Singapore, leaving one side of the triangle missing.

Therefore, this latest phase of Singapore's political economy has seen the PAP-state moving to overcome the limitations of its EOI strategy by strengthening its regional cooperation with foreign capital. At the same time Singapore still depended on foreign money for 90 per cent of its manufacturing investment (*FEER*, 23 May 1990, p. 55). This indicates no shift away from the close political alliance with foreign capital and no substantial growth of a local industrial capitalist class.

SINGAPORE'S POLITICAL ECONOMY AND SOCIAL CONTROL

The phases of Singapore's political economy since 1959 show that economic strategy has always been an expression of the PAP-state's political relationship with foreign capital. These phases also indicate in a general way the importance of political conflict and social control in the history of Singapore's economic development.

In the colonial period when the economy was little more than an adjunct to imperial plunder, Singapore society moved from a system of self-regulation by ethnic communities to a more integrated system administered by a civil service under the colonial state. Underlying tensions relating to ethnicity, nationality and class emerged during the nationalist struggle for political independence. These tensions and the overt conflicts arising from them were contained or suppressed by a mixture of military violence, security police tactics and the extension of state administrative control.

The ISI strategy represented the compromise reached by local class forces and foreign capital. Singapore's successful emergence from Malaysia as an independent state was predicated on the defeat of a popular movement opposed to this alliance. The EOI strategy was the economic form of the new relationship with foreign capital and facilitated the restructuring of Singapore society to entrench PAP supremacy.

The unilateral attempt by the PAP-state to upgrade the technological level of the economy required higher productivity from the newly formed and tightly disciplined working class. Despite the Singapore government's firm regulatory hold on the populace, this initiative failed. The PAP-state had to confront the limitations of this path to industrialisation.

However, as it had done in 1965, the government was able to recoup its political and economic losses in the short term and to take advantage of the global development of capital. By emphasising the regional role of its services sector it was able to adjust to the new forms of capital export from the advanced industrialised countries and adapt to the change from US economic dominance to a multipolar economy in which Japanese and European capital have greater prominence than before.

Thus, the interrelationship of economic strategy, political conflict and systems of social control have been broadly established. But exactly how does social control work in Singapore? How, in particular instances, is it influenced by accumulation strategies, political alliances and social conflicts? How does it influence them? How are the forms of social regulation related to the PAP's lack of a strong domestic class base? Do mechanisms of social control reflect social tensions, resistance and political dissent? These questions underpin the detailed examination of central institutions of social control in the following chapters.

3 Public Housing: The Working-class Barracks

The provision of public housing for approximately 86 per cent of Singapore's population by the construction of half a million apartments (GOS, 1989a, p. 158; Yeh, 1989, p. 826) is generally agreed to be *the* outstanding achievement of the PAP-state.

> Indeed public housing in Singapore is the single most visible index of the government's outstanding performance; it is the *de facto* monument to the PAP government's success. (Tay, 1989, p. 860)

> In Singapore, housing is a symbol of pride, of nationhood, of the political achievement of the People's Action Party, and of government benevolence towards the public interest. (Pugh, 1989, p. 837)

But the political function of public housing as a mechanism of social control is not widely understood. Yet it is one of the main mechanisms by which the PAP-state has guaranteed labour power for its economic strategy and cemented its political supremacy. A periodisation of the public housing system's development shows how it has worked as a regulatory mechanism and how different functions have predominated at different times according to the economic strategy and the nature of political conflict.

VIOLENCE AND FORCED RESETTLEMENT, 1959–66

The Lee faction's strivings to maintain its political pre-eminence between 1959 and 1966 provide the context for the early development of public housing in the post-colonial period. The early 1960s is often characterised as a time of leftist violence. This PAP-promoted view which focuses on a few street demonstrations in Singapore or on the military atrocities of one side in the Malayan Emergency often succeeds in diverting attention from a more sober consideration of state violence. The British held on by means of large-scale military violence against the independence movement in Malaya and by police repression in Singapore. In 1959 the Lee faction, which had cooperated with the colonial authorities in this repression, inherited the repressive apparatus for its own use.

This inheritance included British housing policies of forced resettlement, especially the 'master plan' to relocate a large part of the central city's population in a programme of 'forced suburbanisation' (Yeung, 1973, pp. 14–15, 78). This was a civilian version of the military tactic of establishing militarised 'new villages' in Malaya. Both were aimed at disrupting as far as possible the social base of opposition political organisation (Hua, 1983, p. 96). The master plan involved forcing resettlement of inhabitants from the two major Chinese quarters and the Indian quarter into satellite new towns beyond the city's green belt. It aimed to drain the pond in which the opposition fish swam. The lush, rolling gardens and lawns of the British bungalow belt would have provided easier land for clearance and resettlement, but clearly neither the British nor the PAP had any intention of disturbing this preserve of the senior civil service and the rich (Gamer, 1972, p. 169).

Hence, rural land had to be cleared. But most of the suitable areas were already settled or under cultivation. This was not so much an obstacle as a positive benefit for the PAP because these areas were also often opposition strongholds. In the 1960s the only major population centres outside the inner city were the British military bases (Wong and Ooi, 1989, p. 794). But much of the work force which serviced them and also the overflow from the downtown area, lived in rural villages or squatter settlements. In fact more than half the population lived in rural or semi-rural areas even though only approximately seven per cent derived their livelihoods mainly from agriculture or fishing (Chang, 1976, pp. 283, 287–8). This meant that farms and squatter settlements had to be demolished and the inhabitants rehoused in multi-storeyed concrete blocks. Resettlement involved the destruction of the homes and livelihoods of semi-rural people who actively resisted the process and the suburbanisation of urban poor who were unaware of the social implications of public housing.

Housing resettlement gained greater urgency from the departure of almost the entire PAP party structure and grass roots organisations in 1961 to set up the *Barisan Sosialis*. The PAP remnant had to undermine both the urban and rural bases of the left in order to survive. The Lee faction also came to realise the value of forced resettlement in state-controlled housing in destroying traditional social organisation which it could never hope to control.

> ...compulsory urban resettlement provided the PAP with the opportunity of breaking up established and potential opposition electoral communities by dividing up old ethnic, working-class communities for resettlement in dispersed locations. (Linda Lim, 1989, p. 183)

> The HDB [Housing and Development Board] has been Lee's effective instrument in altering the political demography of Singapore – breaking up natural communities based on affinity of race, clan, religion, language and dialect or on generations of friendly contact and shared work, and transferring the fragments into compact areas that are easy to monitor and easy to isolate should the need arise.... (Minchin, 1986, p. 249)

Public Housing: The Working-class Barracks

In 1962 and 1963 the PAP-state used demolition teams accompanied by police riot squads against farmers and rural dwellers who resisted. Large crowds blocked the bulldozers in the Kallang Basin and Toa Payoh. But public protests faded with the mass arrest of *Barisan Sosialis* leaders in 1963 and the government's dissolution of the Singapore Rural Residents' Association, the Singapore Country People's Association and many hawkers' associations. The PAP labelled them all communist front organisations. A year later, the largely rural Malay population appeared to recognise that the destruction of their social and economic base was a special aim of the resettlement process. Race riots in July 1964 broke out in a district targeted for demolition (Chan, 1976, pp. 166–7). All Malay objections were ignored (George, 1984, p. 102).

Any extended period of passive resistance to demolition and resettlement by a community invited another method of clearance. Serious fires broke out on several occasions. Coincidentally, few fire-engines would be available, the water pressure would be low and the firefighters would have defective equipment and engage in 'rather odd target selection'. During the 1960s, these incidents became known as 'fires of convenience' (George, 1984, p. 102; Pugh, 1989, p. 849).

By 1966 this aggressive state housing policy had enabled the Housing and Development Board (HDB) to build 55,430 dwelling units which housed 23 per cent of the population (Pugh, 1989, p. 848; George, 1984, p. 101). Traditional social organisation in both urban and rural settings was fundamentally threatened and the social base of political opposition increasingly undermined.

Imposition of PAP-State Social Organisation

To consolidate the political gains of the forced resettlement policy, the PAP-state instituted a parallel process of imposing state social organisation on the new settlements. This was an attempt to regain a mass base and prevent the regrowth of political opposition. Government agencies replaced the grass-roots organisation that the *Barisan* had taken away.

In 1960 the People's Association (PA) was established as a statutory board to oversee the Community Centres previously set up by the British. Vastly expanding the network of Community Centres, the PAP-state used the PA to consolidate its power after the split with the left. Over 130 Community Centres were established in *Barisan* strongholds before the 1963 elections. Besides the usual social and recreational functions of the Community Centres, the People's Association was charged with combating communism and inducing loyalty to and identification with the government (Bellows, 1970, pp. 101–2). *Barisan* community organisations were deregistered and similar services provided through the Community Centres. Each Community Centre had a television set and a radio. The Community Centres became 'institutionalized channels where the norms of the new political community envisaged by the PAP leaders would be fostered' (Seah, 1985, p. 177).

The PAP government was inconvenienced by the 11-month strike by People's Association employees sympathetic to the *Barisan*. But, after a purge, the government was able to expand the network and use the centres as a channel of political communication. The merger proposals with Malaya, military conscription and many other government initiatives were conveyed to the public via this network. It was a crucial means of PAP campaigning for the 1963 elections which the Lee faction desperately needed to win.

After the elections and the incarceration of the left leadership, the PAP-state consolidated its organisation in the community by linking it to public housing. Community Centres were constructed within the new public housing estates. In 1964 Management Committees were appointed to run the centres. Members were nominated by their PAP Members of Parliament, vetted by the security police (Seah, 1985, p. 179) and appointed by the Prime Minister's Office. Many subcommittees were also established involving ordinary members of the community. Thus, by providing a limited response to basic community needs and involving the community in providing them, the government laid the foundation for an extensive network of communication and control which was more and more used for direct political indoctrination (Bellows, 1970, p. 105). The People's Association and the Community Centres soon began to coordinate the petitionary-style 'meet-the-people' sessions of PAP MPs, thereby further blurring the distinction between party and state. The Community Centres were often the site of the PAP branch headquarters. The PAP branches also set up kindergartens, youth activities and sports clubs (Linda Lim, 1989, p. 184).

Citizens' Consultative Committees or Constituency Committees were set up on a constituency basis also as a channel of political communication and control. By 1966 they were established in all constituencies. They incorporated influential local figures into the PAP government machinery, gathered political intelligence and defused local problems before they became points of political mobilisation. Again nominations by PAP MPs were security vetted and appointments were made by the Prime Minister's Office. By 1989 there were 81 Constituency Committees (one for each MP) and they coordinated all the other government 'grass roots' organisations (GOS, 1989a, p. 215). PAP members became paramount in the leadership of these government organisations, although they did not necessarily publicise their affiliation.

> the webs of relationship and interaction between the PAP party branch and these grassroots institutions are strong. This aspect also explains why during periods of political campaigning, these grassroots leaders are usually found actively working with the other party members. (Seah, 1985, p. 191)

This imposition of state social organisation represents a takeover by the PAP-state of organisation and communication where workers live in the public housing estates. The PAP's strategy of monopolising all social space outside the workplace in its quest for a mass base, destroyed alternative organisation and precluded the possibility of new autonomous non-state social organisation.

The public housing programme did coincide with a genuine need for substandard housing to be replaced, but the need was met in such a way as to neutralise opposition and induce political loyalty. The PAP housing policy did have popular support when it came to power in 1959. However, the way this policy was violently implemented quickly became unpopular (Minchin, 1986, p. 128) and reflected the primary political goals it acquired: the supremacy and legitimacy of the Lee faction. The strategy was simple: opposition leaders were put in prison, their followers were put in government housing.

CAPITAL FORMATION AND PROLETARIANISATION, 1966–78

After 1966 and the separation of Malaysia and Singapore, the PAP-state had to strengthen its power base within Singapore and its relationship with foreign capital. It proceeded to do this through the EOI policy.

In order to secure foreign investment and technology for production, the PAP-state had to guarantee a disciplined, obedient supply of wage labour. But, despite its destruction of the organisation and leadership of the opposition, there remained a militant labour force experienced in trade union struggles. The government boosted the level of housing welfare as one means to achieve its objectives.

The PAP-state enlisted the cooperation of local capital. Construction was an industry in which local capital could compete because importing houses is not usually an economic proposition. The contribution to GDP of the housing construction sector more than doubled to 5.4 per cent between 1960 and 1970. Investment in the sector constituted almost half the gross domestic capital formation (Hassan, 1977, p. 15; Quah, 1983, p. 204). Large-scale public housing construction therefore enabled the government to stimulate and control domestic class forces even while embarking on an industrialisation policy which relied on foreign capital. As the local capitalist class was organised, the working class was disorganised or fragmented in order to make it available for wage labour.

The main political effect of the housing policy was the production of a working class dependent on the PAP-state for housing and dependent on wage labour to pay for it. The former was achieved through the physical destruction of all other forms of cheap housing and through forced resettlement. The latter was achieved through the elimination or restriction of traditional means of subsistence and the imposition of a comparatively high HDB rental. The PAP-state's housing programme was a kind of forced proletarianisation by means of the extended denial of alternative subsistence and housing.

In this regard it is important to remember that in Singapore there was no large rural population ready to flood to the cities as in other Southeast Asian countries. There was a finite population to rehouse and one which, initially at least, expected improvement to their lives through the rapid changes proposed by the PAP (Hassan, 1977, pp. 11–14). These positive factors enabled the PAP-state to develop public housing in tandem with its expansion of Singapore's industrial infrastructure and achieve remarkable results (Lee Soo Ann, 1973, pp. 41, 117).

One of the main ways that public housing rendered the lower class available for wage labour was through the isolation of the nuclear family as the basic social unit.

Isolating the Nuclear Family

Forced resettlement in HDB flats not only split up communities but, as the flats were designed for nuclear families, also split up generations and ensured that the nuclear family became the basic social unit. Thus, HDB residents were moved from an extended family context with an active community life of mutual support and a sense of local identity and security into seried ranks of self-contained concrete boxes. 'It was argued that what the citizen gained in running water, electricity, and a better roof, he lost in mutual, neighbourhood, support groups and community spirit' (Austin, 1989, pp. 918–19).

A detailed study of HDB residents in the 1970s revealed the extent of the isolation of the nuclear family and the loss of community. Hassan noted a sharp decline in relations with neighbours. He noted that less than ten per cent of children under ten years of age were allowed to play outside the flat and its immediate corridor. Approximately 60 per cent were not even allowed to play in the corridor but remained indoors (Hassan, 1977, p. 136). He recorded a prevailing sense of insecurity especially among the poorer families (Hassan, 1977, p. 200) and the constriction of social life to the social confines of the nuclear family and the physical confines of the flat.

> The most meaningful activities take place within the confines of their 'flat' which they perceive as 'safe', and less meaningful and more artificial interaction 'outside', that is, at the 'neighbourhood' level which is perceived as impersonal if not hostile and constricting. Their perception of the 'outside' environment is that of increasing constraints which are gradually narrowing the margins which they can manipulate in order to obtain a certain degree of freedom. As these margins become smaller and smaller as a result of increasing fixed expenditures and cost of living, it imposes upon them a cognition of the environment which is ever restricting and over which they have little control.   (Hassan, 1977, p. 201)

Hassan confronted a pervasive fear that his survey would somehow be communicated to the government (Hassan, 1977, pp. 203, 206). Would the government find out that there were more people in the flat than officially approved and take it away? Would the fact that a son is in prison affect the family? Was the survey a way of identifying household consumer items which could be taxed? Was this a check to see if electricity was being used illegally? Most residents also expressed a sense of isolation and fear: they were afraid to seek help for their problems, they did not want others to look down on them by revealing their financial hardship, they did not know anyone to ask for help in an emergency. They felt powerless and that they had to accept whatever the government offered (Hassan, 1977, p. 203).

Hassan found high levels of anxiety and stress along with the health problems associated with these conditions: 20 per cent of adults had frequent severe headaches, 40 per cent had trouble sleeping and 44 per cent had children who had trouble sleeping. The suicide figures in housing estates soared and became politically embarrassing (Hassan, 1983, pp. 161–2). The isolation, fear, fatalism and sickness in HDB estates have been related to the social dislocation, the weakening of parental control (Pugh, 1989, p. 851) and the sharp increase in crime (Austin, 1989, p. 919).

But these problems were primarily related to increasing inequality. Resettlement in public housing did not decrease poverty. A 1958 study noted 25 per cent of the population below the poverty line. Twenty years later, when approximately 60 per cent of the population were in HDB housing (Chen, 1983, p. 15), a similar study found poverty had increased to 35 per cent (Pugh, 1989, p. 850). The evidence suggests that the very poor were the worst affected by forced resettlement (Austin, 1989, p. 919).

HDB residents could not continue to supplement their incomes through raising pigs and chickens (Hassan, 1977, p. 203) or through planting their own gardens (Salaff, 1988, p. 30). New regulations forced them to pay for hawker licences and they were unable to undertake any occupation requiring a motor vehicle owing to their increasingly high cost (Austin, 1989, p. 924). An early comparative study of what were considered the 'worst' slum area and the 'best' HDB housing estate revealed that half the 'slum' interviewees preferred to stay where they were and that many lived in adequate housing or better housing than they were being forced into. A third of those already in the estate said they could not afford the HDB rents (Gamer, 1972, pp. 167–8). Another study showed that the standard of housing in the estates depended on the ability to pay. Poor families, often the largest, were concentrated in one-room flats. This pattern became associated with growing juvenile crime and low educational achievement (Hassan, 1976, p. 253). Poorer families, the majority, found HDB flats more costly, transportation more difficult and child rearing more problematic than the better-off families (Austin, 1989, p. 924).

some conditions worsened when the poor were rehoused from squatter dwellings and shophouses to HDB flats. They had lower room-occupancy rates in some pre-modern housing with 3.6 persons, but this increased to 5.0 persons when they were rehoused in HDB flats. The housing conditions in HDB housing and the poverty led to severe constraints on the chances of children, who prematurely left the education system to take low-paid jobs. The poverty also meant that for this section of the population, homeownership was not a realistic opportunity. (Pugh, 1989, pp. 850–1)

The increasing poverty and the social isolation of the nuclear family in public housing combined to produce a closed, self-protective, atomised community.

> For the poorer families the advantages and facilities available in the new housing environment are cancelled out by the increasing household expenses and ever increasing anxiety produced by this increase. The main solace for many of these families is that by living in flats among people they know little about, they can 'hide' their poverty by keeping themselves aloof from their neighbours and the surrounding environment. (Hassan, 1977, p. 199)

The welfare institution with the ostensible purpose of ameliorating the most miserable inner city housing conditions actually reduced the entire working class to a position of dependence on the PAP-state's system of centralised welfare thereby providing highly controlled wage labour for the EOI strategy. The move from *kampung* (village) or urban community life to housing estate made the nuclear family the basic social unit. By forcing this unit to bear alone all the economic burdens of this transformation, its continuing consumption of state welfare was assured. The way this proletarianisation functioned to fragment the working class on ethnic and gender lines and between citizen and migrant worker, creating a dual labour market, became very obvious in the following period.

HDB: Focus of Dissent

The government's political control was experienced most directly through the process of flat allocation by the HDB. The centralisation of access to welfare in the hands of the state and the decline in self-reliant subsistence alternatives obliged Singaporeans to compete for housing. Therefore, although much resettlement was forced in the early years, the cheaper cost of HDB housing in comparison to private rental or purchase and the lack of any alternative soon led to long waiting lists for HDB flats. This gave the HDB enormous power through flat allocation (time of delivery, choice of neighbourhood, size and location of unit).

The government was also able to integrate HDB allocations with its political goals in a highly explicit manner. In addition to breaking up ethnic and traditional social organisation, it was able to advance its family planning objectives. For example, large families had to wait longer for flats in the 1970s because of the policy of encouraging small families. But in the 1980s, three-generation families were given priority as the PAP-state sought to relieve itself of the responsibility for housing the elderly (Linda Lim, 1989, p. 183).

The changing regulations for flat allocation were highly sensitive political matters for the community at large. Public housing policy and the HDB itself became the focus of much discontentment during this period. Public feeling over state housing was to emerge as a major factor in the 1981 by-election which returned the first opposition member to parliament since 1966.

Blocking the Exits

Having put people in their places physically, the government had to ensure that they stayed there. This was done in at least two ways. First, the government made sure there were no alternatives to HDB housing for the working class.

By means of the Land Acquisition Act 1966, the PAP-state gave itself the power to expropriate private rights in land titles. The PAP-state could acquire land not just for specific public purposes but 'for any residential, commercial or industrial purposes' (Yeung, 1973, p. 38). Together with other legislation (for example, the Planning Act 1970 and HDB legislation), this Act has enabled the PAP-state to increase its ownership from 26.1 per cent of Singapore's land area in 1968, to 67 per cent in 1980 and to 75 per cent in 1985 (Linda Lim, 1989, p. 185; Wong and Ooi, 1989, p. 791). This legislation may have been enacted initially to control land prices and facilitate the rapid development of industrial zones, housing estates and infrastructure. Nevertheless, its application also had the effect of ensuring that the working class had no access to cheap freehold land. In short, there was no prospect of returning to a semi-rural subsistence life-style. The only way out of the HDB estate was to increase the family income exponentially in order to meet the very high cost of private housing.

The second way that the PAP-state tied people to public housing was through the state pension scheme, the Central Provident Fund (CPF). This forced saving scheme linked domestic capital formation (through the construction industry), forced housing and the supply of labour power.

Forced Housing, Forced Saving

The Central Provident Fund was established to receive compulsory contributions from workers and employers (Table 3.1). The worker's contribution to the CPF represents that part of the wages paid by capital for the reproduction of labour power in the present but diverted by the state for delayed payment. The contribution by the employer is a state tax taken from the value generated by the workers themselves in production. The combined workers' and employers' contributions along with the remaining portion of the wage comprise the total wage (immediate and delayed) necessary for the workers' subsistence.

The CPF is a state system of forced saving. But, since these savings are deducted directly from the workers' wages, it is more accurately described in the first instance as a scheme for withholding wages.

Table 3.1 Contributions to CPF
(percentage of wage)

	Worker	Employer
1955	5	5
1970	8	8
1980	18	20.5
1984	25	25
1986	25	10
1988	24	12
1990	23	16.5
1991	23	17.5

Sources: Linda Lim (1989) p. 188; *STW* (12 May 1990; 20 April 1991).

The function of the CPF is to ensure that retired workers can continue to be consumers and not become a charge on future capital expenditure either by the state or the corporations. It forces them to pay in advance to support themselves (housing, health care, pension, family responsibilities) when they are no longer productive. Ideologically, workers understand the CPF as a prudent means of providing for their future security.

The CPF is also a scheme by which you get what you earn – eventually. There is no interclass or even intraclass transfer of welfare schemes which guarantee a minimum income to all retired persons. The CPF reproduces social inequalities and reinforces social divisions thereby maintaining working-class fragmentation.

This forced saving mechanism with its contribution level of approximately 40 per cent of the net wage provides the government with immense control. It works on several levels. First, it is not possible for an employee to avoid the CPF. As noted before, the progressive elimination of traditional means of subsistence and housing has forced the working population to rely on wage labour just for survival. Singapore has no hinterland where workers can go and subsist when unemployed. This lack of alternative subsistence renders them susceptible to many forms of regulation mediated through the practice of wage labour including compulsory membership of the CPF.

Secondly, the CPF has become the only practical means for the working class to provide for their retirement. The options of reliance on government welfare or family support are far less attractive. The government welfare budget is very small and very hard to qualify for: 90 per cent of recipients are single, elderly, unmarried and without family, while the other 10 per cent are handicapped, widows, orphans or abandoned wives or children. Welfare payments cover 50 per cent of minimum household requirements of a single person which, for most, means reliance on a charitable institution for survival. In 1985 the Ministry of Social Welfare was abolished and merged into the Ministry of Community Development (Linda Lim, 1989, p. 187). In addition, the traditional reliance on offspring during old age is severely restricted. For most of the PAP's administration, there have been strong disincentives to having more than two children. These disincentives largely remain in place for working-class families, making support of elderly parents devolve on to one or two low-waged young families.

Thirdly, the PAP-state controls access to the forced savings. It possesses and administers each worker's withheld wages, the only major financial asset each worker has to guard against penury in the future. This gives the PAP-state enormous regulatory power. Non-cooperation with the PAP's economic and political objectives through labour militancy or other forms of dissent jeopardises not only workers' present subsistence but also their future security in retirement.

The legitimacy of the PAP-state has been enhanced by workers having a financial investment in its stability and continuance. The PAP-state has not been slow to play on this electorally, pointing out its own trustworthiness and efficiency as against the dubious reliability of opposition parties.

The direct connection between public housing and the CPF came when the right to use CPF credits as down payments and to repay instalments on public housing was granted in 1968. Less than a third of HDB flats were owner-occupied in 1970 but the proportion rose dramatically in the next period.

In contrast to the way the CPF has been used to fragment workers and to force their cooperation through dependence on the state, it has also been used to consolidate local capital behind the PAP. Workers' delayed wages have provided a huge amount of cheap capital to fund other living costs (such as public housing), infrastructural development and to invest in income-earning enterprises. That is, withheld wages have been used to assist domestic capital accumulation and, thus, to consolidate the power of local capital.

In 1966 there were 417,000 contributors to the CPF, which stood at more than $440 million. By 1985, 1.89 million contributors had total forced savings of $26.8 billion (Ho, 1989, p. 677) and by 1988, 2.06 million contributors had forced savings of $32.5 billion (GOS, 1989a, p. 293). As government surpluses in the late 1970s became sufficient to finance public sector expenditure, CPF funds were increasingly used to boost Singapore's huge foreign reserves (Linda Lim, 1989, p. 188).

Through the provision of housing and retirement welfare (and by connecting them) the PAP-state was able to obtain workers' cooperation or at least acquiescence in meeting the demand for a disciplined labour force. Workers were induced to respond to new demands for production and to submit to cuts in wages and conditions as required. (For example, the 15 per cent wage cut in 1986 represented by the reduction in the employers' CPF contribution.) They were thereby mobilised to provide the labour power for foreign capital to generate large surpluses from Singapore production sites. At the same time local capital benefited from its involvement in housing and other infrastructural projects.

In summary, the period from 1966 to 1978 was a time when the PAP consolidated its political gains over the broad opposition movement it had confronted in the transition from colonial rule. Political resistance during this period was manifested through institutions which the PAP had acquired the power base to co-opt or suppress one by one. It had consolidated the local capitalist class through the domestic construction industry. It had reformed the lower classes into an urban proletariat physically located in government housing which it could pay for only by working in the nearby factories of the transnational corporations.

PUBLIC HOUSING AND EMERGING DISSENT, 1979–85

By the launch of the Second Industrial Revolution in the late 1970s, the PAP had succeeded in housing over 80 per cent of the population in HDB flats. The entire working class (estimated at 80.2 per cent of the total population in 1976) (Chan, 1976, p. 34) and much of the middle class was dependent on the state for its housing. The early 1980s saw a sharp rise in CPF withdrawals for home-ownership, with 28 per cent of CPF contributions for 1983 being withdrawn for this purpose. In the 1974–85 period, housing absorbed from 4.8 to 15.9 per cent of gross domestic product and some 11.6 to 34.1 per cent of gross capital formation. Public housing amounted to 92 per cent of all residential construction by the mid-1980s (Pugh, 1989, p. 842).

But by the late 1970s the PAP-state began to face the contradictions of its success with housing welfare and the results of the increased pressure placed on workers by the shift in economic strategy. The government's comprehensive grip on the majority of the populace through the HDB not only gave it enormous powers of social control but also ensured that public housing became a focus of non-cooperation and dissent. New forms of political opposition emerged to block its economic growth strategy.

The move to upgrade the economy required higher spending on industrial infrastructure and technical up-skilling in order to boost productivity and less social expenditure. This change in budgetary priorities was mirrored in the PAP's switch from social justice rhetoric to the elitist ideology of meritocracy. The ideological hangover of the nationalism (touted as Singapore-style socialism) which had sanctioned the ISI strategy could no longer be sustained when such an obvious bid was being made for foreign investment at the expense of the majority of the populace.

Having stabilised the living conditions of the work-force in the immediate post-independence period, the PAP-state moved to cut the costs of housing. The state grant to the HDB was cut from $68.5 million in 1977–8 to $32.9 million in 1979–80. At the same time there was building sector inflation, with price increases reaching 38 per cent in 1981 (Pugh, 1989, p. 849). The HDB continued its high-handed treatment of its tenants, notably by evicting some residents from their flats in the Anson area to make way for a container port. Evicted residents were given no priority on the HDB waiting list. In addition, the government also continued the destruction of adequate non-HDB working-class housing (Pugh, 1989, p. 846), adding more disgruntled citizens to the waiting list. There were still 76,509 families on this list and they were now faced with sharply higher prices for HDB flats (Quah, 1985, pp. 248, 254).

The many grievances surrounding HDB policy and the lowering of state support for welfare led to a degree of political dissent the PAP had not anticipated. This was expressed most obviously through the by-election victory in 1981 of opposition leader J. B. Jeyaretnam, a result which broke the PAP's parliamentary monopoly for the first time since 1966. Voters sent a message of protest which shocked the government out of its complacency. It quickly increased HDB funding.

However, the sudden release of CPF funds for private housing and the increase in HDB construction then led to oversupply and a decline in home values. This was also unpopular 'in a nation where more than three-quarters of the population consists of "home owners" whose homes constitute the bulk of their savings' (Linda Lim, 1989, p. 186). This displeasure, along with other grievances, was reflected in a continuing trend against the PAP in the 1984 general election results and the election of another opposition member.

The Politics of HDB Ownership

It might be expected that the political sensitivity of public housing would be lessened by the rising incidence of HDB home ownership in the 1970s and early 1980s. By 1985, more than 85 per cent of Singapore's population lived in public housing and more than three-quarters of them were owner-occupiers (Linda Lim, 1989, p. 183; Yeh, 1989, p. 826). This high incidence of home ownership has been touted internationally as symbolic of the PAP-state's success (Quah, 1985, p. 248). The government promoted home ownership as a sign of a migrant community showing a sense of permanence and of commitment to the nation by investing in a home (Ong, 1989, p. 937).

But HDB ownership heightened the politicisation of public housing because it did not lead to greater independence for householders but less. HDB home ownership in fact increased the PAP-state's social control. HDB apartment owners are not owners in the sense of a private freehold sale. Rather they purchase equity in the flat in the form of a 99-year lease which reverts to the HDB upon expiry. Owners are little more than tenants. But the HDB's hold over them is greater than over tenants because of the size of the investment that purchase involves and which owners do not wish to jeopardise.

There are many rules and regulations which owners must follow.

For example, the HDB imposes limitations on the number and family status of people who can live in the units, has to approve their renovation, rental and

> resale, forbids the conduct of business in the units, and has the right to evict residents found guilty of morally inappropriate behaviour, not necessarily with compensation for their equity in the unit. (Linda Lim, 1989, p. 183)

Therefore, owners are not only subject to the same petty regulations as tenants in terms of restrictions on the colour they can paint their front door, the type of pets allowed and noise curfews. They are similarly liable to eviction (and imprisonment) for offences such as dropping dangerous litter over their balconies or for offending against the morality of the state. But, in addition to sharing these regulatory burdens with tenants, owners may or may not be compensated for their investment if evicted.

Secondly, although the increasing availability of CPF funds for housing has latterly enabled poorer families to follow the better-off in purchasing flats, this has also had the effect of easing the majority of the working class into a long-term financial commitment requiring long-term fulltime wage labour. Families have to keep their jobs if they are not to miss regular payments and lose their homes.

Thus, HDB ownership puts many in long-term debt to the state and ensures a disciplined labour force at home as well as in the factory. Even those who pay off their debt do not have exclusive rights over their equity and may be deprived of it at the government's discretion. The fear of losing one's own home, which is usually also one's major asset, remains a fact of life for most Singaporeans. Under this constant threat, most Singaporeans are constrained to behave in their own homes as if everything is forbidden except what is expressly allowed. This fear and the mechanisms which tie people into it have become one of the central pillars of the PAP-state's social control.

Furthermore, the PAP-state's launching of its Second Industrial Revolution in the late 1970s could not have been contemplated without already having approximately 80 per cent of the population within the grip of the HDB welfare system.

Increasing Inequality

Another apparently contradictory trend which emerged during this period was the role of a public housing system which was the envy of other Asian countries in again intensifying poverty and inequality.

> Poverty was hidden but it existed. According to one estimate, it was probable that over 30 per cent of Singapore's households were below the poverty line, thanks to HDB policies that had unwittingly promoted 'shelter poverty', that is, poverty brought about when households had to deprive themselves of non-shelter basic necessities in order to meet the high costs of housing. (Bello and Rosenfeld, 1990, p. 331)

Salaff (1988) studied poor and 'secure' families before and after the initiation of the move from labour intensive to capital intensive industrialisation or what she calls the 'early development' stage and the 'advanced development' or second stage. Salaff's observations show that the PAP-state failed significantly to upgrade the skills of the labour force while deepening the social alienation of the majority of workers and their families.

Many families she met in public housing estates during 1974–6 'exhibited the profile of Third World poverty' (Salaff, 1988, p. 3) as well as many of the characteristics also noted by Hassan. By the mid-1980s, Salaff noted that the poor had been drawn more deeply into the wage economy and that 'the income gap by social-class group remains virtually unchanged. Despite the uplift of some of the poorest, poor men still average about half the wages of secure men' (Salaff, 1988, p. 226). Further, she notes that the increase in wages during this second stage had the effect of increasing control over the nuclear family and of reproducing the class structure while differentiating the working class into a minority of better paid workers in core industries and a majority of poorer workers (Salaff, 1988, p. 262).

Salaff's study noted an increased consumption of welfare (for example, housing and education) by all families. Most families had risen above the poverty line and, although still poor, were now consumers. However, while the outward appearance of family life had become more uniform, Salaff found that the divide between rich and poor had not narrowed and the class structure was maintained (Salaff, 1988, pp. 249, 261–2). That is, through the system of withholding wages in conjunction with the housing system, working-class subsistence had been stabilised.

These conclusions have been verified by other scholars who noted the persistence of poverty in housing estates despite the improving standard of flats and the growth in average incomes. This poverty remained concealed, mainly in one-room HDB flats. The poorest ten per cent of the population still received only two to three per cent of total income compared to the 30 per cent received by the richest ten per cent (Pugh, 1989, p. 842).

The increase in poverty in the 'early developmental stage' and its persistence to the present indicates that the reproduction of the class structure and the destruction of traditional working-class organisation are not incidental but integral to the operation of housing welfare. The increased consumption of welfare was one of the social conditions necessary for the extension of wage labour. The isolation of the nuclear family and of the working class as a whole from its existing social and political organisation in the first stage was developed into further integration into the market economy and wage labour in the second. This integration involved further differentiation among the working class with regard to workers in industries targeted for up-grading. However, the HDB welfare system also enabled differentiation of other fractions of the working class throughout the two periods.

Housing and Patriarchy

The added burdens of nuclear family life in HDB flats have already been noted. These strains primarily devolved upon women as part-time wage labourers and housekeeper–child rearers who were now isolated at home without other adult company. Further, the physical design of HDB flats was not related to women's needs in these roles nor to their values. Low-rise, high-density housing would have been more appropriate to the tasks now loaded almost exclusively onto women (Pugh, 1989, pp. 840–1, 853).

However, the increasing pressures from the involvement of families in the money economy meant more and more women were compelled to work to buy consumer goods or furnishings and to help meet the increasing family financial obligations (Salaff, 1988, p. 233; Linda Lim, 1989, p. 186). The location of small manufacturing plants in flatted factories in housing estates encouraged women into part-time, low-paid wage labour.

In the 1980s, Salaff found that the increasing involvement of women in wage labour during the 'advanced development stage' had brought the whole family under the social control of welfare mechanisms in a way that the wage labour of male workers had not yet achieved (Salaff, 1988, p. 263).

Women workers became a differentiated, low-paid sector of the workforce. A full-time woman employee earned three-fifths of the comparative male wage (Salaff, 1988, p. 236). More than this, women were increasingly employed in even lower paid part-time jobs. Those women not already employed when the second stage was launched were further marginalised. Home-making became even more the sole work of the wife and mother and child rearing became even more time-consuming (Salaff, 1988, p. 269).

The PAP-state later began to show concern about this burden on women, not because work in the home was completely unpaid, but because, with the shortage of Singaporean labour, it wanted to force more women into part-time employment. By this means it could extract more labour from the nuclear family unit without an increase in the reproduction costs of that labour.

A speech by Lee Kuan Yew revealed that the PAP-state wanted to push more women into wage labour without raising the level of welfare. He called on men to 'change their cultural attitudes' and help out in the home. 'Wives have jobs, wives have social lives of their own, wives cannot alone carry the burdens of managing the home and bringing up the children,' he said. However, he stated it was 'too difficult for the state or private enterprise to help lighten the load by providing domestic help or good child-care services' (*STW*, 7 July 1990). Soon after, the government said only 33,000 employees or three per cent of the workforce were part-timers and that it wished to increase this to ten per cent (*STW*, 18 August 1990). It had previously noted that 540,000 women were 'not working' (*STW*, 9 September 1989).

Thus, the forced restructuring of social organisation through the HDB and related welfare systems turned working-class women into poorly paid wage workers as well as unpaid workers at home, while increasing the burden of family responsibilities. The patriarchal relations of the nuclear family were reinforced by the capitalist relations of wage labour.

Housing and Voting

Although it failed in its economic objectives, the Second Industrial Revolution did achieve significant social results. The construction industry with public housing as its major activity acquired a new prominence in boosting domestic capital accumulation. With the delayed wages of workers channelled through the CPF as its main financial resource, the construction sector boom continued to consolidate local capital behind the government's economic strategy.

At the same time the integration of forced saving and forced housing through the provision of CPF credits for HDB flats proved its worth as a powerful welfare mechanism of social control. Working class subsistence was stabilised and the working class further fragmented. Social divisions of class, gender and race were sharpened.

But the sudden increase in social inequality and the exploitation of workers induced by the attempted economic revolution also led to both middle-class and working-class dissent. Women were especially under pressure not only from increased domestic responsibilities and low wages but also from state breeding and educational policies (see Chapter 4). Middle-class women established their own organisations such as the Association of Women for Action and Research (AWARE) and the Singapore Association of Women Lawyers (SAWL) and became active in others such as the Singapore Law Society and Catholic community organisations. Also minority-race resistance became stronger as Malays managed to congregate as residential communities in certain HDB estates.

The PAP attempted to overcome this crisis of legitimacy by feigning equality. To this end, as later chapters will detail, it gerrymandered the electoral system, marketed parliament as a forum of genuine political contest and boosted the meritocratic ideology of equal opportunity in education. With regard to public housing, the PAP-state encouraged home ownership as a symbol of the way that its economic policies were supposedly benefiting every social sector.

The most public evidence of dissatisfaction and of non-cooperation with the new economic strategy was the 1981 and 1984 election results. These demonstrated that the PAP-state had become complacent about its ability to convert submission into consent through the electoral process. It had severely misjudged the level of welfare required when it launched its Second Industrial Revolution in the late 1970s. The political lesson for the PAP was that to ensure the optimal level of social control through state social organisation, a sufficient level of welfare needs to be available from the state.

> If housing problems are not solved, those affected might demonstrate their dissatisfaction by not voting for the ruling party. This was demonstrated in the 31 October 1981 Anson by-election. Accordingly, the PAP government must continue to ensure that Singaporeans will be satisfied with public housing otherwise its legitimacy might be further eroded in the future.   (Quah, 1985, p. 254)

To maintain its absolute political hegemony, the PAP requires the legitimacy conferred by a high level of electoral consent. It faced the contradiction of having made HDB flat ownership such a central part of its social control mechanisms. The working class was unable to build its own political organisations but it could exercise with relative impunity its prerogative to withhold electoral consent as an expression of individual dissatisfaction. The one political action the PAP-state cannot make illegal if it is to derive legitimacy from the forms of liberal democracy is casting a vote for the opposition. It therefore had to change the growing perception by Singaporeans that they had nothing to lose by casting a protest vote. Closing off this loophole in the system of social control became a priority once the government reassessed its position after the 1985 recession.

RESTORING LEGITIMACY AFTER 1985

The growing resistance to the PAP-state's social policies contributed to the failure of its economic policy. The 1984 election results shocked the PAP into the realisation that Singaporeans' outward obedience and conformity to the requirements of social regulation could no longer be taken as indicative of political acquiescence. The 1985 recession subsequently undermined the government's main claim to legitimacy: its record of uninterrupted economic growth. This sudden dent in its reputation for economic infallibility potentially put the PAP's political supremacy at risk.

As part of its response to this crisis of legitimacy, the PAP, from 1986 onwards, began to implement measures to link housing welfare more closely to political loyalty. It tied public housing values to the PAP's electoral success through introducing a tier of local government. It changed HDB flat allocation regulations to remove demographic threats posed by ethnic and class concentrations. It strengthened PAP political organisation within the housing estates and it acquired new powers to enforce social discipline.

Town Councils

An early indication of this tightening of the welfare–loyalty link came during the 1984 election campaign when Lee Kuan Yew threatened that constituencies which returned an opposition member might lose some government services. He was responding to Jeyaretnam's 1981 election and to the groundswell of opposition against raising the age for withdrawal from the CPF, against the HDB's flat allocation policies and against family planning schemes which discriminated against the poor. After the election, in which two opposition members were elected, he said 'the government would not be blackmailed' by the people and that, 'to make sure the excesses [votes against the PAP] were not carried too far...it is necessary to put some safeguards into the way in which people use their votes to bargain, to coerce, to push, to jostle and get what they want without running the risk of losing the services of the government' (*Asia Yearbook*, 1986, p. 226).

By 1988 the government had worked out that Singaporeans were voting tactically to put pressure on the PAP. Prime Minister Lee, at a 1988 election rally, put the issue in this way:

> We are now facing a new problem. With every election, a growing realisation spreads across the population that, yes, we need a PAP government which is good, but there is also that itch to say let's put in a few sticks of chili and we will get a quicker response from the government.... If you vote for the wrong man then I wish you well. You will soon find out. (*Asiaweek*, 2 September 1988, p. 34)

What such threats might mean had become clearer in March 1985 when the minister of national development announced that the Housing and Development Board would give priority to PAP constituencies in providing maintenance for lifts, water pipes, drains, roofs, etc. He stated in parliament, 'This is a very practical political decision.... I make no apologies for it. As a PAP government we must look after PAP constituencies first because the majority of people supported us' (*FEER*, 11 April 1985). The PAP-state carried out this threat against dissenting voters by instituting town councils.

Legislation to form town councils in housing estates was introduced on 25 May 1988 and passed the next month. The idea had developed in tandem with the multiple member electorates (called Group Representation Constituencies, GRCs) proposal after the 1984 election (see Chapter 5). It was proposed that the three elected MPs in a GRC would automatically lead the town council, one of them as chairman. In the end, despite the hurried separation of the rationales for these schemes, the final legislation followed this initial proposal.

The power of the HDB to administer and maintain the estates was devolved to the town councils which would be formed according to the parliamentary boundaries. There would thus be town councils formed on a single member constituency (SMC) basis as well as the GRCs. Town councils would be formed in all GRCs and SMCs by February 1991. Each council would be allocated a budget (SMCs $3 million and GRCs $9 million) and have the right to set maintenance fees, make investments, decide on new amenities and raise rates. The government would not subsidise deficits.

In parliament the PAP represented the town council proposal as giving residents more say in the running of their estates, an example of grass-roots democracy. However, the three trial town councils, begun in September 1986 and covering nine constituencies in the Ang Mo Kio area, were hardly democratic in their membership. Each had a PAP MP as chairman with the other two PAP MPs from the GRC as members. It would appear that the fact that MPs were elected to parliament gave sufficient licence to the PAP-state to claim that their appointment to other bodies was a democratic procedure. The other 18–21 councillors were selected by the MPs and were mostly from the government-appointed Residents' Committees or Citizens' Consultative Committees, the strongholds of PAP members and sympathisers (*ST*, 14 September 1986).

Deputy Prime Minister Goh Chok Tong explained the town council legislation in terms of the government's two main concerns after the 1984 election: encouraging Singaporeans to participate in 'building an even better Singapore' and providing 'stabilisers to our democratic political system' (Quah and Quah, 1989, p. 7). More bluntly he earlier stated this latter objective as forcing Singaporeans 'to think a little more carefully before they cast their votes'. This would neutralise the threat of 'protest votes' being registered as in 1984 (*Asia Yearbook*, 1988, p. 223).

Thus, HDB residents were left in no doubt about the implications for their welfare of voting in an opposition Member of Parliament. The enormous task of administering the estates includes maintenance, renovation, regular repainting of the blocks, collecting rubbish, looking after the environment within the estate including parks, car parks and roads and formulating the rules and regulations about what one can and cannot do 'not only in the estate but also within the inside of one's own flat' (*SCMP*, 5 September 1988). The majority of councils, being PAP-dominated, have the back-up of the state administrative apparatus. The extent to which any opposition-controlled council has this support may depend on whether the government wants it to succeed or fail in the eyes of its constituents. The PAP-state has established town councils to reflect national electoral results and has not allowed a local electoral contest in order to be able to show the contrast between PAP and opposition councils.

> A well-run estate can flourish, while negligence and poor service will result in run-down flats, poor facilities, not to mention the dangers of corruption. Property values of such estates will rise or fall depending on how well or how badly they are run, the Government explains.... Opposition parties which are financially weak and lacking in human expertise view it as a serious threat to their political aspirations.... Politics will be an entirely new ball game in Singapore. (*SCMP*, 5 September 1988)

The sole elected opposition MP after 1988, Chiam See Tong of the Singapore Democratic Party (SDP), may well succeed in running the council in his SMC. The resources of his party can be focused on the single constituency. The PAP-state has regarded him as an acceptable opposition and it would benefit from allowing his town council to develop as an opposition show-case in order to authenticate its good faith in establishing the scheme. It would also benefit because the SDP would spend most of its energy on local administration rather than mobilising citizens nationally on national concerns. But it is unlikely that the PAP-state would permit any future Workers' Party MP to be as successful because of the potentially broader appeal of that party to the working class.

The town council scheme therefore introduces a new level of threat against HDB residents. The PAP-state, faced with individual actions which cumulatively could threaten its electoral legitimacy, has responded with a scheme which ties continuing welfare (in this case the value of flats and adequate servicing of them) to political loyalty. If residents lose out, they only have themselves to blame. The PAP-state has introduced the strategy of the military reprisal into its welfare mechanisms: if the enemy is assisted, the whole village is punished.

In addition to this initiative, the PAP-state continues to reassure HDB residents that it will deliver improved property values to those who support it. In his last National Day Rally address as Prime Minister, Lee Kuan Yew promised Singaporeans that 'the Government could double the value of their assets in 20 years provided they treated life like a marathon and stayed the course' (*STW*, 1 September 1990). He was referring to the HDB's renovation and upgrading programme for existing flats which could eventually double their value.

Removing Demographic Threats

Having split up and resettled traditional communities in HDB estates in the early years, the possibility arose by the early 1980s of informal, non-state forms of community affiliation emerging within the estates. Electoral voting patterns indicated opposition strongholds which could eventually tip the balance against the PAP. The government took steps to undermine any growing sense of neighbourhood identity and security arising from minority ethnic affiliation which might be translated into an opposition bloc vote. It achieved these aims by imposing racial quotas, by extending state community organisations and by further militarising the housing estates.

The Singapore Malay community, although a dispossessed and discriminated-against racial minority, has had to be handled carefully owing to the geopolitical location of Singapore between two much larger Malay states. Malay resentment of their political and economic marginalisation and their cynicism about PAP Malay leaders (*STW*, 6 October 1990) has been reflected in a consistent anti-PAP Malay vote. This began to concern the government after an easing of the rules governing HDB flat allocation and their resale resulted in Malays gradually moving back to their favourite districts, concentrating the anti-PAP vote.

This problem was addressed by introducing HDB sale and resale regulations which discriminate on grounds of race in order to prevent or break up what the PAP-state calls 'racial enclaves'. This has been justified as a move to prevent racial conflict. According to the minister of community development, 'To allow the races to regroup now would be to go back to the pre-1965 period when there were racial enclaves and racial riots' (*STW*, 18 February 1989).

The HDB's post-1982 prototype new town is 625 hectares with 40,000 dwelling units (du) divided into neighbourhoods of 6000–7000 du which are further divided into precincts of 400–800 du (Yeh, 1989, p. 826). The precincts generally consist of a number of high-rise blocks. In 1989, the PAP-state set racial limits for HDB estates (Table 3.2).

Table 3.2 HDB Racial Limits
(maximum percentages)

Race	HDB Neighbourhoods	HDB Blocks
Chinese	84	87
Malay	22	25
Indians/Others	13	13

Source: *STW* (18 February 1989).

The limits are described by the government as non-discriminatory and as 'a balanced racial mix' (*STW*, 18 February 1989). By this logic a block which has 87 per cent Chinese residents is not a racial enclave but a block which has 26 per cent Malay residents is a racial enclave. The purpose of the limits is to prevent the growth of strong Malay community organisation, even at an informal level, which would adversely affect the PAP-state's electoral legitimacy. Also a bloc Malay vote against the PAP which became too obvious would expose the institutional racism of the essentially Chinese PAP-state.

It should also be noted that the growing (mainly Chinese) middle class has not been quite as susceptible to the threats of dispossession and criminalisation aimed at the Chinese working class. The HDB's attempt to bring the middle class within its social control mechanisms has been quite successful (Linda Lim, 1989, p. 191). However, its initial elitist policy of building executive class flats together had the effect of concentrating professionals willing to vote against the PAP in particular blocks or estates.

> With the move to providing more middle- and upper-income units, the HDB first segregated these units in like clusters, but more recently preferred dispersal – some believe in part to allow for the possibility that members of a like-income group (educated professionals, for example) might vote in a like manner, resulting in housing patterns biasing voting results.   (Linda Lim, 1989, p. 183)

Thus, the demography of housing remains thoroughly politicised despite the early forced resettlement dispersals of the 1960s and the imposition of exclusive PAP-state social organisation.

Party Control of the Labour Camp

From the late 1970s another level of PAP-state social organisation was added to suppress opposition and induce residents to cooperate with the new accumulation strategy. In a bid to draw the middle class further into PAP-state organisation, Residents' Committees were launched in 1978–9 by the now familiar process of appointment through the Prime Minister's Office. By 1988, 359 Residents' Committees had been set up 'to promote neighbourliness, harmony and community cohesiveness' involving more than 5600 residents, usually the 'better educated among the population' (GOS, 1989a, p. 216). Each Residents' Committee covers one zone of apartment blocks varying from 500 to 2500 flats. Residents' Committees are officially categorised as part of 'Social Defence and Community Relations' (GOS, 1989a, p. 215).

> As Singapore's population was increasingly relocated in HDB estates, the need to create new communities and monitor and resolve the problems of this large constituency of voters became paramount. By 1985, when 84 per cent of Singapore's population were living in HDB flats, housing problems had every possibility of developing into major political issues. Thus in addition to the Citizens' Consultative Committees (CCCs), the Community Centre Management Committees (CCMCs), and the PAP party branches, 261 RCs were set up in constituencies with HDB populations. Each RC has responsibility for a zone of 500–2500 housing units. Without this sensory system of the body politic, it is unlikely that the PAP could have provided effective and stable government for over two decades.   (Chan, 1989, p. 81)

The value of imposing this social organisation on the HDB estates was attested to by Prime Minister Lee Kuan Yew:

> Look at our new towns with community centres, parks and stadiums. Think of their channels of communication for the constituents to reach the HDB, PUB [Public Utilities Board], TAS [Telecommunications Authority of Singapore], the government ministries, and the administrators who manage them. They have their MPs, RCs, MCs [Management Committees], CCCs, who act like the network of nerves and sensors which monitors signals and feedbacks [sic] and sends out messages in return. It is these invisible ties that make for the sense of belonging, a sense of security of life in Singapore.   (*ST*, 20 August 1984)

Housing estate political control was further reinforced by integrating policing with the activities of Residents' Committees. From 1983, Neighbourhood Police Posts (NPPs) were introduced to housing estates, with a total of 91 NPPs expected to be in operation by the end of 1989 (GOS, 1989a, p. 178). Modelled on the Japanese *koban* system, NPPs have generally been sited on the ground floors of public housing blocks and staffed with 25 or more police officers. Constables are required to make personal contact with every family in an NPP's area and to join the activities of local community organisations (Austin, 1989, p. 920).

The NPPs have close cooperation with the Residents' Committees which, as noted already, are appointed through the Prime Minister's Office. The Residents' Committee office is often located near or next to the NPP. Working with the NPPs, the Residents' Committees had established 71,974 Neighbourhood Watch Groups involving 288,217 households by October 1988 (GOS, 1989a, p. 178; Ong, 1989, p. 943).

The formation of Residents' Committees indicates a trend towards implicating the middle class in the administration of the working class where they both live as well as at a distance through the civil service. The integration of policing and PAP-state political organisation within estates represents a tighter linkage between the provision of housing welfare, political loyalty and the apparatus of state violence.

Enforcing Discipline

That capital produces and reproduces not only its social environment but also its physical environment (Harvey, 1982, p. 403) is certainly attested to by the architectural style and physical lay-out of HDB estates. The position and design of public housing renders workers vulnerable to surveillance and control, as well as making their labour power conveniently available. Often sited near the factories of transnational corporations, housing blocks are arranged in ordered rows on open land. There are long empty corridors with one door for each flat. This barrack-style design enables two or three police in the groundfloor lift lobby and stairwell of a twenty-storey block to seal off several hundred people. This may be a major reason why the PAP-state resisted low-rise, high-density housing long after it had been shown to be cheaper, use space more efficiently and be more conducive to a sense of community (Pugh, 1989, p. 852).

> Placing a major segment of the population in barrack-style blocks provided the police with an opportunity to scrutinize citizen activity more efficiently from a distance. (Austin, 1989, p. 919)

Residence in an HDB flat renders a worker vulnerable to surveillance. Details of who is living in which flat are centrally computerised. Citizens must report a change of address to the authorities within two weeks or be subject to a $5000 fine or up to five years imprisonment or both. This monitoring is backed up by electronic surveillance.

For example, all citizens on reaching the age of 12 years are fingerprinted. This print is centrally recorded and is also placed, along with a personal photograph and signature, on an identity card (IC) bearing a personal number. Any citizen must be able to produce their IC when officially requested. Its number is used in all dealings with the state (CPF, HDB, utilities, telephone, educational authorities, hospitals, income tax, driving licence, passport). During 1990 new ICs began to be issued to coincide with the introduction of a computerised, automatic fingerprint identification system. Eventually all citizens will have their prints in this computer which is accessible to the police and security authorities (GOS, 1989a, p. 178; SAWL, 1989, p. 36; *STW*, 18 August 1990).

Physical surveillance was also upgraded when, in 1988, the Criminal Investigation Department (CID) acquired 'a sophisticated video system...for better and more extensive crowd surveillance' (GOS, 1989a, p. 178). In addition to the various types of police surveillance, other state agencies also help regulate the estates. For example, in 1989 there were 24 anti-litter squads, each of four officers, patrolling the estates watching for residents who drop litter from their flats (*STW*, 20 May 1989).

Furthermore, the PAP-state occasionally admits (Parliment of Singapore, 1986, B154) its bugging of private meetings and telephones, interception of mail, reviewing of personal records, use of a very large network of informers, shadowing of citizens and the harsh incognito interrogation of suspects by its secret police, the Internal Security Department. This much-feared force is just one of the government's internal security and intelligence organs. Its organisation and operations are kept largely secret except on such occasions that a mass arrest is conducted to suppress political threats (GOS, 1989a, p. 177).

With the induction of all males into military service and the encouragement of paramilitary organisations in secondary schools and the community, the estates are also highly militarised through the inclusion of the working class itself in the repressive state apparatus.

> it is highly unlikely that many residential blocks are without a number of police-orientated citizens nearby (for example, retired officers, reserve officers, voluntary constables, or prospective recruits) to aid citizens or the regular police in time of need. (Austin, 1989, p. 922)

In 1968, approximately 15 per cent of Singapore's land area was taken for defence and security, much of this occupied by the British (Wong and Ooi, 1989, p. 791). Today, worker–soldiers live under discipline in the barrack-style HDB estates. In this sense, since independence from colonial rule, the perimeter of militarised areas has expanded to become congruent with the borders of the country.

Workers without Housing

The absorption of labour into the public housing construction programme and industrial production from the mid-1960s enabled Singapore's unemployment problem to be solved by the early 1970s. However, the rapid growth of the economy then required more workers, skilled and unskilled, than Singapore could supply itself. Hence, the approximately 150,000 unskilled and semi-skilled foreign workers from neighbouring countries allowed into Singapore as of early March 1990 and the intention to allow more (*STW*, 3 March 1990). Foreign workers on short-term permits constituted more than 12 per cent of the work force.

The PAP-state, like its colonial predecessor, has found it useful to have a labour source it can turn on and off like a tap without any domestic political consequences. When unemployment rose from 2.8 per cent in December 1984 to 6.1 per cent in March 1986, the government reacted to the recession by repatriating foreign workers (Lim Chong Yah, 1989, p. 213). There were no repercussions for the housing market (already in oversupply by 1985) because these workers were largely housed in company-built and government-approved squatter camps on or near building sites.

Furthermore, neither the PAP-state nor foreign investors bear any cost for the generational reproduction of this cheapest source of labour. These workers are not members of the CPF and do not have the same labour rights under law as Singaporeans. The sensitivity of these workers' conditions is attested to by the detention without trial of community workers in 1987 who had begun to expose their misery. But their poor housing eventually came to the surface with the health problems of the 20,000 Thai construction workers. Since 1982 at least 220 Thai workers have died suddenly in their sleep possibly due to their habit of cooking rice in plastic pipes lying around the building site (Singapore's official explanation) or due to the bad living conditions, stress and exhaustion (*The Economist*, 15 September 1990). The official explanation sought to blame the workers but in so doing also revealed their plight.

Poverty and unemployment in neighbouring countries ensure a ready supply of unskilled labour and there is no need to invest in these workers' welfare either to reproduce their labour or to control them. If they get sick or die, there are more where they came from. If they are foolish enough to agitate for better conditions, they can be expelled immediately.

The visible existence of a class of workers on very low wages and deprived of the benefits of the HDB housing welfare system no doubt serves to remind Singaporeans of how lucky they are. Not being in an HDB flat and not being forced to save under the CPF scheme is definitely worse than being the recipient of these state welfare schemes. But the political value of this dual labour market no doubt lies more in its function as a buffer in times of recession and as a block against pressure from local unskilled workers to raise wages. As the most exploited section of the work-force, foreign workers have no vote, few civil rights and can be physically excluded from the nation at will. If there had been any possibility of these workers without access to housing welfare being mobilised politically against the PAP-state by opposition parties then the PAP would have had far more difficulty shoring up its legitimacy after 1985.

PUTTING PEOPLE IN THEIR PLACES

The development of public housing was essentially a process of physically putting people in their places. The early period from approximately 1959 to 1966 saw opposition leaders put in prison while the lower classes were forced into public housing ostensibly to improve their standard of housing but also to isolate them from political mobilisation. It was a time of routine state violence and the regular use of secret police tactics against political opponents. State violence was also mediated through the forced resettlement programmes of public housing.

In the second period from 1966 to 1978, housing estates were rapidly expanded and transformed into labour camps for transnational corporations. The focus of social control became keeping workers in their flats (using the CPF) and blocking all alternative forms of subsistence.

The main task in the 1980s was neutralising new forms of protest arising from more than a decade of industrialisation and the intensified exploitation and inequality of the Second Industrial Revolution. The emphasis of social control moved to welfare, especially housing and education, as the PAP-state sought the means both to camouflage social reality and to enforce political obedience. The restoration of PAP legitimacy since 1985 therefore required a new degree of regulation.

This exposition of public housing as a social control mechanism is not meant to imply the conception and implementation of a master political strategy by the PAP-state. Rather, as it struggled for political hegemony and then to build a successful alliance with foreign capital, the PAP-state used the welfare mechanisms at its disposal to realise its objectives. It seized the opportunities as they presented themselves. It made mistakes. Some policies had unforeseen consequences. The PAP misjudged the level of dissent in the early 1980s, cutting welfare expenditure at the time most likely to undermine its own support. It did not comprehend the politics of Malay resettlement patterns early enough to avoid explicitly racist countermeasures. The PAP-state did not always comprehend the dynamics of its own systems of social control.

Nevertheless, public housing has undoubtedly been a powerful regulatory mechanism to reconstitute and stabilise the work force. More specifically, the institution of public housing has facilitated the following:

- the consolidation of local capital behind the PAP;

- the forced disorganisation of the working class by physical isolation and creating dependence on wage labour for welfare access, thus guaranteeing the reproduction of obedient labour power;

- the differentiation of the working class into grades according to race, gender and national origin with varying access to welfare and wages, in order to raise the level of exploitation without raising the level of welfare;

- the suppression of political resistance or non-cooperation by tying housing to loyalty to the PAP-state;

- the long-term control of the working class outside the factory by imposing state social organisation and linking it more closely to the apparatus of state violence.

These may be controversial conclusions for Singaporean scholars who have disputed the findings of Buchanan (1972), Gamer (1972) and Hassan (1976, 1977) which relate to the problems experienced by HDB residents. Chan Heng Chee (1976) referred to a government survey in order to prove how happy residents are with the HDB and to refute Buchanan. Quah (1983, 1985), in two similar articles, used an HDB–university survey of 1968 and a 1973 survey by two Singapore academics to rebut Buchanan, Gamer and Hassan. While there may be room for improvement of the latters' research methods or refinement of their conclusions, these criticisms of them appear as little more than apologetics for the PAP-state.

For example, Quah claims the benefits of resettlement include ethnic integration, equating forced dispersal of minorities among the overwhelmingly dominant Chinese population with a move towards national unity (Quah, 1983, p. 206). However, the beneficial effects of this process for the Malays or Indians (as opposed to the greater control accruing to the state) have been widely questioned (Willmott, 1989, p. 589). Also, the persistence of Malay antagonism towards the PAP admitted by the regime itself would place this in question.

Furthermore, some Singapore scholars have attempted to minimise the social effects of high-rise living (Quah, 1985, pp. 250–2) or to enhance the political legitimacy of the housing policy and the PAP-state by pointing to the correspondence between the high levels of satisfaction expressed to HDB survey teams and the general election results (Stephen Yeh and Pang Eng Fong, 1973).

However, my conclusions are not predicated on a denial that the HDB has supplied a comparatively high material standard of housing. Rather, it is necessary to place approval or disapproval ratings gathered in official surveys in their proper political context: the alliance between the PAP-state and foreign capital. When Yeh and Pang quote 70 per cent approval for HDB housing and for the PAP-state, this figure can be seen to sustain the central argument of this study: public housing has enhanced the PAP-state's powers of social control for the purposes of political hegemony and the development of capitalism in Singapore.

There are some goods that industrial workers anywhere must have if they are to survive: housing, education, health, pensions and other social services. Through the way these welfare items are provided and alternative means of subsistence to wage labour are eliminated, control of workers can be increased. The provision of essential wage goods through state welfare can be seen as the collectivisation of consumption in order to manage consumption in a manner consistent with accumulation (Harvey, 1982, p. 91). That is, welfare is provided in such a way as to maximise profitability and also control of workers.

Where welfare is provided largely through companies, workers are bound to them; where a great deal of welfare is obtained through the state, as in Singapore, political loyalty to the state is induced. Singaporeans have been forced to purchase a large proportion of their subsistence requirements from the state. This has given the PAP-state considerable power to ensure profitability on behalf of foreign capital, to manage crises by lowering or raising the level of welfare and to generate political loyalty.

The PAP-state's consolidation of an effective system of welfare provision also has rendered less and less necessary the use of overt state violence to cement control. Furthermore, the way welfare has been provided by the state has the ideological appearance of philanthropy from which the PAP has also gained legitimacy. Institutions such as housing and education have managed the provision of welfare so as to minimise the contradictions between the PAP-state's functions of guaranteeing accumulation and of social control and thereby to legitimise both the state's role and the entire economic system.

Regulation through the welfare system has therefore paralleled the effects of the wage system. The PAP-state's control of wages (through the National Wages Council) and welfare enables it to stabilise working-class subsistence to ensure a level of material security that minimises political dissent. The government's economic strategy has facilitated the extension and reproduction of the wage relation in Singapore. As elsewhere, the extension of the wage relation has been 'to the detriment of all other relations of production, and transforms the mode of life of the wage-earning class by destroying all communal conduct. New social norms must be centrally instituted, and these take on a state form' (Aglietta, 1979, p. 32). One of the main mechanisms for reshaping and regulating social relations has been the centrally instituted state welfare system. The working class is tied into this system which links the need for a livelihood to the necessity to engage in wage labour and to be loyal to the state.

By this means the PAP-state has been able to convert the forced submission of the working class into a high degree of formal consent. This has been a major ideological effect of public housing. When consent has not been forthcoming, housing welfare has also been linked to the coercive apparatus of state violence.

But new social contradictions have emerged in this process. New forms of opposition have emerged resisting state racism, resisting the reinforcement of patriarchy by capitalism and opposing the intensifying exploitation of the lower classes. These conflicts have permeated other regulatory institutions, such as education, which also have powerful ideological effects. An understanding of social control in Singapore comes not from examining one institution, but from seeing the links between institutions and how they function together as a whole.

4 Educating for Submission

Just as housing has been the main social control mechanism for putting people in their places physically, the education system in Singapore has functioned as the premier institution for putting them in their social places. But unlike public housing, education deals with all classes. It has therefore regulated the contradictions of class, race, language, religion and gender across the whole of society. It has had to repress, divert or co-opt many forms of political opposition or social conflict.

In studies of Singapore's education system it has often been observed that changes in the PAP-state's education policy have been determined by the requirements of the economy. Linda Lim has said that the PAP-state followed the 'human capital' theory that investment in the improvement of the quality of labour is investment in future high growth rates (Linda Lim, 1989, p. 172). Tham has noted that the post-1965 educational policies allowed 'the full play of economic forces in determining educational outcomes' (Tham, 1989, p. 480) and Gopinathan has stated that educational objectives have been tied to industrialisation (Gopinathan, 1976, p. 74).

True as far as they go, these observations overlook the fundamental social relations which are being maintained by the practices of the education system. What are the pressures arising from class, ethnicity and gender which determine the nature of social control and limit economic strategy? What changes in these social relations necessitate changes in education?

A notable characteristic of the Singapore education system is the frequency with which it has undergone substantial change. It was undoubtedly a difficult task for the PAP-state to bring a racially and linguistically complex society under centralised state control in order to guarantee the provision of a cheap, disciplined labour force and be able to respond to the changing needs of the alliance with foreign capital.

The rigorous control required to achieve such a result should not be underestimated. Singapore's population of 2.65 million (June 1988) consisted of 2.01 million Chinese (76 per cent), 401,200 Malays (15.1 per cent), 171,800 Indians (6.5 per cent) and 62,800 others (2.4 per cent) (GOS, 1989a, p. 25). Traditionally, the Chinese population has been socially differentiated according to language groups, mainly Hokkien, Teochew, Cantonese, Hakka, Hainanese, Foochow, Malay (Straits Chinese) and English. Although there are regional variations among the Malay community, the mother tongue of Malays can be taken as Malay. The Indian population includes a large Tamil-speaking community and also smaller communities speaking Malayalam, Punjabi, Telegu, Hindi, Bengali or English as their mother tongue.

It seems the task of social control in such a complex society took precedence over a higher increase in educational attainment because Singapore has been unable to achieve the increase in educational levels reached by Hong Kong and South Korea (Table 4.1).

Table 4.1 Comparative Educational Levels (Asian Newly Industrialised Countries)
(per cent)

	Year	Singapore	Hong Kong	S. Korea
Literacy	1978	75	90	93
Secondary school enrolment	1965	45	29	35
	1983	69	68	89
Tertiary (20–24 year-olds in tertiary education)	1965	10	5	6
	1983	12	12	24

Source: Linda Lim (1989) p. 179.

Education has been required to regulate so many tensions and struggles in Singapore that it has achieved a less than impressive increase in educational levels.

This chapter and the next focus on the development of the education system and on the social relations behind the statistics. Education's crucial institutional function in the reproduction of labour power is analysed in detail. This chapter examines the way that the state education system was used to defeat the PAP's political opponents and to sort Singaporeans into their class positions for industrialisation. The following chapter concentrates on the attempt to build a new education system to overcome increasing domestic non-cooperation and to meet the new requirements of a shift in the PAP-state's political relationship with foreign capital. But initially it is necessary to outline the legacy inherited by the PAP-state from the colonial period.

THE EDUCATIONAL LEGACY

Before 1939 the British colonial government did not need to establish a structure of universal education to secure social control. The Chinese capitalist class was largely dependent on the British-controlled commodity trade.

Unskilled, migrant workers were adequate for commerce and services. Most of the Chinese were not British subjects and could be disposed of through deportation when not required. In short, the absence of an independent national bourgeoisie or ruling class in Singapore and the plentiful supply of migrant labour meant the British did not need to rule in alliance with local political forces. The colonial government simply imposed its will.

The system of elite schools established by Christian missionaries provided an English education 'largely to supply clerks for Western commercial houses and the government' (Busch, 1974, p. 28). The Chinese education system set up by language groups or clan associations along traditional lines emphasised cultural identity and Chinese nationalism. After the Chinese Revolution of 1911 these schools became increasingly nationalistic and anti-colonial. The emphasis on Mandarin as the unifying language of Chinese nationalism dates from this period (Shotam, 1989, p. 507). In the 1930s the schools were ideologically influenced by the rise of the Communist Party in China. The schools in Singapore were self-governing, self-funding and provided their own textbooks and teachers (Busch, 1974, p. 29). The British colonial government had very little control over them and had no apparent desire for it until, on its return in 1945, it faced a highly organised independence movement. The rudimentary educational infrastructure which had developed during the first decades of the century then became the site of serious conflict during the post-war anti-colonial struggle.

Education and Communalism

The pre-War communalist strategy of building links with the Malay aristocracy in Malaya and largely ignoring the welfare of Chinese migrant labour in Singapore had to change when confronted with the popular surge towards self-government. British educational policy in Singapore after the war must be seen in the context of its broader strategy to defeat the left throughout Malaya and Singapore by manipulating communal factors of race, language and religion to prevent the further development of unity among the lower classes.

> The British in Malaya had to solve the problem of how to hand over political power and simultaneously keep its economic interests intact. But as we have seen, the only credible and consistent force leading the nationalist movement was that rooted in a militant left-wing working class.... Consequently, it was essential for British imperialism to find an alternative to these class forces. The Constitutional talks after the war represented the limit of the colonial state's communalist strategy; namely, the 'institutionalisation' of communalism in the country. (Hua, 1983, p. 76)

The separation of Singapore from its Malayan hinterland and emphasising its special character as a predominantly Chinese city-state was an important part of the British strategy to keep Singapore as a separate strategic colony.

The post-War colonial education policy has been euphemistically described as aimed at obviating 'the threat of social and political divisiveness' (Tham, 1989, p. 495). On the contrary the British administration aimed to maximise communal divisions so that the strong left movement in Singapore would have minimum impact on the peninsula and the Singapore Chinese working class could be isolated and suppressed. Within Singapore itself this strategy meant maximising the divisions within the Chinese community and between Chinese and other races.

It is true however that the British worked to consolidate pro-British forces and to minimise the contradictions between them so that the suppression could be effected over the long term after the end of direct colonial rule.

The colonial state therefore had two aims in education. First, it wished to take control of the Chinese education system in order to remove a major institutional base for Chinese ideological formation and anti-colonial mobilisation. Related to this objective were the plans emerging during the 1950s for an Import-Substitution Industrialisation (ISI) policy. The post-independence Chinese working class would gain citizenship and the franchise and would change from being a migrant labour force to a stable, permanent majority of the population. A state system of education would be required to regulate this class for wage labour.

Secondly, the colonial government aimed to improve the system of English education to consolidate a local capitalist class sympathetic to British commercial interests (Wilson, 1978, p. 240). As the colonial administration began to accept the inevitability of passing state power into local hands, it began to test out local political forces and to attempt to shape them.

This communalist strategy meant deepening the already wide gulf between the English-educated upper class and the Chinese-educated upper class and eventually destroying the social base of the latter. It was obvious after the war that the English-educated upper class had a monopoly on good jobs and that an English education gave access to and the support of the British administration (Shotam, 1989, p. 507). Government favouritism towards English-medium schools and their graduates added to the grievances of the majority Chinese-educated community. Discrimination against Chinese education and culture became a major political issue for both the Chinese-educated upper class and the Chinese lower class (Wilson, 1978, pp. 114–78).

The government advanced its aims by such administrative devices as the application of the Registration of Schools Ordinance which empowered the Department of Education to close any school used for 'unlawful purposes' (Wilson, 1978, p. 159). In addition, Chinese schools became eligible for government grants if they accepted government control However, aided Chinese schools on average were given 30 per cent of the amount per pupil received by English schools (Wilson, 1978, p. 210). These tactics were bitterly resented by the Chinese community.

In 1954 however, when this conflict was at its height, the number of enrolments in English-medium schools overtook those in Chinese-medium schools (Shotam, 1989, p. 510). This reflects the new education strategy to consolidate an English-educated industrial working class in Singapore and to widen the social distinction from Malaya.

The vernacular-educated (Chinese, Malay and Tamil) were being systematically directed to technical and vocational training and were unable to break into higher status and higher paid jobs. But this method of sorting people into two opposing classes by means of language medium was being progressively replaced. The fact that English-medium schools had a majority of enrolments meant that, not only was an English-educated middle class being formed, but also that the English-medium state education system would increasingly put all classes of Singaporeans in their respective class positions. The criteria would remain the same: linguistic facility in English would still determine class position. The difference would be that the process would be completely in the state's control through a centralised, English-medium education system.

But the Chinese education system still had considerable political power to mobilise the lower classes. Therefore, this policy could not be made explicit in the face of a highly organised left movement espousing a Malayan nationalism.

The Pretence of Accommodation

In 1955 the partially elected Legislative Assembly appointed the All Party Committee to review education policy and recommend an appropriate policy for an independent Singapore. The origins of the PAP-state's education policy lie in the report of this committee. Lee Kuan Yew was a member of it. In 1956 the Committee recommended the following.

- the equal treatment of the four main language streams (English, Chinese, Malay and Tamil);
- the introduction of bilingual education (for most, mother tongue and Malay) in primary schools and trilingual (plus English) in secondary schools;
- the use of Singapore–Malaya-oriented textbooks and syllabuses;
- the designation of Malay as the national language;
- priority be given to science and mathematics as the basis for an industrial society (Tham, 1989, p. 478).

The government agreed to much of the report which, in effect, was recommending two common languages, Malay and English. But, in line with its policy of keeping the politics of Singapore separate from that of Malaya and maximising the chances of the English-educated, the colonial government in practice declined to give higher status to Malay, to implement the suggested bilingual and trilingual policy in full or to open up better jobs for the vernacular-educated. While pretending otherwise, it stuck firmly to English as the priority language. It yielded to the appeal for equal treatment for all language streams only in order to lower the political temperature and enable it to acquire more complete control of the Chinese education system. This was achieved by a new funding policy: Chinese schools had to accept full government funding (and complete control) or none at all (Wilson, 1978, p. 220). This policy was successful in bringing almost the entire Chinese education system under the Education Department within a few years. Malay- and Tamil-medium education remained virtually ignored. There were no Malay- or Tamil-medium secondary or tertiary institutions.

In this way the colonial administration used the ideological cover of a multilingual education policy to move towards its goal of a centralised, state-controlled education system which would be most likely to produce a cooperative English-educated capitalist class (mainly Chinese but including a few Indians and fewer Malays).

The Appearance of Choice

This centralisation process enabled the state to begin putting the Chinese working class in its place. By emasculating vernacular education systems (Gwee, 1975, pp. 89–91) and excluding their graduates from social advancement, the vast majority of the population could be transformed into wage labourers, an industrial working class.

But it did not appear this way. Parents were told they had the right to choose an English, Chinese, Malay or Tamil education (Wilson, 1978, p. 218). If their choice was not possible it was because they were not rich enough to afford the fees or their children were academically or linguistically deficient or their community had not been sufficiently far-sighted in providing the schools or the Education Department had not yet caught up with the demand.

As it became clearer that the job market increasingly favoured the English-educated, resistance to education policies became increasingly vociferous. But the government refused to take steps to provide better opportunities for the Chinese-educated, saying that employers had the right to choose whom they wanted to employ and their preference happened to be those who were English-educated. The government ignored the fact that it was the largest employer on the island and therefore was able to establish the main linguistic criteria for employment. On the contrary it encouraged schools 'to abandon curricula and syllabuses which are politically and pedagogically outmoded' (Wilson, 1978, p. 220). As the increasing enrolment in English-medium schools showed, more and more people were moving towards the state education system in a pragmatic assessment of the better chances they perceived it offered for their children. Thus, the ground was already moving from under the Chinese educational lobby as it fought to survive.

Wilson states that educational policies of this period were 'a determined and partially successful attempt to remove the cause of considerable social injustice' (Wilson, 1978, p. 231). The official education policy may have given this impression, but the actual effect of the practices of the restructured educational system was in the direction of greater social control and the undermining of existing social organisation based on ethnic affiliation and working class solidarity. It was obvious that social advancement was open only to the pro-British, English-educated who previously formed a tiny minority.

Contradictions of the Contest for Power

Although the PAP was led by an English-educated faction, there was a contradiction between the PAP policy of the time and that of the government. The PAP, which then also included the legal left, was pushing for Singapore's independence as part of Malaya and therefore emphasised Malay as a future common language. This was a logical policy for a party committed to a programme of import substitution industrialisation in a region where Malay was the *lingua franca* and in which the predominantly Chinese PAP had aspirations to be a major political force in a federal Malaysian polity.

The British, however, were still planning to keep Singapore as a separate strategic colony. Hence, the policy of making English the primary language. As noted above, the colonial government largely ignored the All Party Committee proposals on bilingual and trilingual education which amounted to recommending two common languages, Malay and English. On coming to power the PAP pursued this latter policy with its emphasis on Malay in order to establish its Malayan nationalist credentials. After its expulsion from Malaysia, there was no political gain to be had from the policy. Its primary interest in its alliance with foreign capital was an English-educated work force. It thus reverted to the British colonial communalist strategy: official recognition of all four languages as mediums of instruction but practical provision for only English as people 'chose' this 'option'.

Lee Kuan Yew indicated he understood the logic of the British position if Singapore was kept a separate state from Malaya when he said in the Assembly in 1956:

> If we had to solve the language problem in Singapore alone, I think the solution [would] be somewhat different from that which would be arrived at if [we] solved it on a Pan–Malayan basis. And I still wish to talk on a Pan–Malayan basis because the other alternative is uncomfortable. (Legislative Assembly Debate 1955/56 col. 1900–9, 12 April 1956)

In short the communalist education policy of the British colonial state was determined by its interest in maintaining it as a strategic colony. It failed to achieve this. The PAP's policies were determined by the political alliances it hoped to make: first with the Malayan ruling class and subsequently solely with British capital. It failed with the first and succeeded with the second.

Colonial educational practices, with their manipulation of language and race for political control, therefore formed the legacy which the PAP-state refined to suit the contingencies of its political ambitions and its alliance with foreign capital. The ascendancy of particular practices and their ideological effects varied according to the phases of this alliance and the strength of resistance against them.

THE PAP'S COMMUNALIST TACTICS, 1959–65

While the colonial state had aimed to control Chinese education, the PAP-state sought to destroy it. Initially, the PAP government had the advantage of not being seen as an alien regime in the way the British were. But the 1961 split and the formation of the *Barisan Sosialis* left the PAP bourgeois nationalists exposed culturally as well as politically. The English-educated Lee faction faced the problem of not appearing authentically Chinese in comparison to the *Barisan* leadership which had emerged from the Chinese community's own institutions. Also, with internal security still in the hands of the British, the PAP risked appearing as their puppets when it cracked down on the left.

The Lee faction therefore pursued a two-pronged strategy to consolidate its political hegemony and ensure the survival of its class. First it used the criminal law and police-state tactics in a concerted attempt to destroy the movement comprising an alliance between elements of the Chinese merchant class, the Chinese working class and the intellectual left. Secondly, to deny this movement one of its major institutional bases and to prevent continuing doubts about the PAP's cultural legitimacy, the Lee group set about destroying not only the autonomy but also the cultural integrity of Chinese education. This was done by replacing the traditional elements of Chinese education with the standardised state-approved syllabus. The PAP-state was still able to claim that the option of a Chinese-medium education remained; a claim which obscured the rapid vitiation of its content. Malay and Tamil vernacular education, not nearly so highly developed nor so politically pivotal, suffered a similar fate.

This policy proceeded as part of a broader educational initiative to ensure that the state education system became a primary sorting mechanism across the whole society. Primary education was made universal. Increased access to state education began as part of the socialist welfare programme of the PAP and proceeded after 1961 as a means to wean the lower classes away from the *Barisan*.

Extending Educational Welfare

Apart from its emphasis on Malay, the PAP-state pursued the destruction of Chinese education and the extension and centralisation of the state education system under an official policy very similar to the previous government's. It had four aims:

- equal treatment of the four streams, namely, Malay, Chinese, Tamil and English;
- establishment of four official languages with Malay as the national language of the new nation in an attempt to unify the multiracial community;
- emphasis on the study of mathematics, science and technical subjects designed to equip youth with requisite skills, aptitudes and attitudes for employment in the industrial sector;
- building of loyalty to the nation (Seah and Seah, 1983, p. 241).

During the 1959–65 period the PAP-state built up the state school system to provide universal primary education, improving facilities, classroom resources and teacher training (Wilson, 1978, p. 235). As a demonstration of its sincerity in aspiring to be part of a Malayan nation, the PAP-state introduced Malay as a second language throughout the English and Chinese streams. In 1960 it announced a scheme to provide free education for Malays up to university level (Gopinathan, 1976, p. 72). It also began to provide secondary education for the Malay and Tamil streams. In 1960, education took 23.5 per cent of total government expenditure, the largest item. By 1963–4 education expenditure reached its peak of 32 per cent of government expenditure, a level it has never again attained (Linda Lim, 1989, p. 178). The PAP-state had to deliver on its election promises to provide higher levels of welfare, especially in housing and education, to attract popular support to itself and away from the *Barisan Sosialis*. The PAP's political survival also rested on the success of the broader British communal strategy for the formation of Malaysia and the launch of the ISI policy. PAP-state educational policies were therefore framed within the parameters of this communalist policy.

> The 'merger' solution in 1963 was a realisation of imperialist strategy which completely ignored the democratic demands of the masses in the respective nations. Once again communalism was employed by British imperialism in the application of this neo-colonial solution to incorporate Singapore and the North Bornean states.
>
> The inclusion of Singapore by itself would, in numerical terms, have tilted the communal equation in favour of the Chinese, but this was unacceptable to the Malay rulers. Now, with the new possibilities for gerrymandering by the inclusion of Sarawak and Sabah, the time was ripe for merging Singapore with the Federation. It was the ideal solution to enable British imperialism to maintain its hold on the rich resources of the North Bornean states (oil, timber, pepper, tobacco, gas) and at the same time deal with the left-wing threat in Singapore. (Hua, 1983, p. 135)

The extension of educational welfare gave the ideological appearance of multiracial equity but in reality the transition to independence saw the exacerbation of communalism as a conscious policy of divide and rule by the British and the PAP. The extension of state education was an important extension of social control.

Control through Standardisation

To destroy the political influence of the Chinese education system, the PAP-state continued the British policy of funding only schools which accepted state control and of arresting the main anti-government leaders. But it had to go much further.

In 1961 Chinese schools were instructed to follow the English-medium school pattern of primary, secondary and tertiary education. Examination boycotts by Chinese-medium students followed but failed (Arumugam, 1975, p. 63). By 1963 there was a standard system of education to which all language streams had to conform: six years primary, four years secondary and two years pre-university.

> In addition, the government undertook a crash programme to build public, Chinese-language schools so that no longer would parents desiring this type of education have to send their children to radical schools. Rules of accreditation were also arranged so that schools defying government control could not provide the same benefits to students of more compliant Chinese-medium institutions. More (though still not enough) job opportunities were provided to Chinese-medium graduates so that potential opposition leaders were increasingly drained away from communist-affiliated organisations. Finally, the structures surrounding the school system were also attended to. School committees that had provided funds for Chinese education and had managed the schools had also afforded a means whereby local elites could have their status recognised and where they could exercise leadership. Similar committees were organised by the government to perform these functions – but under government control.... The point emerging from all these developments is that the government breached the structural integrity of the Chinese community, undercut its radical leadership, and established a far-reaching organisational basis for its support. (Busch, 1974, pp. 128–9)

The cruellest blow to Chinese education was the frontal attack on its premier institution, Nanyang University. Established in 1956 as a Mandarin-medium university for Southeast Asian Chinese, Nanyang became a vibrant centre of classical Chinese learning and left politics. Funded by wealthy Chinese entrepreneurs, the Hokkien clan association and even by taxi and trishaw drivers who contributed a day's earnings to its foundation, it was the symbol of Chinese educational achievement (Turnbull, 1989, p. 241; Chew, 1982, p. 65).

In the process of its humbling, students and faculty were arrested, expelled or deported for their political activities. The imposed curriculum reorganisation of Nanyang in 1964 led to widespread protest which was summarily suppressed. The citizenship of its prime benefactor and millionaire founder, Tan Lark Sye, was revoked because, said the government, 'out of extreme racialist sentiment he knowingly allowed himself to be used by his associates to advocate the communist cause in Malaya'. In fact Tan helped to finance some *Barisan Sosialis* candidates in the 1963 elections (George, 1984, pp. 131, 138). Ngee Ann College, another Chinese tertiary institution founded by the Teochew association in 1963, was quickly brought into line with similar imposed changes in 1966 (Arumugam, 1975, p. 63).

Class Discrimination and Communalism

Under its multiracial educational policy the PAP-state claimed to be building a just, multiracial society. But even apart from its outright assault on Chinese education, the measures it took were not aimed at upholding the cultural integrity of vernacular education. In 1959 a government programme began which integrated two or more language streams within a single school ostensibly to aid the intermingling of races (Gopinathan, 1976, p. 72). But the main effect of integrated schools was to bring all vernacular education under state control and thereby open all language streams to standardisation and centralisation.

In 1960 the introduction of the Primary School Leaving Examination (PSLE) assisted the enforcement of a standard syllabus across all four language streams. It was a standard national state examination which all students, regardless of language medium, had to pass in order to continue their studies.

The First State Development Plan 1960–4, with its agenda of industrialisation, brought an immediate emphasis on mathematics, science and technical subjects and bursaries were made available to those willing to take subjects, in the words of the education minister, 'considered desirable by the Government' (Wilson, 1978, p. 234). The need for vocational and technical streams was officially recognised and it was recommended that only 20 per cent of primary school graduates be channelled into the academic stream (Gopinathan, 1976, p. 74; Seah and Seah, 1983, p. 242). The academic stream consisted overwhelmingly of the English-educated.

The policy of equal treatment for all language streams appeared fair and came to be accepted as a political principle by the public. But the racial integration policy was in fact an ideological cover for an all-out attack on Chinese education and for the reproduction of a Chinese-, Malay- and Tamil-speaking industrial working class and an English-speaking capitalist class.

In addition, the apparently non-communal policy commitment to Malay as the national language and to bilingual and trilingual education disguised the fact that English would continue to be the language of business in Singapore (Tham, 1989, p. 478). To those being sorted by these practices, it seemed fair to be learning two or three languages and that all language streams received standard treatment. This provided the ideological legitimation the PAP-state needed.

Since there was already an efficient Chinese education system to a high level, equal treatment for all streams would more logically have involved increased state funding to set up autonomous education systems for the Malay and Tamil streams. But the political interest of the PAP-state was to undermine the autonomy of Chinese education and, as a side product, to attempt to win Malay support by portraying itself as genuinely multiracial. Chinese educationalists therefore were lambasted as communalist chauvinists and as antagonistic to the interests of a multiracial society (George, 1984, p. 138).

There was equal treatment of all language streams in that all were brought under a standardised, centralised PAP-state education system. The vernacular-educated, regardless of linguistic background or ethnicity, were channelled into a class-specific education which prepared them for wage labour. This was the actual effect of educational sorting designed to exploit the contradictions of communalism for political purposes. It was not yet obvious to the ordinary citizen that a deeply discriminatory, meritocratic education system was being established.

Failure of Communalist Tactics

On one level the PAP's communalist tactics failed. In federal Malaysian politics, the PAP was using the same strategy of heightening communalism for political ends under the guise of preaching the merits of multi-racialism.

But instead of threatening Chinese educationalists for their alleged chauvinism as in Singapore, in Malaya the PAP played to Chinese chauvinism in its attempt to supplant the Malayan Chinese Association (MCA). The MCA was the party through which Chinese entrepreneurs had built a political alliance with the Malay ruling class to form a governing federal coalition which itself ruled in cooperation with British capital. In the federal parliament the PAP was in opposition but aimed to replace the MCA in the governing coalition. It therefore sought to attract Malayan Chinese support by increasingly communalist appeals.

> It was quite evident that the PAP's challenge of 'Malay Special Rights' was basically an appeal to the communalist sentiments of the non-Malays in its attempt to extend its interests in the mainland.... [T]hroughout 1963–65, Lee and the PAP created a highly charged atmosphere of communalism within Malaysia. (Hua, 1983, pp. 142–3)

Lee was hardly advancing the cause of multi-racialism when he threatened the Malay leadership in Kuala Lumpur: 'Supposing we real, virile Chinese unite, there would be trouble in five or ten years, because there are five million Chinese, 42 per cent of the population' (George, 1984, p. 78).

But the PAP miscalculated by raising the political temperature in Malaya to the point that the Malay ruling party, the United Malay National Organisation (UMNO), expelled Singapore from the Federation.

The PAP's extension of social control through a system of state universal education had aimed to produce both political supremacy within Singapore and the labour power for import-substitution industrialisation in a federal Malayan polity.

While rather successful in these objectives, the more blatant communalist tactics at a federal level failed. The PAP-state was unable to use the strength of its newly achieved domestic control in Singapore as a springboard to political dominance on a wider stage.

FROM COMMUNALISM TO MERITOCRACY, 1966–77

Singapore's expulsion from Malaysia did not mean the end of communalist education policies. Rather it led to their incorporation into a more sophisticated meritocratic sorting process. Education played a major role in restructuring political relationships in the island-state in accordance with the new economic strategy necessitated by separation.

The political alliance behind the EOI strategy between the English-educated, mainly Chinese, PAP fraction of the Singapore capitalist class and foreign capital (increasingly from the United States rather than Britain) brought a new emphasis to the importance of English literacy, to being Chinese and to loyalty to the PAP, attributes that had begun to acquire a certain relativity in a Malaysian polity. Without the large Malay population of Malaysia, the PAP had a simplified task in sorting its majority Chinese population.

The PAP-state jettisoned one of the major educational objectives it was previously required to meet as a Malaysian state. The emphasis on Malay as the national *lingua franca* and the upgrading of Malay-medium education was dropped in practice although regional geopolitical sensitivities required continuing lip service to it.

The shaping of the education system for centralised control and people-sorting according to the needs of foreign capital and PAP-state hegemony could thus proceed with simplified criteria of merit. English, the language of foreign capital, would be the indisputable and sole language of merit. Facility in English (or the lack of it) would be the ostensibly neutral criterion for placing Singaporeans in their social places. But since English was the language of the Chinese and Indian middle and upper classes, an educational system which favoured English would continue to reinforce the connections between class, language and race. English would unite the middle and upper classes across ethnic divides while excluding the working class of all races. In this way the 'neutral' criterion would ensure the reproduction of the capitalist class and the consolidation of an industrial proletariat.

This reassertion of meritocratic educational practices also involved the intensification of control over the newly centralised, standardised education system and the mopping up of the remnants of the Chinese education system. By 1965 much of the groundwork had been done. The period of merger with Malaysia had achieved one of the PAP's objectives: the final rout of the left and the destruction of its political organisation. It remained for the PAP-state to institutionalise its political gains by refining the mechanisms of meritocracy and systematising their ideological effects.

Bilingual Strategy for English Dominance

With the complications of Malaysian political life behind it the PAP-state was able essentially to revert to the 1956 colonial educational prescriptions: the reproduction of an English-educated capitalist class and the formation of a technically skilled working class with sufficient facility in English to perform the labour required of them. The promotion of bilingualism and technical education put the mechanisms of social control in place to bring this policy to fruition.

> The post-Malaysian period formed the watershed in the history of education as the emphasis on both bilingual and technical education was stressed with political independence and the resulting need to restructure the economy so that Singapore could become economically viable as an island state. (Seah and Seah, 1983, p. 242)

The bilingual policy meant that one of the languages learnt by every student would be English which would then become the common language. In other words the policy ensured that English would eventually gain almost complete supremacy as the first language of the education system and the national language of intercommunal communication. In 1966 all first-year secondary pupils were required to learn a second language. From 1969 all students had to offer a second language in the school certificate examinations. By that time over one-quarter of primary and three-quarters of secondary schools were of the integrated type which combined language streams within one school. These schools failed in their stated aim of fostering better inter-racial contact and of ensuring students became effectively bilingual. Furthermore, non-integrated exclusively English-medium schools were seen to maintain higher academic standards (Arumugam, 1975, pp. 64–5). As a result the bilingual policy actually encouraged parents to send their children to English-medium schools because they could be assured of a higher standard of English learning and, thus, better job prospects, while still being taught their mother tongue as a second language. By 1968 57 per cent of Chinese students were in the English-medium stream and 43 per cent in the Chinese-medium stream.

Mathematics, science and technical subjects were emphasised by the PAP-state as the basis of education for nation-building and industrialisation. In 1966 mathematics and science were required to be taught in English in the first-year classes of non-English-medium primary schools (Seah and Seah, 1983, p. 242). By 1969 all pupils were streamed into academic, technical or vocational schools after their primary education, essentially on the basis of their aptitude in English.

By 1975 all schools, regardless of language medium, were required to teach mathematics and science in English at all levels while other subjects such as history, civics and geography could be taught in the second language (Arumugam, 1975, pp. 66–7).

The emphasis on English and science effectively downgraded both a vernacular-medium education and a liberal arts education. Not only might these latter social formations render students susceptible to political mobilisation against the PAP-state but they also enabled students to avoid the core 'language' of industrialisation: science and technology. English was the way to this deeper 'language'.

The speed with which English gained ascendancy as the *de facto lingua franca* was justified by the government on the grounds that it was an international language and the language of modernity, of science and technology. Apparently no longer the hated language of colonialism, it was, according to the English-educated PAP leadership, a neutral language for use by all racial groups. The PAP justified English on the basis that it was the language of investing industrialists and that its continued use would mean continuity in records, administration and law in Singapore (Gopinathan, 1976, p. 76; Wilson, 1978, p. 236). But it strove to characterise its policy as intercommunal and internationalist rather than as favouring what had been popularly regarded as the international language of imperialism.

> Singapore thus appears unique, in Southeast Asia, in encouraging the use of the language of its former colonial rulers, and it is tempting to suppose that, although nowhere clearly stated as a matter of policy, this has been the aim of the Government. By 1970, enrolment in English-medium schools was considerably in excess of that in all other schools combined. (Wilson, 1978, p. 237)

Within a few years of independence the educational system which claimed to be giving equal weight to the four language streams was in fact becoming a single stream favouring English. The language of merit and of Singapore's political economy was indisputably English. The subjects of merit were mathematics and science. The priorities and needs of the EOI policy had defined the route to educational success and upward social mobility.

Mandarin: The Second Language

The bilingual policy helped the government to avoid any community's last-ditch resistance to the loss of their vernacular by promising that it would always be available as a second language in the education system. This was a comparatively simple matter with the minority Malay and Indian communities who spoke mainly Malay and Tamil and could be forced to fall in line with state policy.

But the bilingual policy raised some contradictions for the majority Chinese community with its entrenched dialect affiliations (Hokkien, Hakka, Teochew, Cantonese, Hainanese, Foochow and Malay). As the mother tongues of the Chinese working class they exerted a powerful political force in terms of kinship and other primary social relationships. These linguistic affiliations stood in the way of rendering the Chinese working class more susceptible to direct political control. The bilingual policy attempted to disorganise dialect communities by unilaterally laying down that the mother-tongue of every Chinese was Mandarin even though less than one per cent of Singapore Chinese had Mandarin as their mother-tongue (Chew, 1982, p. 66).

Mandarin had been the symbolic language for uniting Chinese linguistic communities around the political agenda of the left. The cultural integrity of the Chinese education system which nurtured this tradition had been destroyed by the PAP. But the language itself remained in a few prestigious Chinese-medium institutions which were potential bases for a cultural resurgence. The bilingual policy provided both the rationale for finally dismantling the institutional remnant of Chinese education and the means of co-opting the symbolic significance of Mandarin for the PAP-state's political purposes. From 1969 the bilingual policy made it possible for the PAP-state to appease Chinese public opinion with the encouragement of Mandarin as a second language to English while, at the same time, completing the demolition of the Chinese education system.

For example, the government stated that students of Nanyang University must be effectively bilingual in English and Chinese (Mandarin). Using this as justification, all first-year classes were conducted in English from 1975. In 1978 first-year classes were combined with the English-medium University of Singapore. The same year the real agenda was stated by a PAP minister: 'The medium of instruction at all tertiary institutions is and will be English' (Chew, 1982, p. 65). By 1979 only Chinese language and literature were taught in Mandarin. In 1980 Nanyang was forced to merge with the University of Singapore to form the National University of Singapore. As final ignominy, Nanyang's prestigious campus was made into a technical institute as had that of Ngee Ann College before it. By this time Nanyang had already been starved of the highest calibre of faculty and students and its financial base had been eroded.

The previous destruction of the left and this systematic dismantling of the Chinese education system now made Mandarin available for the political agenda of the PAP-state. Some observers have seen the second language policy of Mandarin as having the objective of building up ethnic solidarity and pride among Chinese. By making all Chinese equally proficient in Mandarin, the PAP-state may have hoped to ensure their loyalty and negate the entrenched Malay resistance to PAP rule (Busch, 1974, p. 112). There may be some truth in this observation that, once again, the PAP was engaging in communal tactics to ensure its own political longevity.

But a more important reason may have been the PAP's determination to open Chinese communities to the use of English by denying them their own mother-languages at any point in the education system. The mandatory Mandarin bilingual policy immediately restricted actual Chinese mother tongues to domestic use within each community. These languages were progressively eliminated as children were schooled in English and Mandarin, languages unknown to their parents and grandparents (*FEER*, 20 June 1991, p. 17). In addition, the Mandarin policy gave the PAP-state added power to put Chinese in their social place. Instead of using Mandarin as a unifying language, the PAP used it as a weapon to break down Chinese social structure and to reconstitute the community as an atomised working class. This led to the historical irony of the English-educated PAP wielding the cultural authority of Mandarin and, in its own political interests, imposing the language as the sole language of intracommunity communication.

Contradictions of Promoting English

Following the linguistic agenda of foreign capital also brought contradictions especially in administration and political control. The administrative complexity of promoting English, while pretending otherwise, in such a linguistically diverse society inevitably brought confusion and resistance. In the early years of its rule the PAP-state found that some of the changes it imposed on the education system failed to achieve the expected results and had to be changed. Sometimes changes were obstructed. Often those most involved in the process of education, such as principals and teachers, were not consulted and subsequently disagreed with or did not understand the point of the changes.

The government therefore formalised the channels of 'consultation' under its control through which educational advice would be acceptable, thus rendering other responses *ad hoc,* unacceptable and politically hostile. For example, the Advisory Committee on Curriculum Development was set up in 1970 for the 'harmonising of subject objectives with overall objectives' (Wilson, 1978, p. 238). But such actions merely contained dissent in the short term. The contradictory effects of policies which aimed to reconstitute the whole linguistic configuration of the population demanded frequent changes to educational practices. This instability, as noted at the beginning of the chapter, undermined the overall increase in educational levels.

Just as worrying for the PAP was the fact that English is an international language which increasingly opened the local community to outside influences as more people learned it. The PAP leadership knew that English gave access to liberal democratic values, having themselves been introduced to parliamentary politics by this route. The ferment of student and worker uprisings in Europe and the anti-Vietnam war movement in the USA at the end of the decade, as well as the counter-cultural movements, no doubt added to their fears that these social and political traditions would become more widely accessible within Singapore as English usage spread. This introduced a major problem of political control.

This concern was focused on Chinese students more than Malays and the PAP framed the problem in terms of losing Asian culture and values under the onslaught of Western permissiveness. Malays were less likely to lose their culture because of their residence within the geographical area of their cultural heritage. Also the PAP had already consigned the Malays to a vernacular-speaking underclass who had little access to Western political traditions anyway. But having demolished the Chinese education system, the PAP-state's real concern cannot have been the preservation of Chinese culture. Rather its project was to consolidate a larger English-speaking Chinese governing class while restricting its politicisation to the PAP programme.

To achieve this end the government suppressed the local media, restricted the foreign media, controlled local non-government organisations and prevented international NGOs (such as Oxfam) from locating regional headquarters in Singapore (Asia Watch, 1989). In education it attempted to use the mother tongue strategy to portray outside political influence as alien and un-Asian and to prevent the development of non-government international links.

As early as December 1966 the Ministry of Education began to plan a comprehensive programme for moral education and social discipline (Chan Heng Chee, 1971, p. 52). From 1972 the learning of the mother-tongue was promoted as reinforcing traditional Asian values. The latter appeared to be the PAP-state's answer to questions of morals and discipline. While English was necessary for economic success, the mother tongue, according to Lee Kuan Yew, was necessary for 'the ethics, values of work and discipline in an orderly society' (*The Mirror*, 20 November 1972). In this way the mother-tongue emphasis was used as a political prophylactic.

In 1974 as the English-educated students at the University of Singapore were demonstrating in support of retrenched workers from TNC factories, the PAP-state launched its Education for Living (EFL) and Civics courses into primary and secondary schools, respectively (Chiew, 1983, p. 257). These courses aimed to instil Asian moral values of thrift, filial duty, obedience to authority and loyalty to the government.

These traditional values, supposedly absorbed through the device of language lessons in the mother-tongue, were termed 'cultural ballast' by the government (Gopinathan, 1976, p. 77), a revealing term that it has continued to use (GOS, 1989a, p. 187). Ballast, while assisting the navigation of a steady course, is also, by definition, dispensable and unimportant in itself. This reinforces the analysis that English, mathematics and science were the core of education, while the 'mother tongue' (relegated to the position of 'second language') and Asian values were merely dispensable weightage for controlling the course set by the priorities of the alliance with foreign capital. Thus, from the early 1970s schools were enjoined to supply an English education geared to serving export-oriented industrialisation while simultaneously being required to build into the minds of students the supposed means of psychological control and political legitimation. The outbreak of political dissent in the 1980s would appear to mark the partial failure of this initiative.

Controlling the Centralised System

In suppressing dissent within educational institutions, the PAP-state was aiming to control three forms of political opposition which were often related: socialism, communal self-determination and liberal democratic parliamentarism. The PAP had crushed the left movement, demolished educational institutions nourishing communal independence and co-opted linguistic and cultural traditions. But the existence of strong, English-medium, liberal democratic institutions like the parliament and the university provided possible institutional avenues for an eventual resurgence of all these dissenting forces.

Between 1966 and 1977 the PAP-state therefore tightened its grip on these institutions. It mainly used the criminal law in combination with administrative restructuring and personal intimidation. These direct methods of control were used during the decade to make sure that the meritocratic educational system was set in place and loyally administered. Direct political control of all educational institutions prevented obstruction of restructuring by unsympathetic professional educationalists and prevented opposition forces and an alternative political leadership from emerging through the newly centralised education system.

On one level this intensified control ensured that the benefits of conformity to the criteria of merit were explicitly connected to political loyalty through the introduction in 1966 of a flag-raising ceremony, recitation of an oath of loyalty and the singing of the national anthem every day at every school. The expansion of uniformed cadet units at schools followed in the late 1960s (Gopinathan, 1976, p. 74) along with the introduction of military education for all males in the form of National Service which began in 1969 (Chew, 1982, p. 196). These innovations not only assisted the PAP-state to generate a sense of crisis concerning the survival of the nation. In focusing on nationalistic loyalty to the PAP-state, they also ideologically obfuscated the reality of the subordinate relationship of the PAP-state to foreign capital.

On another level the government went to considerable lengths to ensure that the education system could never again become the base for political opposition. Entrance to university was made conditional on the issuance of a political suitability certificate issued by the internal security police. Individual dossiers were maintained on all students by the security authorities which were referred to at the time of employment (Wilson, 1978, pp. 238–9; George, 1984, p. 137). In 1970 Lee Kuan Yew told students not to take political science, philosophy and sociology but to take more useful subjects (such as science, medicine and law). The following year the Public Service Commission stopped all bursaries for students taking these subjects. Since that time the arts and social science subjects have attracted those who could not get in to the more prestigious, officially approved subjects (Clammer, 1985, p. 160).

PAP operatives and infrastructure were inserted at all levels of the system. PAP members were introduced into the university administration, faculty and student organisations. Expatriate faculty were marginalised: all were forbidden to be involved in local issues and some were expelled. The University of Singapore Vice-Chancellor resigned over state interference in the university. In 1968 he was replaced by Dr Toh Chin Chye, Deputy Prime Minister and Chairman of the PAP, who continued to hold his government posts concurrently. The departments of history and political science were combined and headed by another cabinet minister (George, 1984, pp. 137–8).

University students were severely warned about the inadvisability of opposition.

> [Prime Minister] Lee personally saw to it that students were left in no doubt that they were sticking their necks out if they took an interest in what did not directly concern them. Whenever he addressed a student meeting his tone was intimidating. If a question rose from the floor, he would first insist on knowing the student's name, citizenship and subject of study. If a questioner said he was Malaysian, Lee would say he had no right to ask questions. If the questioner said he was studying chemistry, Lee would chastise him for asking questions on politics. It did not take students long to realise that silence was golden. (George, 1984, p. 141)

When Lee received an unfriendly reception during an address at the university in 1969, he ordered a subsequent meeting of first-year students to be held. At this meeting he warned the students against their seniors and their teachers and said that the government knew everything that happened inside and outside the classroom. He said he would not allow dissent on the fundamental issues of national security, National Service, multi-racialism, economic survival and the political system. Lee met the executive of the students' union beforehand and threatened that any student who stepped out of line during the following meeting would be called up for two years' National Service immediately (George, 1984, p. 199).

By means of its Senior and Junior Pyramid clubs on campus, the government monitored faculty and students in discussion programmes and recreational activities, using these clubs as recruiting grounds for the PAP and government service. Alternative political societies were suppressed, especially the long-established Socialist Club which came under attack from the PAP-state as early as 1963 when its journal was banned. In 1964 the Democratic Socialist Club, patronised by Cabinet Members, was established as an officially approved counter-organisation. In 1971 the Socialist Club was finally suppressed through deregistration.

The internal security police kept the universities under close surveillance to the extent of recording lectures and watching the extra-curricular activities of lecturers and students (Wilson, 1978, p. 239; George, 1984, p. 139). Some student activism was still possible through the students' association as evidenced by the student protests over retrenchment of workers by foreign companies in 1974. This linkage between the increasingly significant English-educated middle class and workers was clearly too much for the government. It resulted in a stage-managed trial of student leaders on fabricated charges, imprisonment and deportation (Tan Wah Piow, 1984, 1987a, b).

Legislative changes then removed the last vestiges of autonomy from the students' association.

> The significance of these events lies very much in the fact that they represented a direct attack on essentially middle-class institutions, and a firm recognition of the extent of middle-class disenchantment and potential for political opposition. The government was attacking not only the radical left, but also the liberalism of English-stream students, and the assertion of Chinese culture among Chinese-stream students.... To repress the left wing, and minimise its influence among the lower classes, the government has extended tight control over areas of life which are middle class in character. In doing so, it has alienated important sectors of the intermediate middle-class – for whom repression of the radical left wing is perfectly legitimate, but repression of liberalism is quite another matter, and so too is repression of culture. (Buchanan, 1972, p. 215)

Busch noted the tendency of English-educated students to regard the *process* of politics to be as important as the benefits it provides. The alienation of this emergent middle class from the PAP, he observed, 'may be a serious problem for Singapore' (Busch, 1974, pp. 90–1). The leadership of liberal democratic dissent in the mid-1980s by these same students and also their emigration in large numbers has proved him correct.

Recruiting Failures through Meritocratic Education

By the end of 1977 the political effects of the centralised system of state education were very clear. Social relations had been restructured according to the criteria of merit most congenial to the PAP's political hegemony and the needs of its alliance with foreign capital. The capitalist class being consolidated was to remain English-speaking and pro-Western. The working class was left in no doubt that learning English and a technical education were necessary qualifications for access to the material benefits of industrialisation.

To these ends the education system deprived all except the capitalist class of a formal education in their own cultural and linguistic traditions. Communal factors of race and language were systematically correlated with class position through the bilingual policy and the emphasis on science and technology.

> That the Government of Singapore makes deliberate use of the education system for purposes of social engineering can hardly be doubted.... The shape of society which is beginning to emerge seems not so very unlike Plato's perception of the ideal city-state in which 'the wise shall lead and rule, and the ignorant shall follow'. Certainly, the school system is rigorously competitive and selective, with a series of examinations resulting in the channelling of the

overwhelming majority into one or other of the technical/vocational streams. (Wilson, 1978, pp. 238–9)

The schooling selection process of universal examinations ensured that the working class were denied significant opportunities for upward mobility, thus remaining available for training for wage labour. Only 71 per cent of pupils passed the Primary School Leaving Examination according to a 1978 Ministry of Education report. Of these only 35 per cent completed secondary school while the remaining 36 per cent failed or dropped out. That is, 65 per cent of primary school entrants did not successfully complete a secondary education. From the 35 per cent who completed, only 14 per cent gained entrance to pre-university level and only 9 per cent then went on to tertiary study (four per cent to university, five per cent to polytechnic or teachers' college) (Gopinathan, 1976, p. 75; Seah and Seah, 1983, pp. 246–7).

The education system was fulfilling the political function of ensuring that all citizens were subject to the sorting process by extending access to state education. The working class and ethnic minorities acquired only a minimal level of education necessary for the reproduction of labour power. The education system then failed this majority in order to make their labour power available.

This political function is a widely recognised task of meritocratic education in industrialised countries:

The main reason why schools do not seriously attempt to undermine the process [of discriminatory education] is that the upward and downward cycles of brightness training and dullness training actually facilitate the schools' task of reproducing society's class structure.... Their task is to produce in each age cohort a differentiated body of graduates who can be fit[ted] into existing occupational roles and statuses with a minimum of friction. In this way, the basic structure of social classes is recreated even though particular families may rise or fall in the hierarchy from one generation to the next. (Blum, 1978, p. 176)

In Singapore the education system had been successfully extended and restructured to recruit failures. These political results indicate what people were constrained to do by the education system. But they do not reveal how people thought about what they were pressured to do.

The Ideological Effects of Meritocratical Education

The Draconian labour legislation of 1968, the drop in average wages in 1967–9, the loss of 75,000 jobs and more than 13 per cent of GDP with the departure of the British military at the end of the decade (Buchanan, 1972, pp. 83, 87) would not seem the ideal time to intensify educational practices which fail the majority of students. The reason this process assisted the PAP-state's social control rather than undermined it lies in the ideological effects of the practices. The education system ensured that people blamed themselves for their failure to raise their class status.

The experience of being processed by the mechanisms of educational social control produced ideological effects that students and their parents internalised as explanations for what was happening. It appeared that the criteria of merit were neutral objectives available for all to satisfy by means of their own efforts. Students who were literate in English and did well in academic examinations in mathematics and science were the most meritorious and deserved the success they so quickly attained in terms of status and jobs. Those who did not succeed could only blame themselves. Even the realisation that the English-educated Chinese upper classes were overwhelmingly the most meritorious did not lead to questioning of the basis of the definition of merit. Rather it encouraged the trend towards English-medium education.

> English is regarded by all ethnic groups as providing the best job opportunities, a belief justified by the socio-economic disparities that continue to exist between the English and the non-English-educated and which has led to reduced enrolments in the non-English streams. (Gopinathan, 1976, p. 76)

The PAP-state's policy of maintaining the pretence of four equal language streams, its promotion of second languages and its imposition of streaming and universal examinations fostered the belief that there was real choice and real opportunity: that the success of a student was up to the parents' judgement and their child's personal intelligence and application. This perception has been shared by academics who have also failed to see that the practice of providing choices conceals the real selection functions of education.

> The wisdom of governmental non-interference with the existing educational provisions was never more dramatically revealed than when more and more parents *voluntarily chose* to have their children educated in English-medium schools. (Tham, 1989, p. 481; my emphasis)

Seah and Seah are more circumspect in their observation, indicating that choice is constrained by political considerations.

> The flow of command in the overall education system is thus unidirectional from the political leadership down to the Ministry of Education, to the principals and teachers and finally to the parents of the schoolchildren. Ironically, democracy is still practised at the tail-end of this chain of command in that parents supposedly can decide or choose ultimately between the options available in the education and school system. (Seah and Seah, 1983, p. 257)

As part of making parents and students feel personally responsible for their educational success or failure and, thus, their social position, the experience of educational practices actively shapes students' perceptions of themselves.

[Schools] attempt to align students' self-conceptions with their eventual job prospects so those in lower-class occupations will feel they are capable of nothing better and will not feel cheated. All this can be achieved more easily if students are quickly stratified into ability levels and trained in such a way that those in the higher levels learn more than those in the lower ones. An interactive process which has this effect may diminish the learning capacities of many students, but nevertheless be functional for reproducing the class structure.... Since schools are expected to display no favoritism toward any particular group, they tend to recruit their failures from among the children who are initially hardest to teach; these being the ones who lack familiarity with middle class lifestyles and speech patterns. (Blum, 1978, pp. 176–7)

In Singapore those selected to fail and then ideologically conditioned to accept this are the working class and racial minorities. Salaff noted that the poor 'accept the authorities' evaluation of their children's abilities.... By accepting the power of the school system to determine their children's occupational future, the working-class becomes further involved in the new industrial order' (Salaff, 1988, p. 246). Their ideological formation assists their proletarianisation.

This derivation of self-worth and vocational prospects from educational practices also produced an insidious internalisation of racism by its victims. In his study of legitimacy and ethnicity in Singapore, Busch concluded that ethnic self-denigration among the Malays was severe, many of them regarding themselves as inferior to Chinese. Malays tended to see the reason for educational failure in culturally acquired laziness rather than in educational practices which discriminated against them or in the worthlessness of Malay-medium education within the PAP-state's economic plan (Busch, 1974, pp. 85–6).

Therefore there was a difference between the actual political effects of what people were pressured to do by the education system and what people thought about educational practices and themselves as a result of being involved in them. In this sense ideology was produced by concrete practices; the way people came to think about what they did was a major ideological effect. Thus, the experience of meritocratic educational sorting processes produced the ideological effect in students that they were being sorted correctly according to their own abilities.

This means that the education system should not be understood simply as a specialist ideological institution imposing a state ideology. This essentially idealist understanding of ideology lies behind observations that Singapore's education system is 'the most important item in the programme of thought control' (George, 1984, p. 136) and the instrument of 'elite ideology and mass indoctrination' (Busch, 1974, p. 32). This view of education assumes that ideological imposition is necessary because people do not otherwise perceive educational practices to be in their interest. But this way of comprehending the relationship between ideology and action takes insufficient account of the most striking characteristic of the PAP-state's educational system which was not the opposition to it but the extraordinary degree of cooperation it achieved across the whole of society. This suggests that an increasing majority of people began to see it as working in their interest.

But this effect has definitely been reinforced through the way that the ideology produced by educational practices has been systematised or formalised by Singapore's institutions and political leaders. Politicians, technocrats, teachers and the media constantly provided students with the ideological categories which appeared to accord with what they were experiencing.

The Formalisation of Ideology

The systematisation of the ideological effects of Singapore's education system had its own characteristics but was by no means unique. Similar practices have produced similar effects elsewhere which have been formalised into meritocratic ideologies. In addition, Lee Kuan Yew and many of his peers in the PAP leadership were ideologically formed by their experience of the colonial and elitist educational practices of Britain. They naturally interpreted the practices they introduced in the same ideological terms.

Equal Opportunity and Merit
A crucial ideological principle was that of equality of opportunity regardless of race, religion, class or linguistic heritage. The ideological perception of choice legitimated the PAP-state's role as apparent neutral guarantor of meritocratic advancement. This became ideologically formalised in the rhetoric of equality of opportunity. What an individual did with this opportunity was dependent on personal merit.

> There was constant emphasis on merit as the criterion for upward mobility and privilege. It was asserted that Singapore had to be achievement-oriented and that the island could neither afford nor tolerate shirkers in its quest for progress – 'from each his economic best, to each his economic worth'. (Gopinathan, 1976, p. 75)

According to this reasoning, equality of opportunity logically leads to social inequality since individual abilities differ. The recognition of individual merit leads to a just society. A just society is an unequal one.

> [M]ore and more the young are showing that they want to be equal in order that they can strive to be unequal. What they want is not to be equal throughout life but to have equal opportunities, so that those whose ability and whose application are better than the average can become more equal than the others.... Our immediate task is to build up a society in which man [sic] will be rewarded, not according to the amount of property he owns, but according to his active contribution to society in physical or mental labour. From each according to his ability. To each according to his worth and contribution to society. This is the

first step to a more equal and just society. (Lee Kuan Yew in an address to the Socialist International, quoted in Josey, 1980, pp. 68–9)

Because there was no legal bar preventing the working class and ethnic minorities from entering elite institutions, Lee and other PAP leaders claimed that equal opportunity existed for all classes and races. They clearly felt their role as arbiters of a person's worth and contribution to society according to such criteria as their facility in English, their loyalty to the PAP and to capitalism, to be a neutral one. Failure to take advantage of 'equal' opportunities could therefore, in their view, be due only to the weaknesses of those who failed in the attempt.

As noted before, this ideology is not new.

The general notion of meritocracy uses two related arguments to depict the class structure of western capitalist societies as natural and socially desirable. First, it pictures society as providing opportunity for all to rise in the occupational hierarchy. Inequalities of wealth, power, and status exist because people differ in how intelligent and industrious they are. *Such differences are the cause of inequality*, and since they themselves are the product of nature, the inequalities which exist must also be natural.

Secondly, it contends that society benefits by recruiting the most capable individuals into the most responsible jobs. These jobs must offer much greater prestige and salary than others as a way of attracting capable persons. Hence, the existing inequalities perform the necessary function of conserving scarce talent and directing it where it is most needed. Individuals employed in upper class occupations deserve their wealth and privilege because their contribution to society is especially valuable.

Conversely, the poor are poor because they are lazy and unintelligent. They merit nothing better than bare subsistence living because they contribute little to society, and it is in society's interest not to improve their position substantially. (Blum, 1978, p. 162; my emphasis)

The ideology of natural differences determining merit and *causing* inequality sanctifies the concentration of wealth and power in the hands of a few on the basis that they individually merit it. The blame for being poor and powerless correspondingly is laid squarely on those who are. This ideology dissolves the issue of class.

However, the PAP came to power with a socialist programme and the Lee faction faced the problem of switching from a public commitment to egalitarianism to outright capitalist meritocracy. It also confronted the need to consolidate a technocratic capitalist class around the PAP-state since the Lee faction had no mass support and did not represent a strong bourgeoisie. Lee was equal to the task. He stated that the socialist aim of 'putting the economic power of the State into the hands of the people as a whole' could be achieved by an elite providing 'the direction, planning and control of this power in the people's interest' (Josey, 1980, p. 69). Lee then set about consolidating this elite.

Class Ideology of Meritocratic Leadership

Between 1966 and 1977 it became obvious that Lee Kuan Yew's understanding of his own educational formation accorded with the kind of people-sorting mechanisms that the PAP-state was introducing into the education system. It seems he concluded from his experience at the elite local Raffles College and then at Cambridge University in the 1940s that such institutions for reproducing the ruling class act as neutral sorting mechanisms for advancing to their proper level in society the most intelligent and those most gifted with leadership qualities. Since many of those with whom he studied later became the political leaders or the senior bureaucrats of Malaysia and Singapore, such a belief is perhaps understandable. However, by 1967 Lee had generalised this ideological perception to a belief that, in any society, there is an elite of 'no more than five per cent' who are 'more than ordinarily endowed physically and mentally'.

> It is on this group that we must expend our limited and slender resources in order that they will provide that yeast, that ferment, that catalyst in our society which alone will ensure that Singapore shall maintain its pre-eminent place in the societies that exist in South East Asia – and the social organisation which enables us, with almost no natural resources, to provide the second highest standard of living in Asia. (Lee Kuan Yew quoted in *Eastern Sun*, 26 June 1967)

The year before in a speech to school principals Lee indicated that he expected the education system to unite Singaporeans in support of the state regardless of their race, language, religion or culture. Yet, at the same time, it functioned to divide them according to class, race, language, religion and culture. Therefore, he required the education system to perform its customary role of both reproducing social relations and legitimising the process. But his emphasis was on the formation of a paternalistic, technocratic, governing class.

> Our community lacks in-built reflexes – loyalty, patriotism, history or tradition.... [O]ur society and its education system was never designed to produce a people capable of cohesive action, identifying their collective interests and then acting in furtherance of them.... The reflexes of group thinking must be built to ensure the survival of the community, not the survival of the individual, this means a reorientation of emphasis and a reshuffling of values.... We must have qualities of leadership at the top, and qualities of cohesion on the ground.... The ideal product is the student, the university graduate who is strong, robust, rugged, with tremendous qualities of stamina, endurance and at the same time with great intellectual discipline and most important of all, humility and love for his community. (Lee Kuan Yew, 1967, in George, 1984, p. 136)

A decade later Lee observed that all the top people in Singapore could be accommodated in one jumbo jet and that, if it crashed, that would be the end of

Singapore (Caldwell, 1979, p. 14). In his last National Day speech as prime minister, Lee Kuan Yew returned to the theme, saying that only the top three per cent of Singapore are capable of political leadership.

> It's a small place, no more than a total of those within the ages thirty to forty-five, at the most 800 people. We can put them all into one little lap-top computer, all the basic data. (*STW*, 1 September 1990)

Of the current PAP leadership, he stated:

> Our right to govern is based on merit. We have to show that we are manifestly qualified to govern by our abilities, our training, our character, our ability to deliver the goods, and that we exercise power for the common good. (*STW*, 8 September 1990)

These statements are but echoes of an early address by Lee given at Chatham House in London in 1962.

> At a time when you want harder work with less return and more capital investment, one man one vote produces just the opposite.... [In Asia this system] has been superseded by systems which give power effectively to one man or group of men for an indefinite period. Government to be effective must at least give the impression of enduring, and a government which is open to the vagaries of the ballot box when the people who put their crosses in the ballot box are not illiterate but semi-literate, which is worse, is a government which is already weakened before it starts to govern.... If I were in authority in Singapore indefinitely without having to ask those who are being governed whether they like what is being done, then I have not the slightest doubt that I could govern much more effectively in their own interests. That is a fact which the educated understand. (George, 1984, p. 114)

It is therefore hardly surprising that the PAP-state's educational initiatives produced meritocratic ideology. Lee's 1965 proposal for 'the establishment of an Eton-style boarding school in which Singapore's brightest students would be groomed for future command' (Buchanan, 1972, p. 290) is an early example. This proposal met with considerable opposition (*ST*, 4 May 1965) but eventually came forward in 1969 in the modified form of four elite pre-university colleges.

> It was stressed that such schools were not for children of the wealthy and privileged in society – bright children would qualify, so long as they satisfied certain requirements, regardless of what stratum of society they came from. (Buchanan, 1972, p. 291)

The 'certain requirements' were, of course, the criteria set by the PAP-state's definition of merit. These elite establishments accordingly filled up with the children of the wealthy, the English-educated, the capitalist class and the emerging middle class (George, 1984, p. 186).

The Ideology of Class Hatred

If equal opportunity enables individuals to achieve the level they merit, then it is a short step to claiming that people actually do reach the level of their ability. Therefore, once meritocratic sorting practices are spread across the whole of society, it is only a matter of time before the whole of society is sorted according to their natural ability. Thus, some proponents of meritocratic education, including Lee Kuan Yew, claim moral justification for it on the grounds that it overcomes hereditary class divisions and leads to divisions based on actual ability.

> Singapore is a society based on effort and merit, not wealth and privilege depending on birth. There is nothing in the life-style of the employer which is not open to the worker. (Lee Kuan Yew, *STW*, 14 October 1989)

The moral impact of this ideological position can be seen when the implicit connection between intelligence, biological heredity and race or class is made explicit. Herrnstein, an American scholar, has given academic comfort to those who argue that social inequality is a necessary consequence of hereditary meritocracy.

> The privileged classes of the past, based on religion, title, property, race, even physiognomy, were probably not much superior biologically to the downtrodden, which is why revolutions had a fair chance of success. By removing artificial barriers between classes, society has encouraged the creation of biological barriers. When people can take their natural level in society, the upper classes will by definition, have greater capacity than the lower. (Herrnstein, 1971, pp. 201-2)

This ideology has been soundly criticised as nothing more than 'a bare assertion that the ideology of capitalist society accurately expresses universal traits of human nature, and that certain related, implicit assumptions of behaviourist psychology are correct' (Chomsky, 1972, p. 29). In Singapore it soon became clear that the lower classes and minority races failed overwhelmingly in the education system. The PAP leadership concluded that they are therefore naturally lacking in ability. Lee revealed his view of working-class Singaporeans in his frequent public references to them as 'digits' (George, 1984, p. 132). He made his view of education for the poor rather clear in a 1967 address to a community centre meeting:

> We will be to blame if youngsters ten years from now become hooligans, ruffians and sluts. They can be trained to be otherwise. Even dogs can be trained as proved by the Police Training School where dogs, at a whistle, jump through a hoop, sit down or attack those who need to be attacked. (George, 1984, p. 194)

Dressed up with the pseudoscientific principles of intelligence levels (IQ) and eugenics (Chee and Chan, 1984), this ideology has legitimated class hatred and racism in Singapore.

The Ideology of Eugenics

Eugenics theory makes explicit in an extreme form the underlying assumptions of neo-classical economic theory that people are the product of their genes rather than their circumstances. Lee Kuan Yew has often espoused such notions but their origin in capitalist political economy gives them wider significance as the ideological product of capitalist social relations rather than as the idiosyncratic theories of a dominant personality.

Many of the government's actions which have been justified by eugenics are more prominent in the next developmental phase of education where they will be dealt with in detail. It is sufficient to note at this stage that once society is properly sorted and if intelligence (or the lack of it) is hereditary, then it makes no sense to let the lower classes and minorities increase the proportion of meritocratic failures in the population by irresponsible breeding. Hence, when the PAP-state wanted to maximise its skilled human resources in the late 1960s in order to launch the export-oriented industrialisation policy, it introduced abortion and voluntary sterilisation laws aimed at the poor and ethnic minorities. In Lee's words:

> Free education and subsidised housing lead to a situation where the less economically productive people in the community are reproducing themselves at rates higher than the rest. This will increase the total population of less productive people.
>
> Our problem is how to devise a system of disincentives, so that the irresponsible, the social delinquents, do not believe that all they have to do is to produce their children and the government then owes them and their children sufficient food, medicine, housing, education and jobs.... Until such time when moral inhibitions disappear and legislative or administrative measures can be taken to regulate the size of families, we must try to induce people to limit their families....
>
> One of the crucial yardsticks by which we shall have to judge the results of the new abortion law combined with the voluntary sterilisation law will be whether it tends to raise or lower the total quality of our population. We must encourage those who earn less than two hundred dollars per month and cannot afford to nurture and educate many children never to have more than two. We will regret the time lost if we do not now take the first tentative steps towards correcting a trend which can leave our society with a large number of the physically, intellectually, and culturally anaemic.   (Abortion Bill, Third Reading, 29 December 1969, Select Committee Report, pp. 321–3)

The reality that the social control mechanisms of the education system, together with socio-economic conditions, actively discriminated against the educational achievement of the working class, women and minority races, had been ideologically concealed. Meritocracy was the formalised ideology for the institutionalisation of class hatred and racism. Lee Kuan Yew's ideological position has a disturbing affinity to that of a previous political leader:

Since the inferior always outnumber the superior, the former would always increase more rapidly if they possessed the same capacities for survival and for the procreation of their kind; and the final consequence would be that the best in quality would be forced to recede into the background. Therefore a corrective measure in favour of the better quality must intervene. (Adolf Hitler, 1942, pp. 161–2)

Racial Hatred and the Ideology of Multi-racialism

The formalisation of the application of eugenics to Malays was done explicitly by a Malay politician, Mahathir bin Mohamad, now the prime minister of Malaysia, in a book entitled *The Malay Dilemma* (1970). He 'proved' that inbreeding has made Malays intellectually inferior to Chinese. For this reason, he concluded, Chinese control the economy. His book was essentially aimed at explaining the economic subjugation of Malays and at motivating them to do something about it.

But in Singapore where Dr Mahathir studied and where racist educational and other practices continue, their ideological effect is to legitimate Chinese dominance and enshrine racism against Malays as a scientific principle of genetic inferiority. As Busch states, 'Repeatedly, I heard this theme from Malays in Singapore, even from secondary school pupils who had never heard of Dr Mahathir and his book' (Busch, 1974, p. 59; see also Nasir and Chee, 1984).

Lee Kuan Yew has also never attempted to hide his racism, since he also regarded it as scientific reasoning. He has accounted for the superiority of East Asians (over Malays) in terms of 'innate ethnic qualities' (*The Mirror*, 21 October 1968). He has isolated other factors as well:

> Climate and diet may have given East Asians a cultural edge over Southeast Asians in coping with modern economic development. They may account in part for the intense, thrifty, and largely secular societies of China, Japan, Korea and Vietnam. (Lecture at Columbia University, New York reported in *Eastern Sun*, 23 December 1968)

Lee frequently made reference to his 4000 years of cultural history in comparison to equatorial races who would go to sleep in the afternoon (George, 1984, p. 168).

But the predictable failure of Malays in a racist educational system established for highly competitive, individualistic, English-educated Chinese has needed and acquired more sophisticated ideological legitimacy than thinly disguised racial hatred.

The legitimation of the results of educational sorting by meritocratic ideology has been complemented by an ideology of multiracialism which portrays Malay failure as being for the common good. It might be expected that the principles of a multi-racial policy would emphasise the right of all racial communities to order their own affairs in culturally appropriate ways. However, the PAP-state advanced principles of multi-racialism which emphasised the reasons why minority racial communities may not have this right.

The official PAP policy after independence was to recognise Malay rights as equal to those of other races and to note that their educational needs were greater. But the PAP-state no longer had to accommodate the Malay politics of the peninsula. It merely had to contain the politics of its own Malay minority. Therefore, despite specific constitutional guarantees to the Malays, it stood by the principle that 'there can be no distinction between majority rights and minority rights' (*Parliamentary Debates*, cited in Betts, 1975, p. 136) and that the greatest danger to minorities is 'not tyranny by the majority, but pursuit of minority rights' (*Straits Budget* cited in Betts, 1975, p. 137). Furthermore, the PAP held that if the Malays objected to the principle of equal rights, the Chinese majority was automatically released from adherence to this principle (Chew, 1982, p. 206). Just as the policy of multi-racialism had been used against the Chinese education system, it was now turned against the Malays as an ideological weapon which would label objections to the high rate of Malay educational failure as communal and subversive of multi-racialism.

However, because of the glaring racial inequities of meritocratic education in Singapore, academic apologists have had to claim that racial injustice is fair and that doing anything about it would be unfair. In justifying the ideology of meritocracy as 'a denial of the norm of equity in favour of the norm of efficiency', Tham proceeds to state:

> First, it ensured that critical areas of the economy would have men and women of proven ability and performance; and secondly, it suggested to the public at large fairness and justice irrespective of ethnic differences. Seen in this context the underlying logic of meritocracy seems unassailable. There was, of course, the question as to whether certain groups such as the Malays should merit special government intervention to ensure their effective participation in the economy. Such a step, if proposed at all, would have militated against the government's thinking concerning how best to improve the Malays' economic status. Any multiracial party in power would have been loath to employ group-focused economic-development policies since it would most certainly have been unpopular with the majority. In any case, there was also the belief that Malays would be better able to compete in future if they developed the qualities of hard work and self-reliance. (Tham, 1989, p. 481)

This ideological rationalisation assists greatly in connecting the ideology of meritocracy with the PAP-state's ideology of multiracialism and of welfare. In fact, of course, 'group-focused economic-development policies' exactly describes meritocratic practices which ensure that, in Lee Kuan Yew's words, 'we must expend our limited and slender resources' on the 'no more than five per cent' of the population who happen to be overwhelmingly Chinese and members of the capitalist class. Consciously or not, Tham has justified the PAP-state policy of not wasting money on those who are genetically unable to improve their intellectual level, the same justification used by Lee for restricting physical reproduction by the poor.

This position accords with the PAP-state's actual fiscal priorities which saw the education budget progressively decline from its peak of 32 per cent of total government expenditure in 1964 to less than nine per cent in 1980 (Linda Lim, 1989, p. 178). Having achieved political hegemony and begun to sort the Chinese working class, the PAP-state did not waste its money on those other races quickly identified as total meritocratic failures. Thus, in Singapore, the ideology of meritocracy incorporates ideologies of multiracialism and welfare which legitimate Chinese domination and a racist state.

Broader Ideological Context

The ideology of meritocracy was systematised in the broader ideological context of a PAP-generated crisis of national survival after expulsion from Malaysia (Chan Heng Chee, 1971, p. 53). There was a call to unity for the sake of survival. This call contained at least four elements: fostering a multi-racial democratic ideal, building a rugged, tightly organised and modern society, developing a sense of Singapore identity and having a commitment to change. With the diplomacy which earned her a term as Singapore's Permanent Representative at the United Nations, Chan notes that:

> There is little doubt that the ideology has been consciously formed and articulated to achieve particular ends but it cannot be asserted with similar certainty that the primary intent of PAP ideology is to ensure the survival of the party, although admittedly, an ideology stressing unity would tend to maximise the ruling party's power.   (Chan Heng Chee, 1971, p. 53)

The implications of this ideology have been noted more emphatically by Rodan.

> This 'ideology of survival'...insisted on the inseparability of economic and political survival and the necessary subservience of all other considerations. Above all else, survival demanded the internalisation of an entirely new set of social attitudes and beliefs which embodied self-sacrifice for the 'national interest'. An important aspect of the new ideology was the acceptance of the PAP's sole right to determine this interest and the belief that the PAP's own political survival was paramount to Singapore's survival.   (Rodan, 1989, p. 88)

In short, the PAP exploited the public insecurity resulting from its expulsion from Malaysia and the later British military withdrawal to systematise an ideological climate favourable to its political survival and the objectives of its alliance with foreign capital. Great emphasis was placed on raising skills, on social discipline and on foregoing short-term benefits for long-term gain. The 'rugged society' was the regime's shorthand for this.

By this is meant the exercise of self-discipline and social responsibility by individuals so that the needs of society can, when necessary, take precedence over individual desires.... Out of such industrious cooperation is supposed to emerge a 'rugged society' able to cope with a different international environment because it has mobilised its human resources – the only resources Singapore has. (Busch, 1974, pp. 33–4)

In this ideological context it was possible to suppress claims for the redress of grievances or attempts at anti-PAP political mobilisation with contemptuous caricature.

When we are trying to survive in a tight situation there is very little place for harmful or even meaningless activities. At best they are irrelevant eccentricities; at worst they lead the young into a world of fantasy and make them unfit for the strenuous exertions that may lie ahead. (Goh Keng Swee in *The Mirror*, 17 April 1967)

Furthermore, the withdrawal of British forces led to a massive militarisation programme with the assistance of Israeli advisers. The decision of the PAP leadership publicly to proclaim that they were building a garrison state on the Israeli model seemed calculated to maintain communal tension in the Malay archipelago and to undermine inter-ethnic cooperation among opposition movements in the region. The aggressively anti-Islamic implications of explicitly imitating Israeli militarism heightened anti-Chinese feeling in Malaysia and Indonesia, providing a distraction from class politics most convenient for foreign capital and local capitalist classes. The PAP-state took over the role of the British in advancing a communal strategy on a regional scale to fragment class solidarity.

This militarisation also ensured domestic stability for the attraction of foreign investment (Buchanan, 1972, pp. 261, 267; George, 1984, p. 192). In 1969, defence expenditure surpassed education expenditure as a proportion of total government spending (Linda Lim, 1989, p. 178). Lee Kuan Yew made it clear that he regarded Singapore as the 'linchpin' for Western interests in Southeast Asia and for the future prosperity of Malaysia and Indonesia (Josey, 1968, pp. 427–8). Furthermore, he made it plain that part of the educational commitment to science and technology was related to military priorities:

We intend to fight for our stake in this part of the world, and [to] anybody who thinks they can push us around, I say: over my dead body.... I don't care if there are 100 million Indonesians of whom 400,000 are armed. So what? What is important, I know in ten, fifteen years I can breed a generation that can man missiles.... We know that some of our neighbours can get this equipment. But can they work it as quickly as we can work it? (*ST*, 10 November 1965)

Later Lee stated:

We opted for the Israeli fashion, for in our situation we think it might be necessary not only to train every boy but also every girl to be a disciplined and effective digit in defence of their own country. (*Eastern Sun*, 21 October 1967)

The ideology of meritocracy was formalised within a highly repressive atmosphere to legitimise not only educational practices but also the entire political programme of exploitation and repression developed in alliance with Western capital. The PAP-state was able to proceed with its undermining of local working class organisation and conditions with justifications of pragmatism and necessity. Its control of educational institutions and the media enabled it to formalise a congenial ideological consensus for the legitimation of its political objectives.

The consolidation of the meritocratic practices of education between 1966 and 1977 greatly assisted the proletarianisation of the lower classes and minorities for export-oriented industrialisation. The formalisation of meritocratic ideology had legitimised the practices which produced it and the PAP-state had markedly increased its powers of social control through educational and housing welfare. But by 1977 some of the contradictions of these practices had become obvious as the PAP-state's economic ambitions confronted intense international competition.

5 The New Education System

By 1978 the state education system had shown itself to be one of the most influential institutional mechanisms for the reconstruction of Singapore society. Singaporeans had been sorted into their social positions in the industrialisation process and this stratification had produced a high degree of political submission. Education had transformed people's perceptions of their place in society, had altered their aspirations and had begun to change their linguistic and cultural practices.

However, the next phase of development put education under so much pressure that it became overloaded with regulatory tasks. It was required to resolve, divert or suppress too many social contradictions and political conflicts. It quickly became necessary to move to a new education system which distanced responsibility for educational sorting from the government thereby lessening the need to feign equity.

THE GREAT LEAP FORWARD, 1978–85

The increasing competition in labour-intensive, intermediate technology production from other Asian countries potentially threatened the PAP-state's ability to deliver the high rates of economic growth which secured its political tenure. Continuous growth had both required and justified increasing social control during the initial period of industrialisation. The decision to upgrade the economy under this pressure to sustain economic ascendancy required yet another qualitative change in the Singapore labour force. As the development of public housing after 1978 has already demonstrated, this change or 'revolution' was attempted by means of a sudden intensification of the social control practices previously consolidated.

To equip its workers for the great leap forward, the government launched educational initiatives to take its work-force to a higher level of skill. This entailed a more rigorous categorisation of people and a more concise targeting of educational resources. It also included the linking of sexual reproduction to educational sorting mechanisms in a remarkably explicit official breeding programme which has achieved international notoriety. The incentives and disincentives for baby production introduced a selection process before birth which connected the chances of being born to the education system's previous categorisation of parents.

However, the PAP was confronted with a resurgence of opposition and non-cooperation as it sought to implement these measures and was therefore severely limited in what it could achieve. The 1985 collapse of the Second Industrial

Revolution indicated a crisis in social relations partly precipitated by this domestic response to industrialisation.

Maximising a Scarce Resource

Even by 1978 there was general recognition that the education system had become clogged up by the simultaneous stress on bilingualism, technical education and English proficiency unmatched by enough highly qualified teachers and adequate facilities (Seah and Seah, 1983, p. 243). It had also suffered from frequent changes to the method of implementing the bilingual policy, changes which were handed down from the top political leadership, often the prime minister himself, to an increasingly demoralised Ministry of Education and, thence, to schools which obediently put into practice directives they knew to be ineffective or contradictory (Seah and Seah, 1983, p. 255). Lee Kuan Yew appeared to recognise that the sorting mechanisms of education were working too well: an English-educated technocratic elite was being created but everyone else was dropping out without achieving even the minimal standard of education required. 'Only the bright rise above all the overload and break through, and the average give up,' he noted (*Asia Yearbook*, 1979, p. 289). In failing people too efficiently, the system itself was failing.

The result was drop-out and attrition (drop-outs plus failures) rates far higher than those of Taiwan (Tham, 1989, p. 488), low literacy levels and ineffective bilingualism. It could not be assumed that completion of a bilingual education had rendered the students effectively bilingual. At one stage the army had to issue badges to national servicemen indicating which languages they understood in order to assist communication (Seah and Seah, 1983, p. 250).

In 1979 an Educational Study Team chaired by Deputy Prime Minister Goh Keng Swee presented a report on the education system along with recommendations for change. While noting many of the problems outlined above, the Goh Report's main concern was expressed in terms of 'educational wastage': failure to achieve expected standards and premature school-leaving (Tham, 1989, p. 488). The team was not concerned that the people-sorting mechanisms of the education system were biased in favour of reproducing the capitalist class by assisting the educationally advantaged to reach their proper station in life. Nor was it concerned that these mechanisms reproduced the working class by discriminating against the Chinese-educated and ethnic minorities. After all the education system was designed to achieve these objectives and was achieving them successfully.

Rather the Goh Report focused on the system's failure to extract 'the maximum potential from a scarce resource' and on the need 'to fill up the education gap in manpower requirements before Singapore can successfully join the ranks of brain and technology-intensive nations' (Seah and Seah, 1983, pp. 248–9). In other words the problem was not that members of the working class were being ejected from the education system as failures. The problem was that when the academic-stream students graduated they had not achieved a sufficiently high educational standard. Similarly when the working-class students were ejected into vocational and technical education and, thence, into the labour force, they were still insufficiently skilled, linguistically (in English) and technically, to sustain the great leap forward into high-tech industrialisation. In the process of launching the Second Industrial Revolution, the PAP-state realised that approximately 600,000 workers of its one million strong labour force had not reached Primary Six level, the final year of primary education (Chiew, 1983, p. 253). In the eyes of the PAP leadership, Singapore was not maximising the use of its major resource, people.

In a sense the PAP-state was facing a form of political struggle. Both working-class and middle-class students were reacting against the alienating educational selection process by not learning. Singaporeans were demonstrating their reluctance to learn the two languages required by industrialisation: the English language and the language of science and technology. The working class was not inclined to learn a foreign language so that foreign bosses would find it easier to order them around. They had to be further pressured to learn the above subjects so that the economic strategy of the alliance with foreign capital could be sustained.

Goh's Education Study Team consisted mainly of systems engineers aged in their thirties or younger, not professional educationalists. It is therefore perhaps understandable that they decided not to continue wasting government expenditure on giving all children the same quality of primary education up to the Primary School Leaving Examination (PSLE) in Primary Six. Instead they decided on intelligence tests to grade children after the third year of primary education at the age of eight or nine years. The government then put in place graded streams of education designed to give each group an education suitable to its expected station in life. In this way the government tailored educational practices to 'the needs of private companies engaged in, or moving towards, higher value-added production' (Rodan, 1989, p. 149). IQ tests, which generally work against working-class children, racial minorities and girls, were used to sort out the future adult members of the various classes at this stage.

This system of early sorting opened the way for education to become even more elitist: a Gifted Education Programme was introduced for the most talented 8 per cent and the best educational resources were directed to them and the next 30 per cent. At the same time more funds were immediately directed to tertiary education. Total enrolments in universities and colleges rose by 49.4 per cent and in technical and vocational institutes by 7.5 per cent from 1979 to 1983. Over the same period, engineering course enrolments rose by 2104 at the National University of Singapore and by 10,232 at Singapore Polytechnic (Rodan, 1989, p. 149).

The lower streams were given a year or two longer to pick up basic English skills (Seah and Seah, 1983, pp. 258–60). This aimed to ensure that more skilled labour could be extracted from the largest part of the 'scarce resource' before it was finally ejected from the system. Between 1979 and 1984 the proportion of those entering the labour force with only primary level qualifications or less declined from 43 to 26 per cent (*FEER*, 25 August 1988, p. 59).

Government expenditure on education rose from $32.75 million in 1978–9 to $374.68 million in 1982–3, a 1044 per cent increase (Rodan, 1989, p. 149) or from less than 9 per cent of total government expenditure in 1980 to 14 per cent in 1985 (Linda Lim, 1989, p. 178; *STW*, 18 March, 25 March 1989). This should not be seen as a reversal of the PAP-state's welfare ideology. Much of the expenditure was targeted at the tertiary and technical levels not at programmes to assist working-class primary students to get into the academic stream. It was also a temporary infusion of state funds to kick-start the economic upgrading process. Towards the end of the 1980s the government reduced the level of educational funding.

Ending the Myth of Equal Treatment

The PAP-state's rigorous campaign to upgrade the education system ended the myth that the four language streams were receiving equal treatment. This period saw the official assertion of the supremacy of the English language as the educational language for all Singaporeans. The PAP-state increased the pressure to learn English and science as it sought to overcome people's reluctance to do so.

In December 1983 the PAP-state announced the 'National Stream' of education. English-medium education would officially overwhelmingly predominate, even for ethnic minorities such as the Malays. All workers were forced to learn some English. Also instead of some Malays failing through their own vernacular-medium education, they would all henceforth drop out of an English-medium system, saving the government the cost of Malay-medium schools.

By 1985 the round figures for student enrolment in the various language medium streams were 97 per cent in English-medium and three per cent in Chinese-medium. Barely recordable were the 0.04 per cent enrolled in Malay-medium and 0.01 per cent in Tamil-medium (Shotam, 1989, p. 510).

> The new system of education appears in total consonance with the economic requirements in terms of manpower provision. With the emphasis in English which will become the first language of 80 per cent of the Primary I cohort and the remaining 20 per cent grounded in at least oral English, the harnessing on to science, technology and international business communication will satisfy the economic needs of the global economy. (Seah and Seah, 1983, p. 262)

At the same time the government had to clear the path of bilingualism for English speakers whose second language was not up to standard. Some were faltering on the thresholds of secondary school and university because they were failing their second language. The requirements for the second language at PSLE (Primary School Leaving Examination) level and for entrance to university were therefore watered down in 1985 (*ST*, 14 July 1985). The government continued to be adamant that it was pursuing a bilingual policy (Tham, 1989, p. 490). The dilution of the bilingual policy was also necessary for a patriarchal state because girls were achieving much higher linguistic standards than boys and, thus, gaining entrance to the university in greater numbers.

As well as intensifying the meritocratic practices of the education system, the government also tried to extract more from the rejects of the education system. It put considerable effort into improving the skills of those who had already been rejected: the 60 per cent of the overall labour force without primary-level education. In 1979 the Skills Development Fund was set up by imposing a levy on employers for each employee (Rodan, 1989, p. 144). Other schemes were also started such as the Basic Education for Skill Training (BEST) programme. This began in July 1982 with an initial intake of 500 workers who were taught English and mathematics up to Primary Six level by means of two 60-hour courses (Chiew, 1983, p. 253).

The Reserve Army of Labour

As already noted, these educational initiatives were part of an attempt to upgrade quickly the quality, in meritocratic terms, of the total population. This process could not ignore the large numbers of migrant workers who had come to Singapore since the early 1970s. They were treated as a latent reserve being admitted for short periods and regularly rotated. They were not permitted to bring their families with them or to have offspring in Singapore to be sorted by Singapore's education system.

Migrant workers had been permitted to come to fill job vacancies created by rapid economic growth and their presence kept wages low in labour-intensive, low value-added industries. They were concentrated in construction and the dirtier, more dangerous or more monotonous jobs.

Officially there were 40,000 foreign workers holding 'work permits' in Singapore in 1978 but there may actually have been more than double that number (*Asia Yearbook*, 1979, p. 292). One estimate of Malaysians working in Singapore was as high as 120,000 (Rodan, 1989, p. 138) but some of these may have been salaried 'employment pass' holders, a category for foreign business people, technicians and professionals who formed a privileged elite. Between 1970 and 1980 the proportion of non-citizen, non-permanent residents went up from 2.9 to 5.5 per cent of the total population (Yap, 1989, p. 466).

Regulations were already in place to prevent migrant workers from having access to PAP-state welfare and, thus, from acquiring a degree of permanence. Any work permit holder wishing to marry a Singaporean had to gain government permission. This was rarely granted. If permission was granted and the worker had been in Singapore less than five years then both husband and wife had to agree to be sterilised after their second child (Yap, 1989, p. 466) to prevent them disproportionately lowering the quality of the population.

In 1978 there was still a labour shortage with approximately 40,000 jobs being created each year and only approximately 30,000 Singapore workers entering the work-force (Rodan, 1989, p. 137). Nevertheless, the PAP-state's high-wage policy from 1978 was aimed at phasing out low value-added industries and it saw this as an opportunity to cut its reliance on foreign labour.

It especially wanted to cut out non-Chinese migrant workers altogether during this industrial restructuring. The government's euphemism to cover its racism was 'non-traditional sources'. The traditional source was Malaysian Chinese to whom many Singapore Chinese are related. The PAP-state aimed to use the upgrading process to lessen its dependence on non-Chinese workers from other neighbouring countries.

But by 1982 it was clear that the attempt to curtail foreign labour was undermining the PAP-state's support within the local capitalist class. The construction industry needed these workers (*Asia Yearbook*, 1982, pp. 232–3). The PAP-state relented but began to introduce ever more stringent measures to control migrant workers and to ensure they did not get a permanent toe-hold in Singapore.

Therefore, from 1978 the PAP-state took major initiatives to improve the level of each educational stream especially the academic and technical tertiary stream. It also took steps to raise the skill level of those who had already been sorted and failed. Furthermore, it tried to minimise the possibility of low-skilled Chinese foreigners contributing disproportionately to lowering the quality of the permanent population through their offspring. It tried to eliminate this possibility altogether for low-skilled non-Chinese foreigners, first by attempting to dispense with their labour altogether and then by ever more rigorous administration of their short-term permits.

Two other sections of the population that the PAP-state decided to target specifically in its intensification of meritocratic practices were women and the generation yet unborn. This policy was the most remarkable feature of the PAP leadership's social engineering initiatives which accompanied the great leap forward.

Ante-Natal Streaming

In his 1983 National Day address Lee Kuan Yew expressed alarm that the well-educated in the population were reproducing at a slower rate that the less-educated. Women university graduates were averaging 1.65 children while uneducated women were averaging 3.5 children. If this continued, he declared, 'levels of competence will decline. Our economy will suffer and the society will decline' (*ST*, 15 August 1983).

Lee elaborated:

> We gave universal education to the first generation in the early 1960s. In the 1960s and 1970s, we reaped a big crop of able boys and girls. They came from bright parents, many of whom were never educated. In their parents' gen-

eration, the able and not-so-able both had large families. This is a once-ever bumper crop which is not likely to be repeated.

For once, this generation of children from uneducated parents have received their education in the late 1960s and 1970s and as the bright ones make it to the top, to tertiary levels, they will have less than two children per ever-married woman. They will not have large families like their parents.   (Lee Kuan Yew, 1983, p. 5).

This view was consistent with meritocratic ideology elsewhere that 'after several generations of meritocratic selection, those left at the bottom are, biologically speaking, the dregs' (Blum, 1978, p. 178). Lee believed that more than two decades of PAP sorting had seen the able and intelligent rise to positions of wealth and power in Singapore society while the rest had found their true level beneath. The divisions between upper class, middle class and working class now corresponded exactly with levels of intelligence. Furthermore, since he regarded intelligence as hereditary, the failure of those in the upper classes to breed in sufficient numbers to reproduce themselves was a threat to the PAP's ambition to build a developed industrialised country. The educational sorting mechanisms needed more high-quality raw material.

Such logic has unavoidably racist implications. Those breeding too much were not only working class but ethnically were also mainly Malays and Indians. Lee must have noted that, while the early family-planning policies aimed at the poor in the 1960s and early 1970s had a devastating effect on the birth rates of Malays and Indians, their rates were moving back up to replacement level (Yap, 1989, p. 462) which they reached in 1985. Meanwhile the Chinese rate continued to decline and had been insufficient for replacement since 1975 (Yap, 1989, p. 457).

A system of incentives and disincentives had been in place since the 1960s to prevent the working class from breeding too much.

> The disincentives were: an increase in delivery charges in government hospitals for each additional child beyond the second; no paid leave for working women expecting their third or subsequent child; no income tax relief for the fourth and subsequent children; large families not to be given priority in public housing and not to be allowed to sublet rooms in their HDB flats; and higher antenatal care fees for those women with two or more children. The incentives were benefits accruing to those who had undergone sterilisation, namely higher priority in the choice of primary school; waiver of delivery fees; paid medical leave, and unrecorded, full paid leave.   (Quah and Quah, 1989, pp. 112–3).

Lee's justifications for the later introduction of abortion and voluntary sterilisation in 1970 have been noted earlier. Abortion on demand was allowed from 1974. By 1983 the production of parents' sterilisation certificates at the start of primary school was a fact of life (Wilson, 1978, p. 239).

Apparently these measures were not enough. The government encouraged educated Singaporeans to breed more in order to replace and even expand 'the talent pool' (*ST*, 15 August 1983). In January 1984 the government announced that graduate mothers with three or more children would receive top priority in registering their children in the best primary schools. In March 'working mothers' with a degree (that is not working-*class* mothers) and a third child were given 30 per cent tax relief (Quah and Quah, 1989, p. 114).

But working-class women were not forgotten. In June the government stated it would pay $10,000 into the Central Provident Fund of any mother under 30 years of age with little or no education who was willing to be sterilised or ligated after their first or second child. Both parents had to be Singapore citizens or permanent residents with a combined income of under $1500 per month. The money could be used towards the purchase of an HDB flat. There were 311 enquiries on the first day this policy came into effect (*Asiaweek*, 7 September 1984, p. 44; Quah and Quah, 1989, p. 114).

This income limit avoided a pitfall of the previous incentives to be sterilised: better educated women had disproportionately been willing to get sterilised and make use of the primary school priority registration. Non-graduate mothers had not been so keen so that by 1983 there were 37,000 non-graduate mothers with four or more children and low incomes (Quah and Quah, 1989, p. 114). The new policy of paying poor women to be sterilised was aimed at reversing this situation and would, at the same time, tie them more tightly into public housing.

This system of incentives and disincentives to breed was a sorting practice which amounted to a kind of ante-natal streaming. Working-class parents were encouraged to choose to have only one or two children so as not to pollute the talent pool too much. Third and subsequent children were streamed out and not permitted to be born by sterilisation, extra taxes and deposits on HDB flats.

To ensure the availability of working-class women for wage labour once they had bred up to the government limit, the suggestion of full-day schools for their offspring began to be raised from the early 1980s (Seah and Seah, 1983, pp. 249, 262). Until then most schools ran two sessions daily. With children away all day instead of half a day, working-class women would be able to go out to work without any child care costs accruing to the state. Middle- and upper-class women employed foreign women, domestics, the lowest paid workers in Singapore to care for their children. Therefore, the change in schooling pattern was primarily designed to obtain the labour power of working-class women in the workplace as well as in the home and to achieve this objective without increasing the costs of education and other welfare expenditure. It was a way to cut the overall costs of reproducing the working class.

The government wanted to spend its resources on high-quality children and therefore encouraged middle- and upper-class women to produce more of them. These children received preferential treatment from before birth and throughout their school careers. It can be said that even before birth they were placed in the academic stream.

From Mother-Tongue to Father-Faith

The intensification of meritocratic practices from 1978 and their extension into the most personal aspects of people's lives, required a new degree of ideological legitimation in the face of continuing forms of non-cooperation in the education system and in the labour force. This realisation surfaced in the 1978 Goh Report which concluded that the teaching of a course 'Education for Living' and of civics in the mother-tongue was, by itself, insufficient to instil traditional values in the young. The more intensive exploitation of their labour involved in upgrading the economy required an ideological basis for forcing people to stay in their social places and not seek escape. The PAP-state searched for a collective ethic to use against those who gave priority to their personal interest in avoiding increased exploitation and exercised their political rights to do so.

This initiative may have been related to a corresponding move in labour relations during the same period when Lee Kuan Yew called for greater 'team spirit' among workers (*ST*, 1 May 1981) and urged that the Japanese system of industrial relations be followed. Since there was a labour shortage in Singapore, workers were able to change jobs in response to marginal incentives offered by rival employers. Politically this represented another form of non-cooperation or resistance. The situation of full employment gave workers who could not escape their class position the opportunity to at least find the most congenial job conditions available by choosing between employers. Job-hopping forced foreign companies to compete with each other for Singapore workers and they objected to it. Since the PAP could not legislate to force workers to stay in their jobs without undermining the whole ideology of its wage labour system, it encouraged an 'East Asian' ethic of company loyalty along with Japanese methods of intensifying work practices by means of more 'collective' work methods such as quality control circles. The government also tried to instil a higher degree of selfless obedience in the next generation of workers through its ideological formation of school students.

The Goh Report stressed moral education in addition to mother-tongue learning while also indicating that something more was needed in the area of cultural education.

> A society unguided by moral values can hardly be expected to remain cohesive under stress. It is a commitment to a common set of values that will determine the degree to which people of recent migrant origin will be willing and able to defend their collective interest. They will not be able to do this unless individuals belonging to the group are able to discern that an enlightened view of their long-term self-interest often conflicts with their desire for immediate gain.

> [W]hile moral education would help to give school children a set of values which could guide them in their adult life, this may not be sufficient to provide the cultural ballast to withstand the stresses of living in a fast changing society exposed to influences, good and bad, of an open society such as ours. With the large scale movement to education in English, the risk of deculturization cannot be ignored. One way to overcoming the danger of deculturization is to teach children the historical origins of their culture. (*Report of the Ministry of Education 1978*)

In 1979 a moral education programme was launched which had been developed by a Catholic priest. It dealt with an individual's awareness of self and of her or his relation to society. It encouraged young people to identify the values underlying the choices facing them, to make the choice they wanted and to accept the consequences. But some of their parents chose to vote for the opposition in the 1981 Anson by-election and the PAP-state decided this choice should not be encouraged. It stopped the programme.

> While the young people were being taught responsibility in decision-making, they were also being initiated in the concept of rights, individual and social. This was really too dangerous. In 1982 the programme which had already been developed for secondaries one and two was stopped. (*Voices from Singapore*, December 1990, p. 3)

The PAP-state then appeared to conclude that a moral and cultural grounding which would minimise the assertion of individual political rights could be supplied by the formal teaching of religion from an academic perspective.

This unsentimental, pragmatic view of religion as a means of social control potentially at the disposal of the state was not disguised. The PAP-state's lack of sentiment for religious tradition had recently been well proven by the demolition of a 120-year-old Chinese temple by the Housing and Development Board to make way for a swimming complex. In 1977 the central Sikh temple had been destroyed for another HDB complex. Both acts had been strongly opposed by the respective religious communities (*Asia Yearbook*, 1979, p. 289).

In 1982 Education Minister Goh Keng Swee introduced compulsory religious education as an examination subject in secondary schools from 1984. Every student had to study at least one subject from a list which included Confucianism, Islam, Hinduism, Buddhism and Christianity. At the same time the general population was subjected to an extended government campaign on Confucian ethics, the use of Mandarin and Chinese identity. This was the government's ideological conditioning of Chinese Singaporeans for the 1984 general elections: an attempt to stem the electoral tide towards the opposition which the Second Industrial Revolution had accelerated. The message was that parliamentary opposition was not merely un-Asian but anti-Asian.

In the third quarter of 1982, eight Confucian scholars were invited by the Ministry of Education to help draft guidelines for the subject of Confucian Ethics. They gave public talks on the subject in English and Mandarin, and held discussions with relevant bodies such as the Faculty of Arts and Social Sciences of the National University of Singapore. The Chinese dailies published, almost every day for months, articles and comments on the subject.... [S]ome of these Confucian scholars (from the United States) expressed their impressions obtained from ethnic Chinese pupils in the secondary schools they visited that most Chinese would *choose* to study Confucian ethics. (Chiew, 1983, p. 257; my emphasis)

The PAP-state let Chinese students know that another subject of merit was Confucian ethics and that there was no doubt at all that this was their cultural heritage. Since it was expected that students would take the subject most relevant to their own cultural heritage, the majority of Chinese were thereby induced to take courses in Confucian ethics which stressed the moral rectitude of loyalty to the patriarchal state even at the expense of one's personal wellbeing.

Confucius, according to Goh Keng Swee, 'believed that unless the government is in the hands of upright men, disaster will befall the country. By the way, in this respect, the PAP also believes the same thing' (*ST*, 4 February 1982). The implication was that if a government is in the hands of 'upright men' like the PAP, then it should not be questioned but respected and obeyed (Rodan, 1989, pp. 172–3). When announcing the scheme, Goh Keng Swee threatened that any parents not wanting their children to study any religion or system of ethics would be personally interviewed by him (*FEER*, 19 October 1989).

This use of religion had a deeper purpose beyond that of undermining immediate parliamentary dissent or inducing conformity in the young. Confucianism and the major religious traditions all sanctify hierarchical, patriarchal familial relations. This ideological reinforcement of male power was also aimed at the increasing opposition of women who were refusing to breed and work at the new intensity required by the PAP.

Political Achievements of Meritocratic Intensification

The more rigorous and targeted sorting practices of the new education system achieved some useful results. Educational levels improved (Table 5.1). However these levels remained markedly behind those of Singapore's competitors. South Korea and Taiwan remained far ahead in tertiary education (*FEER*, 25 August 1988, p. 59; Linda Lim, 1989, p. 179).

Table 5.1 Educational Levels
(percentage of total labour force)

	less than primary	secondary	post-secondary	tertiary
1974	40.3	19.7	6.2	2.4
1985	22.8	29.3	11.0	5.2

Source: Linda Lim (1989) p. 178.

The political effects of this sharp intensification of exploitation and social control were also very clear in terms of the social structure. Salaff's study of Singapore families before and after the launching of the 'second stage' economy showed three major effects: the reinforcement of the class structure, the increased use by the poor of welfare mechanisms, including the education system and further fragmentation of the working class.

She discovered that poor parents used the school system more than previously, but that their children remained at the bottom of it. She noted their disadvantages in planning their children's education, in employing tutors for private tuition and in choosing schools (Salaff, 1988, p. 249).

Salaff's examination of the new skills training programmes showed that the poor 'are least likely to upgrade their jobs through training programmes' and that men without diplomas could not compete for the better jobs (Salaff, 1988, pp. 230, 263). She found that few firms hired women graduates of training programmes and that working class women were generally doomed to low-wage labour (Salaff, 1988, p. 234).

> A family's ability to buy a home in the public sector and the extent of its use of educational and family planning programmes turn on income, education and property.... Thus the Singapore development strategy has changed outward appearances of family life-style more than internal relations.... families retain their distinct positions in the class structure and in wage labour. (Salaff, 1988, p. 262)

With the attempt to upgrade skills, the opportunities for upward social mobility were taken by some better-off elements of the working class and of the lower middle class. According to Salaff this only worsened the fragmentation of the working class.

> [N]ow that sections of the formerly poor are advancing, and with the meritocracy as the overarching ideology, the community of the poor is not cohesive. Families that have bettered themselves contract their ties to a small circle.... [V]ery poor families have lost their supportive community. (Salaff, 1988, p. 268)

Other writers have also noted the sudden increase in poverty and inequality.

> Between 1979 and 1983, income inequality widened between workers in different occupations and between workers with different educational qualifications. By 1983 the average earnings of administrative and managerial personnel were five times more than those of production and service personnel. (Bello and Rosenfeld, 1990, p. 331)

Therefore, in terms of the PAP's political agenda, there were positive developments. Educational and skill levels were improved, though not enough. At the same time the working class was tied more firmly into the educational sorting mechanisms and its capacity for class solidarity was further undermined by increased inequality.

It would appear from early trends that initiatives for ante-natal streaming of the working class were also having the desired effect. But the associated attempt to raise the fertility of educated women failed (Yap, 1989, p. 470).

The imposition of Confucian ethics achieved some degree of legitimation of the PAP-state's welfare objectives. The sudden concern to reassert patriarchal relations through emphasis on the extended family and filial piety, which the PAP-state had previously been instrumental in breaking down, included the pedestrian aim of relieving the government of the increasing cost of welfare expenditure on the elderly. This came at a time when it wanted to increase its funding of infrastructural developments.

> The government's promotion of filial piety was certainly to some extent motivated by the expected shortfall in land available for public housing. It also provided justification for government attempts to curtail welfare spending which would enable increased expenditure on economic development. (Rodan, 1989, p. 173)

This enlargement of the nuclear family by tacking on elderly parents was another attempt to lower the overall cost of welfare by loading more costs on to the primary social unit. This objective was eloquently expressed by Senior Minister Rajaratnam:

> We want to teach people the government is not a rich uncle. You get what you pay for. We are moving in the direction of making people pay for everything.... We want to disabuse people of the notion that in a good society the rich must pay for the poor. (Vasil, 1984, p. 168)

The new emphasis on the extended family was not a genuine attempt to recreate it since that would entail the recreation of autonomous communities with their web of kinship relationships. Not only would such a development be against the interests of the PAP, but it would also be impossible without major changes to Singapore's economic development model. Rather Confucian ethics and religious instruction in schools was primarily concerned with legitimising the new level of exploitation by engendering obedience and loyalty and reinforcing patriarchal relations to overcome the non-cooperation of women. The success of this primary aim was doubtful.

By 1985 it was clear that PAP-state's rigorous control of the centralised education system had indeed enabled it to initiate rapid change to meet the labour requirements of a high-technology economy. But it was also clear that Singapore had fallen short of the objective and new problems had arisen.

A Crisis of Legitimacy

The roots of the crisis faced by the PAP in 1985–6 lay partly in the strategies for reproducing the class structure, for reinforcing the subordination of women and for racial domination which had been implemented within the education system. They had sharpened underlying social conflicts and undermined the ideological legitimacy of the process of social sorting.

Escape from Class
The ideological power of meritocratic sorting comes from its appearance as a natural social ordering process and as being in the interests of all individuals. The Second Industrial Revolution's sudden shift of policy made it difficult to achieve this legitimation. The sharp, ruthless and explicit targeting of different sectors of society for different treatment began to reveal the PAP's real political objectives. Far from negating rising opposition to almost two decades of industrialisation, the Second Industrial Revolution further stimulated it.

For example, the ideological impact of early streaming was to heighten the sense of competition at all levels of education and to increase the fear of failure. The ideological assumption of equal opportunity was undermined when this fear turned into the certainty of failure. Also the priority scheme for children of graduate mothers alienated both educated women, who felt classified as mere breeding machines and working-class women, who felt deeply discriminated against.

The most visible manifestations of the rising alienation and opposition which created this crisis were the loss of the 1981 by-election and a 12 per cent swing against the PAP in the 1984 general election. But there was another damaging indication. By the mid-1980s approximately 2000 families per year were emigrating to Western countries. After 1985 the outflow increased considerably and the government estimate of approximately 10,000 families between 1986 and 1989 is probably a very conservative figure (*STW*, 21 January, 26 August, 16 December 1989). In 1989 itself an estimated 4700 families (16,000 people) emigrated (Elegant, 1989, p. 18), a figure proportionately not far below the exodus of the middle and upper classes from Hong Kong, who faced an uncertain future with China (*The Economist*, 10 March 1990, p. 37).

This loss of educated Singaporeans represented a serious blow to upgrading the educational level of the population. Lee Kuan Yew spent much of his 1989 National

Day address on this issue, making a very emotional appeal for loyalty. *The Straits Times* headline read: 'PM, close to tears, tells nation: Singaporeans must have conviction that this is their country and their life'. Directly addressing emigrants, Lee declared: 'You are a washout'. The foreign media noted, 'leaving is perhaps the cruellest of opposition gestures' (*The Economist*, 11 November 1989, p. 41) and that it constituted a social breakdown of serious proportions because of the significant numbers involved (*The Economist*, 10 March 1990, p. 37).

Escape as a form of dissent reflects the realisation of the middle class either that their or their children's chances of joining the capitalist class were minimal or that the rewards were not worth the effort. As one emigrant said, 'People just get tired of living in the sixth form all their lives' (Elegant, 1989, p. 18). They were escaping the classification system altogether. Mass emigration indicated, among other things, a breakdown in meritocratic educational practice and ideology. There was no choice in Singapore that they wished to choose.

Patriarchy and Capitalism

Upgrading population 'quality' by linking family planning to education had mixed results. The attempts to raise fertility among the better educated had largely failed (Yap, 1989, p. 470). Over the long term, the Population Planning Unit of the Ministry of Health estimated, on the basis of the birth rate, a 25 per cent decline in the 15–29 age group from 816,000 in 1985 to 619,000 by the year 2000. In 1986 60 per cent of clerical workers, 40 per cent of production workers and 30 per cent of all service workers were under 30 years of age. Hence, the manufacturing, financial and services sectors would be hard hit by this decline (*FEER*, 25 August 1988). Combined with the slow rise in educational levels, this trend made the government's short-term aim of having 20 per cent of the labour force in professional or technical jobs by 1995, compared to less than 14 per cent in 1980, look increasingly unrealistic (*The Economist*, 15 August 1987, p. 22). The total population was forecast to peak in 2010 at 2.9 million and then decline by the end of the century to half its present size (*Asia Yearbook*, 1988, p. 223). The PAP-state faced a crisis not only of its attempt to improve the skills of the existing labour force but of maintaining the class structure of that force over the long term.

The refusal of middle- and upper-class Chinese women to reproduce was one of the main forms of non-cooperation behind the failure of this PAP policy. They refused in a number of ways: by not getting married at all, by marrying late and having few children, if any or by escaping the PAP-state's breeding controls altogether. The latter option included emigration, marriage to a foreigner or both. (The social and political sanctions against unmarried women having children rendered the single parent family without patriarchal dominance an almost impossible option.) The openly discriminatory nature of the graduate mother scheme with its explicit connection between class and educational privilege was a major stimulus of this non-cooperation.

Behind this resistance lay a deeper conflict between the imperatives of patriarchy and the requirements of capitalism. The first priority of a patriarchal system of social relations is control of women's breeding: 'the appropriation of the labour of women as *reproducers*' (Lerner, 1986, p. 52; her emphasis). In contrast, the priorities of capitalist social relations are the exploitation of labour power in the work place and of unpaid labour in the home.

Women in Singapore are needed for their reproductive labour, their wage labour and their unpaid domestic labour but in varying amounts according to their class. Working-class women were pressured to provide more low-wage labour and less reproductive labour so as to lower welfare costs, raise the surplus generated and avoid diluting the talent pool too much. Middle- and upper-class women were pressured to deliver more of their high-quality babies as well as to engage in paid work and domestic labour. However, they frequently employ foreign women as domestic workers and have thereby been increasingly freed from such unpaid work themselves. (Through the levy paid to the government, which is in addition to the maids' wages, the PAP-state has ensured that educated women reimburse the cost of reproducing this labour.) Therefore, Singapore women are subject to two systems of power organising in relation to each other and which increasingly came into conflict under the social pressures of the economic upgrading strategy.

As women have internalised the capitalist ideology of meritocracy with its individualistic values through their involvement in education, they have come into conflict with hierarchical male dominance both at home and in the work place. The pressure to work has emphasised the similarity between husband and employer in terms of subordination. The pressure to breed has exacerbated the contradiction between personal achievement through paid labour and the patriarchal state's appropriation of their reproductive labour. These conflicts have undermined patriarchal relations just when the development of capitalism to a new stage needed them.

The government's promotion of patriarchal ethics and religion backfired by sharpening the contradictions between patriarchy and capitalism. The social ethics of Confucianism and major religious traditions are generally based on the pre-capitalist self-sufficient home where the patriarchal family was an integral part of the system of production. However, 'the capitalist patriarchal family is based on the distinction between domestic and wage labour, and hence is represented ideologically as separate and apart from the world of work (wage labour)' (Eisenstein, 1980, p. 50).

Religious education undermined the ideological separation of home and work, as did the explicit PAP demands to produce more children for the work-force. There was a widespread feeling among women that the state had intruded too far into personal matters (Quah and Quah, 1989, p. 114). Many middle-class Chinese women became willing publicly to oppose Confucian ethics as anachronistic, oppressive and alien. Some Chinese Christian women were drawn to liberation theology and Christian feminism as an ideological critique of PAP policy. Since the PAP-state had officially encouraged religious education within the state education system, it could not immediately suppress this dissent which the contradictions of its own policies had stimulated.

Middle- and upper-class women were able to vent their opposition to the linkage between breeding, education and religion because they faced less risk of censure and could do so without directly attacking the PAP's accumulation strategy. Probably their greater investment in meritocratic education made them more aware of these contradictions than working-class women, who were not only more exploited but also subject to greater social control.

But educated women did not connect their dissent to class and race in a fundamental critique of PAP economic policy. For example, the alternative policy of expanding welfare provisions to ensure greater educational opportunities for the disadvantaged after they were born and thereby obtaining the required talent from all sectors of society, was not central to their critique. Therefore, even with regard to a deeply unpopular policy, the government did not lose the political initiative completely. Nevertheless, the contradictions between the requirements of patriarchy and of industrialisation limited the government's ability to extract the maximum potential labour power from women. Women refused to cooperate.

Racism and Class

The intensified social control measures of this period also uncovered the relationship between race and class. Government policies were increasingly experienced and understood as racist as the PAP-state put more and more effort into its priorities of reproducing the Chinese capitalist class and of containing Malays and Indians in the lower reaches of the working class.

The first priority was threatened by the exodus of Chinese professionals and the refusal of the remaining educated Chinese women to reproduce their race and class to replacement level. The second priority was frustrated by the relative success in discouraging poor Chinese women from breeding and the failure to persuade Malay and Indian women to follow suit. The refusal of these minority women to collaborate with state control of their mothering can also been seen as a kind of unorganised non-cooperation.

The linkage of education to reproduction patterns in the graduate mothers was detected as racist by Malays who were aware of their low achievement rate in the education system. Furthermore, the PAP exacerbated these tensions by imposing religious education. This added another explosive factor to the fraught equation between ethnicity and language which the government had already politicised within the education system. Now each student's official classification according to ethnicity, language and religion determined at least two of the subjects taken and also the chances of educational success. Malays were forced to take Malay language as their second language and Islamic studies as their religious subject. Neither had any value in the scheme of the PAP's political economy, a fact made abundantly clear by the PAP's constant and almost exclusive emphasis on

Mandarin and Confucianism, an emphasis experienced as racist by minority communities.

The main ideological effect of these measures was the exposure of the PAP's multi-racialism as bogus. It became more obvious that the PAP policy was one of containing Malays within the lower sections of the working class, including the latent reserve, while accepting a token presence in the top levels of the administration to sustain the PAP's multi-racial credentials. The PAP-state's heightened concern with Chinese breeding patterns was increasingly understood as a fear of Malays increasing their numbers as a proportion of the total population. A declining proportion of Chinese in the population would undermine the legitimacy of a Chinese state in a Malay region. The combination of racism and class discrimination suffered by Malays ensured strong electoral opposition from this community. Their disloyalty did not go unnoticed by the PAP; as we have seen, racial quotas were soon imposed in HDB estates.

Regulation of foreign workers was the other focus of state racist practices. Employment-pass holders, overwhelmingly Caucasian and Chinese middle-class professionals and business people from Malaysia and elsewhere, were able to bring their families to Singapore, to marry Singaporeans, to use the education system and to join the CPF (an incentive to foreigners who could take out the total amount in cash on departure). Work-permit holders, mainly working-class production workers, construction labourers and domestics, from Malaysia, Thailand, Indonesia, the Philippines and Sri Lanka, were stringently controlled and denied the rights accorded employment-pass holders. This fragmentation of the working class, enhanced by racist policies, had advantages in cementing social control over the whole class.

The PAP-state's economic strategy from 1978 involved a regime of intensified social control which exacerbated underlying structural tensions of racism, class discrimination and patriarchal domination. By mediating control of so many social conflicts through the education system the government unwittingly stimulated the growth of new forms of opposition and non-cooperation against itself and ensured the failure of its economic revolution.

PRIVATISING THE POLITICS OF EDUCATION

The shift to a new system of education was prominent among the steps the PAP-state took to restore its legitimacy after 1985. This adjustment is not obvious from the priorities and content of the educational practices. The substantive educational requirements of the alliance with foreign capital remained in place and were further consolidated. However, the education system was made new in the sense that its regulatory role became more confined to its primary roles of sorting and skilling within educational institutions. It was delinked from its explicit connections with the class-based state-breeding strategies which had previously undermined its legitimating meritocratic ideology. The government sought other means to control women's reproductive labour. The PAP-state also distanced itself from direct political responsibility for the educational process by privatising the elite sectors of the education system. At the same time communalist education strategies were realigned to suppress political dissent. The government made another attempt to reassert its ideological hegemony through the formalisation of a state ideology and it gave up the attempt at using religion for this purpose.

These measures did not lessen state control of the education system. Rather by giving the appearance of greater educational autonomy the government aimed to recover its control. Neither did these steps address the fundamental contradictions of PAP policy. They constituted a counter-attack on the forms of dissent and non-cooperation which had arisen and which were the political manifestations of these contradictions.

This effort to revivify the control functions of education was part of a general offensive after 1985. For example, the PAP-state also adjusted the mechanisms for the legal expression of dissent: voting in parliamentary elections (see chapter 6). It further criminalised opposition politics to discourage anyone from standing for parliament. It introduced the Town Council scheme to prevent HDB residents from casting opposition votes without a cost to themselves in terms of services and property values (Chapter 3).

The rest of this chapter examines the initiatives to make a new education system after 1985: the consolidation of educational priorities in accordance with the political economy, the adjusted strategies for reproducing the capitalist class and the working class, the privatisation of education, the realignment of communalist policies and the formalisation of a state ideology.

Consolidation of Educational Priorities

Since 1985 there have been several reports reaffirming the educational priorities of the Second Industrial Revolution. The 1986 Economic Committee report called for a more skilled and creative labour force. This reflected the hard reality that, even to keep at the leading edge of NIC production, something had to be done about the fact that approximately half of the Singapore labour force still had only primary-level education or less. Also National University of Singapore graduates had acquired the reputation in business and industry of being better at following manuals than dealing with concepts or thinking for themselves (*FEER*, 25 August 1988; *STW*, 25 March 1989).

A 1990 report *Building a Firm Foundation* was based on a study of Japan and Taiwan and recommended a more rigorous streaming process, single session schools, teacher upgrading and more moral education (*STW*, 4 August 1990). The Minister of Education went on record stating that 'there was a need for Singapore's education system to move away from the British–American model – which provides a general liberal education for all – to one akin to the German–

Swiss system which stresses technical and/or vocational education for the majority of students' (*STW*, 28 July 1990). He later stated:

> It is clear, therefore, that maintaining and, indeed, improving levels of achievement in Mathematics and English must be a primary task of the Ministry of Education. If levels of achievement in these two subjects drop, we will suffer an overall decline in the educational performance of our children, which will have long term adverse economic consequences for Singapore. (*STW*, 17 November 1990)

These statements and reports show no deviation from previous practices, only refinements and reaffirmations of them. The PAP remained committed to increasing social control through more rigorous sorting and forcing through an educational agenda politicised by its industrialisation strategy.

There were steps to improve the education system in line with these priorities such as the establishment of a second university (*STW*, 7 March 1990) and the awarding of marks to students at the National University for speaking in tutorials as a way to promote creativity (*STW*, 13 October 1990). More worker training schemes were launched such as the Worker Improvement through Secondary Education (WISE) programme set up in 1987 to give the 600,000 eligible workers, 53 per cent of the labour force (including the 23 per cent who had no schooling at all), basic competence in English and mathematics (*Asia Yearbook*, 1987, p. 236; *The Economist*, 15 August 1987; GOS, 1989a, p. 196).

The main innovations in educational content reflected the shift in the internationalisation of capital. The growing importance of Japanese and European capital in a multipolar global economy was recognised in the encouragement of French, German and Japanese language learning. This was the PAP's formal acknowledgement in educational practice of the need to attract more capital from the European Community and Japan (*STW*, 1, 22, 29 September 1990).

Delinking Education from Reproductive Labour

The PAP did not draw back from its determination to reproduce the Chinese capitalist class. Neither did it lessen the pressure on middle- and upper-class Chinese women to have more babies. If anything the pressure increased as a major source of racial replenishment was drying up. Educated Malaysian Chinese now, in Lee Kuan Yew's words, 'leap-frogged' Singapore for the West (*STW*, 26 August 1989).

But in 1985 the government did withdraw the graduate mother priority scheme in the face of sustained public anger. It continued to pursue the same objectives but without the explicit link between class and educational privilege that this scheme demonstrated. Instead of using educational qualifications to target the class of women it wanted to breed and instead of using priority entry for their children as an incentive, the PAP-state switched to targeting them through income levels.

In 1987 the government introduced income-related incentives for baby production. Tax relief for a third child was increased and a tax rebate of $20,000 added. That is, if your household income was sufficient to attract more than $20,000 in tax, then you received that amount back as a rebate. In 1988 tax reliefs for children were doubled to $1500 and extended to a fourth child. The $20,000 rebate was also made available for a fourth child (*STW*, 11 March 1989, 16 June 1990). In 1990 a tax rebate of $20,000 was offered for couples who have their second child early and the five-year claim period for the $20,000 rebate for third and fourth children was extended to seven years (*STW*, 22 December 1990). The child tax reliefs were aimed at maintaining the birth rate of the Chinese working class. The much larger tax rebates could only apply to those on high salaries since only they paid sufficient tax to qualify for the rebates. The rebates were therefore designed as breeding incentives to educated women.

This was a policy switch from targeting class reproduction through educational levels to targeting it directly through income levels. It was a variation on the previously noted income targeting of the poorest in the working class for sterilisation whereby a maximum income level established eligibility for sterilisation cash incentives.

This tax strategy avoided the odium attracted by the graduate mothers scheme. As Lee Kuan Yew pointed out when congratulating the new generation of PAP leadership, the same political objective had been reached by other means:

> Giving them [graduate mothers] preference for their children in school became very unpopular and very objectionable. So do we change? All right, we concede. But the principle to get more educated women to have more children has not changed. And income tax reliefs have been given, which means it's all fair, in accordance with what you pay the government.
>
> If you don't pay, then obviously you can't afford to be given relief. So in that way, they [the new PAP leaders] have been able to get their objectives.... We have given not blanket incentives, not maternity leave for the third child which will encourage people who can't afford the third child to have one. So we give it to those who can afford.... It has produced results. That is the joy of working for Singapore. (*STW*, 1 September 1990)

Differentiation on the basis of class through income was ideologically acceptable to Singaporeans because it accorded with the ideological effect of meritocratic practices. A person's individual economic success was perceived as determined by their individual ability and efforts. The decision as to whether to take advantage of financial incentives was also seen as a personal one, not a discriminatory policy imposed by the state.

Having removed the ideologically damaging link with education, the PAP-state then went on the offensive. In a speech to a university audience on 12 December 1986, Lee Kuan Yew expressed concern about the step before breeding, marriage. Not enough single educated women were getting married: 39 per cent of women with a tertiary education were choosing to remain single. He also produced charts to show the 'lop-sided' birth rate with Malays more than reproducing themselves, Indians nearly doing so and Chinese far behind. He further showed that the children of graduate mothers and graduate fathers were consistently at the top of all educational levels, ahead even of those whose fathers but not mothers were graduates.

The primary, if convoluted, message to the assembled students was directed at male students, telling them to avoid marriage to non-graduate women:

> [R]emember when you get married, be prepared, as Bernard Shaw says to an actress, to have your daughter as stupid as your wife and as ugly as you instead of as pretty as your wife and as smart as you. Now if you're satisfied with that, then marry her and vice versa. If you are not, then think again because there are shared attributes. Some 250,000 genes go into one chromosome. They don't come from outer space. It's the method of biological transmission whether it's fruits, animals or human beings. (*ST*, 16 December 1986, p. 25)

Lee recognised that in a patriarchal society, men can, by marriage, raise women of inferior class status to their own class level. The reverse can rarely happen. This mechanism for acquiring the reproductive labour of working-class women is in conflict with the meritocratic practices of capitalism. It lessened the pressure on educated women to have their reproductive capacities appropriated by men of their own class.

Furthermore, it seemed that middle- and upper-class men were showing an increasing preference for their female social inferiors. Educated men were apparently reluctant to marry women educated to an equal standard as themselves because these women had internalised the individualism of meritocracy. They were a threat to patriarchal relations within the family. Lee sought to close off this form of female escape from social control by paternalistic prescription, by encouraging men to marry within their class.

Lee also reaffirmed that the government would not waste money on an equal standard of education for the working class:

> Do these statistics lie? Every year it can be repeated. The West knows this. But the Western liberal says let's not talk about it, then we won't spend money on those who need that extra help. Well, maybe they can lavish their resources away. We can't. We've got to know what are the profiles. What returns for what investment. (*ST*, 15 December 1986, p. 19)

The encouragement to students to marry within their class (and therefore race) and the statement that the government would spend money on them rather than on the poor were not, of course, particularly offensive to them or the English-educated public. The outcry came when Lee turned to the problem that marriages between educated parents yielded few children. He appeared to endorse an obvious solution.

Three years ago I was talking to some journalists, analysing these figures for them.... And [a woman journalist] said to me, 'But, Prime Minister, if a man wants to marry me for my genes, I don't want to marry him.' And I thought to myself, 'What a silly ass of a girl.'

When the Japanese *zaibatsu* chairman says, 'Find me a son-in-law' to the vice-minister, he is wanting to ensure that his grandchildren will measure up. And the way the old society did it was by polygamy. The successful ... had more than one wife. In fact, you can have as many as your economic status entitles you or can persuade people to give their daughters up to you. In other words, the unsuccessful are like the weak lions or bucks in a herd, they were neutralised.

So over the generations you must have the physically and the mentally more vibrant and vital reproduce. We are doing just the opposite. We introduced monogamy. It seems so manifestly correct. The West was successful, superior. Why? Because they are monogamous? It was wrong. It was stupid.

When Mr Tanaka was asked in the Japanese Diet five, six years ago, 'You've got another mistress with children there?' he nodded in vehement agreement. He said, 'That's quite right.' And the more Tanakas there are in Japan, I have no doubt the more dynamic will be Japanese society. (*ST*, 15 December 1986)

Four years later in his final National Day address as prime minister, Lee again addressed a form of political non-compliance by women which offended his racial sensibilities and raised the spectre of a significant non-Chinese presence in the capitalist class: the marriage of educated women within their class but to Caucasian foreigners. He warned:

The Singapore woman is not stupid. She knows that white men marry you freely, they also divorce you freely. (Applause) And I believe the children will also be a plus because they are going to be highly competent and well-trained persons. Of course, you know there are innate prejudices. And I don't pretend that I don't share those prejudices. I do. If one of my sons had come back and said, "I've got this American lady whom I met in America, my first question is, what colour is she? (Laughter).   (*STW*, 1 September 1990; parentheses in *STW* report)

Despite the racial pollution involved, consistency in its eugenics ideology demanded that the PAP-state recognise that the offspring of such intraclass unions would be highly-intelligent. In order to keep the resultant high-quality babies, permanent residence regulations were relaxed to enable such couples to remain in Singapore (*STW*, 8 September 1990). Nevertheless Lee lamented:

That 50 per cent of graduate girls will either marry down [less-educated men], marry foreigners or stay unmarried, it is a very unhappy position for any country to be in.   (*STW*, 1 September 1990)

That the other 50 per cent of graduate women were marrying graduate men was, however, seen as an improvement over 1983 when only 37.6 per cent did so. The increase was partially due to the establishment in 1983 of the government's Social Development Unit (SDU) which was an officially sanctioned and promoted dating service aimed at overcoming the two main forms of non-cooperation by bourgeois Chinese women: remaining single and marrying foreigners. The SDU provided an education programme in how to have normal personal relationships, an area of knowledge previously denied to many young educational achievers. Educated single women and men in the civil service, statutory boards and major companies were pressured to register with the SDU and to attend its functions. Initially popularly lampooned as standing for 'Single, Desperate and Ugly', the official pressure paid off to the extent that 240 couples were married through its auspices in 1988 (*STW*, 29 April 1989).

While the PAP-state used the category of educational level to ensure intraclass unions, the success rate of its official programmes remained far from solving the problem perceived by the PAP leadership. This was because the trends towards a single life-style and fewer children were themselves a product of economic growth and meritocracy and of upper-class membership. The conflict between patriarchal and capitalist social relations remained.

This conflict reached its most intense when the government arrested 22 middle class professionals and community workers in two security sweeps code-named Operation Spectrum on 21 May 1987 and a month later. They were detained without trial under the Internal Security Act and harshly interrogated, leading to an international human rights campaign for their release (Asia Watch, 1989, p. 18). Twelve of the detainees were women, almost all single and/or childless. This security sweep can be understood politically as mainly directed at women who had risen to professional status in the meritocracy but who had no desire to earn a lot of money and join the capitalist class and who were not under patriarchal control through mothering. Several days of continuous interrogation in underground cells was partly aimed at enabling the government to understand this political phenomenon, as well as being aimed at obtaining the usual forced confessions of complicity in a plot to overthrow the PAP. The PAP-state had minimal means of control over such people and resorted to secret-police tactics to suppress this form of opposition which was subversive of both capitalist and patriarchal social relations. Furthermore, the detainees were involved in legal and welfare assistance to foreign workers and domestics, the most exploited section of the working class.

Adjusted Strategy for Working-class Reproduction

After 1985 the PAP-state changed the structure of the working class and its strategy for reproducing it to accord more closely with its accumulation process. The core of the working class would remain Chinese and male. Women would continue to be pressured into low-paid, part-time wage labour and used as a latent reserve. To help make up for the 120,000 Chinese babies short of replacement level since 1975 (Lee Kuan Yew in *STW*, 26 August 1989), the reproductive labour of the better-off sections of the working class would also be encouraged through child tax relief and adjusted school times. The government followed up on its plans to introduce single session schools to release women from child care during the day (*STW*, 1 September 1990). It also brought in 'full-time benefits' for part-time workers (*STW*, 18 August 1990) in order to draw some of the 540,000 women not in wage labour into the labour force (*STW*, 9 September 1989).

The breeding efforts of working-class Chinese women were to be supplemented by encouraging the immigration of Chinese skilled labour from Hong Kong and elsewhere. Malays were finally consigned to the bottom of the resident working class and little money was to be wasted on the education of this core of political opposition.

Non-Chinese, temporary, foreign workers were accepted as a permanent sector of the working class and, in light of this, were to be even more rigorously controlled to prevent any individuals from gaining permanent residence status. The continuing denial of full-time benefits to this large sector of the working class facilitated their provision to Singaporean Chinese women.

The encouragement of Hong Kong migrants and the acceptance of a permanent, rotating sector of foreign workers were aspects of a racist policy to undermine both the strength of the resident Chinese working class and of the Malay community.

Importing Chinese Breeding Stock
The PAP-state took advantage of the 1997 deadline for British rule in Hong Kong and the post-Tiananmen panic to offer permanent residence to 100,000 Hong Kong Chinese skilled workers (*STW*, 15 July 1989). This was an attempt to acquire pre-sorted and skilled Chinese breeding stock. A year later, of the 14, 500 skilled workers granted permanent residence, only 1300 were living in Singapore. Of them, 950 were already working in Singapore when they applied (*STW*, 24 March, 28 July 1990). The success of this scheme remains open to question since Singapore is not a first choice for most Hong Kong people. Many Hong Kong Chinese see Singapore as a Chinese island in a Malay sea and have doubts about its long-term stability. In addition a Mandarin–English-speaking Chinese society is not especially attractive to Cantonese speakers (*STW*, 16 February 1991).

This immigration scheme was justified as keeping Singapore's racial 'balance' (*STW*, 29 July 1989). Guaranteeing 76 per cent Chinese dominance was more accurately but less often referred to as keeping the racial status quo as in the report of Lee Kuan Yew's 1989 National Day speech:

'Let us just maintain the status quo. And we have to maintain it or there will be a shift in the economy, both the economic performance and the political backdrop which makes that economy possible.' Mr Lee said statistics showed there will be significant differences in the economy of Singapore if the ratio were transposed. 'You look at the educational levels of the performers. It has got to do with culture, nature and so many other factors. But year after year, this is the end result. Let's leave well alone. The formula has worked. Keep it.'

Disclosing that a straw poll had indicated that Chinese Singaporeans favoured the new policy while Malays and Indians were against it, he said race was a human instinct that would not go away. (*STW*, 26 August 1989)

Temporary Workers Become Permanent Sector
Foreign workers are divided by race by the euphemistic categories of traditional source (working-class Malaysian Chinese) and non-traditional source (Thai, Filipino, Indian, etc.). Malaysian Chinese are permitted to work in the service sector although they may not exceed ten per cent of the workers in that sector (*STW*, 10, 24 March 1990). Other races (nationalities) are restricted by government regulation to manufacturing, construction, shipyards and domestic help. To induce employers to restrict their reliance on foreign labour and to upgrade their technological level, employers must pay a levy to the state of $300 per month per worker (to increase to $350 per month from April 1991) (*STW*, 10 March 1990; *FEER*, 21 February 1991). This levy is part of the surplus created by the foreign workers and, thus, can also be seen as their reimbursement of the daily costs of their reproduction. Furthermore, in order to ensure that foreign workers do not acquire roots in Singapore and that the government is not liable for any welfare benefits for them, they are still not permitted to join the CPF.

Draconian immigration legislation was introduced to tighten control of foreign workers (*STW*, 28 January, 4 February 1989). The legislation was first used in 1989 when the government expelled as illegal overstayers 9800 Thai workers and 1900 Indian workers (*STW*, 20 May 1989) on pain of caning and imprisonment. This initial use of the legislation was to clear Singapore of foreigners who had evaded the new level of regulation and to ensure that the more stringent immigration procedures would henceforth exert full control over all migrant workers. Many of those expelled were later permitted to re-enter properly documented.

The regulations covering migrant workers prevent them from bringing their families or from breeding in Singapore. All female workers, especially foreign maids, have compulsory AIDS tests and six-monthly pregnancy tests (*STW*, 14 April 1990). Men may not marry without government permission on pain of immediate repatriation. They have no children to be sorted by the education system and there are consequently no welfare costs to the Singapore state of processing a succeeding generation. Those costs accrue to their home countries.

The acceptance by the PAP-state that a significant and rising proportion of the population will consist of temporarily resident foreigners is a major development of the late 1980s. The move to allow foreign workers into the services sector was a result of the failure of the attempt to upgrade the economy and the subsequent emphasis on services. The racial disadvantage, as perceived by the PAP, of having such a large number of non-Chinese workers has been offset by their political function in fragmenting the working class. They have no political rights to exercise and are only interested in saving their wages to take back home. They also keep down wages in the industrial sector and the government pays nothing at all for their generational reproduction.

This new policy also means that the education system and other welfare institutions no longer extend their regulatory mechanisms across the whole of Singapore society. The primary regulatory mechanisms for foreign workers are the immigration laws and their contracts with employers. This is a reversion to the practices of the colonial state.

Lee Kuan Yew has acknowledged this parasitical role of feeding off the cheap labour and misery of surrounding countries as a permanent feature of Singapore's polity.

In another ten years, we will not get workers from Malaysia or Thailand. In another fifteen years, no more from Indonesia. We may have to go to Burma, Sri Lanka, because I don't think their problems are going to go away that easily. (*STW*, 1 September 1990)

The PAP-state's sale of arms to Burma's military junta appears as some insurance of Lee's veracity (*FEER*, 3 November 1988). The government has also initiated discussions with Burma for the purpose of finalising an agreement for labour supply (*FEER*, 16 August 1990).

Therefore, the acceptance of 200,000 temporary foreign workers as a permanent low-paid sector of Singapore's working class meant the PAP-state no longer had to concern itself with the generational reproduction of this sector of the population or with using welfare regulatory mechanisms to shore up its legitimacy. But these problems remained with regard to the rest of the population.

Privatising Meritocracy

The public anxiety created by the intense competition for education and its manifestation in the 1984 election results precipitated the privatisation of education. The government could not meet the raised expectations of the whole population and, as its graduate mother priority scheme demonstrated, it had no intention of doing so. This politicisation of the state's delivery of this type of welfare was undermining its legitimacy. Since 1985 the PAP-state has drawn back from direct political accountability for education.

Privatisation refers not to the sale of state assets but to the devolution of the final individual selection decisions to schools which have been granted a restricted degree of administrative autonomy from the Ministry of Education. It also refers to the gradual withdrawal of state funding for education and the transfer of school financing to parents in the form of higher school fees. This accords with the PAP-state's policy of lowering the level of state welfare once sufficient educational infrastructure has been put in place to ensure the reproduction of a sufficiently skilled labour force. In 1989 the education budget was 14.6 per cent of total government expenditure and the government wanted to reduce it (*STW*, 25 March 1989).

The competition to enter the top schools remained intense and therefore highly politicised. The government raised the idea of making the top schools 'independent' in 1986 (Tham, 1989, pp. 492–3) and proceeded to grant limited administrative autonomy to the six most prestigious high schools. The stated purpose was to 'shift the focus of education innovation from the Ministry to the school' (Tony Tan, Minister of Education, *STW*, 11 January 1987). To this end, the government assisted the top schools in upgrading their already high-grade facilities. Perhaps as a final realisation of Lee's desire in 1965 for elite 'Eton-style boarding schools', the government also funded construction of hostels at some of these schools (Buchanan, 1972, p. 290; *STW*, 8 September 1990).

Although the Ministry of Education still controls who gets on the waiting list for these independent schools, the final decision on entrance is made by the school itself. Photographs of principals interviewing parents and their families have appeared in *The Straits Times* (*STW*, 22 December 1990). The responsibility for rejecting aspirants to the top educational stream is now seen to lie with the schools, not the government. This ideological effect will be reinforced as more schools become 'independent'.

Soon after gaining independent status, the schools raised their fees by between 300 and 800 per cent within two years. From a common base of $25 per month, fees have risen to as high as $200 per month (*STW*, 2 December 1989, 15 September 1990). These fees do not include the cost of books, uniforms or transport (*FEER*, 17 January 1991).

There has been considerable publicity to convince the public that the schools are open to all who reach the required educational standard regardless of income. The government announced subsidies for 'needy' students among the 4000 combined annual intake of the independent schools (*STW*, 8 September 1990). But this is a public relations exercise which disguises two facts. First, it avoids questions as to the desirability of such an elitist school system. Secondly, it camouflages the role of ethnicity and class in determining merit.

For example, the poor cannot afford the years of private tuition which is now the norm for middle class children from kindergarten through primary school. It is not unusual for a middle-class kindergarten child to be privately tutored three afternoons a week or for a primary school child to have three or four tutors in different subjects at a cost of $200 to $300 per month (*STW*, 14 September 1987). Accordingly the fee subsidies will go to a few lower middle-class children at no great expense to the government which at the same time reaps a huge dividend in terms of making the system appear equitable.

Lowering State Welfare Costs

The justification advanced for the high fee increases was the need to help the schools offer more educational choices and more creative programmes. But creativity will be for the rich. True to its word, the PAP-state is making quality education the preserve of the capitalist class. The fee hike for independent schools (which are still state-funded) was the precursor to lowering state funding for all schools.

This withdrawal of state welfare took a step forward with the announcement of the Edusave scheme in December 1990. The government said it would establish an endowment fund of one billion dollars which would generate sufficient income to pay approximately $100 per year to every school child between six and 16 years of age. Within a decade it is intended that the fund will grow to five billion dollars and that the annual amount remitted to each child's Edusave account will grow accordingly. The money can only be used for payment of school fees and for official extra-curricular activities (not private tutoring). The annual education budget of $1.8 billion can be expected to drop as Edusave takes effect (*STW*, 25 March 1989).

Announcing the scheme as a personal grand gesture after his accession to the prime ministership, Goh Chok Tong said:

> I have come up with the Edusave programme because I want to temper our meritocratic, free market system with compassion and more equal opportunities.
>
> Under the free-market system, the able and talented are encouraged to put their talents to maximum use. They will do better than those less able than them. Naturally, their children will have advantage over others.
>
> With Edusave, all children, rich or poor, are brought to the same starting line. This is the philosophy behind the Edusave scheme. (*STW*, 22 December 1990)

Goh's speech reveals the extent to which political non-compliance and opposition had forced the PAP to compensate ideologically for its educational strategy. No doubt the pretence of humanitarian concern will have some effect in restoring confidence in schooling and the PAP. But the concrete political effect of Edusave will be financially to tie schoolchildren into a state-controlled welfare mechanism. The level of funding and the regulations for withdrawals from Edusave accounts will ensure that each student goes to that part of the education system that the PAP-state wants her or him to be. The amount supplied by Edusave will be insufficient to meet future school fees at any school. As Goh pointed out, Edusave does not mean the beginning of a welfare state or handouts. Parents will still have to contribute to their children's education. It can therefore be anticipated that fees at all schools will increase as Edusave becomes available and the government progressively withdraws its funding. The impression of equal opportunity for every child is created by granting the same amount to every child.

But Edusave will provide just enough support to enable poor parents to send their children to the worst schools. For the upper-class parents who can already afford substantial school fees, the Edusave scheme will be a useful extra, sufficient perhaps to pay for ballet lessons for their children. Income will determine even more the quality of education that each family has access to although the ideological effect is the perception of equality. Maintaining this effect is the reason the government quickly rejected calls to give Edusave to the poor alone (*STW*, 29 December 1990). But, in reality, the working class will retain the equal opportunity to remain unequal.

The PAP-state's objectives in launching Edusave are to shift the cost of education directly onto parents, to restore its legitimacy by retaining control of the sorting practices at one step removed and to entrench meritocratic educational practices on the basis of income now that all Singaporeans have found their proper place in society after the first generation of PAP sorting. The government will not be fully funding the schools and it will appear not to be running them even though it will maintain a tight grip on educational policy. Its political control over education will thereby increase as it escapes direct political accountability.

The Edusave initiative will achieve with regard to primary and secondary education what the PAP-state has already begun to implement in tertiary education by means of fee increases and declining government subsidies. Similar control has already been extended with parents' CPF accounts permitted to be drawn upon for tertiary fees (*STW*, 18, 25 March, 1 April 1989).

Realignment of Communalist Policies

After 1985 part of the PAP-state's response to the rising level of liberal democratic dissent in the population was to reassert a communalist strategy in order to break up the political resistance that had emerged in various forms. It began to use Chinese-medium education against the English-educated Chinese. It persisted with strident 'Speak Mandarin' campaigns which alienated non-Chinese. It also launched a public offensive against Malay educational and political dissatisfaction.

The increasing political activism of the English-educated middle class, especially women, surfaced through opposition parties, the Law Society, church community work and cultural groups. The trend towards liberal democratic dissent was countered with the usual means of repression: arrests under the Internal Security Act, forced televised confessions of a Marxist conspiracy and legislative suppression of the civil and political rights of targeted groups (Asia Watch, 1989). At the same time the PAP-state increased its public ruminations about the values taught through Chinese-medium education and floated initiatives which suggested Mandarin should be taught at the expense of English (*FEER*, 24 January 1991, pp. 19–20). This was an attempt to destabilise the English-educated middle class.

Mandarin Against the Rest

The small number of Special Assistance Plan (SAP) Chinese-only primary and secondary schools were the subject of major debate in parliament during 1990 (*STW*, 21 July 1990). Nine Chinese schools had been preserved by direct order of Lee Kuan Yew a decade previously in order to preserve a remnant of the Chinese education system (Seah and Seah, 1983, pp. 255, 262). These SAP schools were expected to transmit the values of 'hard work, obedience, filial piety, respect for authority, moral rectitude, mutual support and a sense of social duty' (Tham, 1989, pp. 484, 496). Lee's motivation may also have included the maintenance of a sufficiently high standard of Mandarin in one part of the education system in case it was ever needed – as it was, for example, in order to take advantage of long-term commercial opportunities in China.

In 1989 ten primary schools were chosen as 'seed' SAP schools for teaching not only Mandarin but also English at first language levels and for transmitting Chinese values to Chinese students (*STW*, 25 March 1989). Five more schools were added in 1991 (*STW*, 16 February 1991).

In 1990 the Chinese-only SAP schools were the centre of a PAP-sponsored discussion in parliament about the problems of Western influence on the English-educated, the poor standard of Mandarin being achieved in the mainstream education system and the implications of monoracial schools for multiracialism (*STW*, 17 March 1990). A statement by Goh Chok Tong about the possibility of introducing Mandarin-medium primary schools because Chinese teachers 'are very good transmitters of values' seemed calculated to raise fears that the rules were being changed again (*STW*, 29 September 1990). Not only were non-Chinese already disadvantaged by the emphasis on Mandarin and English but the placing of Mandarin at the top of the meritocratic education tree would also disadvantage the Chinese middle and upper classes who had not taken Mandarin seriously.

One government MP, with the clear backing of his superiors, entered the debate to push the importance of Mandarin-medium education, noting that non-English-educated Chinese 'do not champion human rights and do not know much about their own legal rights, but they do have a strong sense of right and wrong, based on traditional Chinese values' (*STW*, 27 October 1990). The aggressive Speak Mandarin campaign of 1990 went beyond the encouragement of Mandarin over dialects to encouraging Mandarin to be spoken instead of English in the work place among Chinese (*STW*, 6 October 1990). These initiatives had a predictably negative effect on the upper and middle classes as well as on minority races who perceived them as Chinese chauvinism (*FEER*, 9 February 1989, 24 January 1991). But the main message was a warning to the upper and middle classes to realise that their interests lay with the PAP and that they were not necessarily secure in their assumption of a place in the capitalist class. The PAP was letting them know it could change the rules. A regional journal pronounced:

[T]he generally younger English-educated segment of the population seems to increasingly hanker after a more open political system.... Some observers say the PAP might have now decided to play its 'Chinese' card against the demands for a greater degree of democracy from the English-educated electorate. (*FEER*, 24 January 1991, p. 19)

The PAP-state was using the communalist potential of its existing bilingual policy rather than implementing a new policy. It was lighting the fuse of the 'Chinese language bomb' (Shotam, 1989, p. 517) to scare those who had shown a tendency towards supporting the opposition.

Ethnicity and Language: Promoting Communalism
By the late 1980s the bilingual education policy had not only promoted English as the *de facto* common language and the language of economic success, it had also produced English–Mandarin as the pre-eminent linguistic combination.

Chinese has penetrated into the magic economic (as opposed to cultural) circle that English has dominated thus far. This opportunity has been provided by the official correlation accorded the language and economic opportunities on the Chinese mainland. Further, there is a growing suspicion that employers discriminate in favour of those who have had an English–Mandarin bilingual education. (Shotam, 1989, p. 512)

The promotion of Mandarin as the symbolic language of all Chinese, whether or not they spoke it, set up a communal equation of ethnicity and language which had not previously existed: a united Chinese population against all others, especially against Malay indigenous opposition. The 1985 Speak Mandarin campaign made this equation explicit with its slogan 'Mandarin is Chinese'. The 1990 slogan offended even more non-Chinese and English-educated Chinese with its slogan 'If you're Chinese, make a statement – in Mandarin' (*STW*, 6 October 1990).

Thus to enforce a neat correlation – between English–Mandarin and ethnic Chinese, English–Malay and ethnic Malays, and *therefore* English–Tamil with ethnic South Indians – is inadvertently to keep the embers of language burning, so that the fires can easily be stoked up again. (Shotam, 1989, p. 517)

However, this policy was far from inadvertent. The PAP-state intentionally pursued a policy to maximise communal manipulation by preventing Chinese students from studying Malay or Tamil as a second language and vice versa. The ethnic distribution of students and their second language options is a classified state secret but the pattern is clear: language choices are officially predetermined according to race (Shotam, 1989, pp. 513, 517). Under the guise of equal treatment of the major languages, the bilingual policy has therefore preserved and entrenched communalism with the second language option becoming a means for determining social mobility according to ethnicity. English–Mandarin is of first importance with English–Malay as a poor second and English–Tamil as a distant third. English–Mandarin is also, now, superior to English alone.

Current educational initiatives can be seen as PAP-state manipulation of communalism to ensure not only preservation of Chinese dominance but also the gradual replacement of an English-educated capitalist class with a Mandarin–English-speaking, Chinese-educated capitalist class. Minority races have put a lot of their resources into attaining a higher level of English proficiency. Now they are being faced with a Chinese–Mandarin ethnic-linguistic bias which excludes them. The primarily English-educated Chinese middle class which has been seeking liberal democratic political rights has also been put on the defensive by the call to Chinese unity under the Mandarin banner. Previously seen as an empty slogan, this call is being backed up by substantive changes to educational practices.

The proposal for a new three-stage primary education system with equal emphasis on English and mother tongue learning (which now means Mandarin for 76 per cent of the population) has to be understood in the context of this communal strategy and of the building blocks already put in place by the SAP and 'seed' schools (*STW*, 17, 24 November 1990). Statements by Lee Kuan Yew and other ministers that English will continue to be the common language and that other races can have exclusive schools if there is a demand, do not preclude this communal strategy (*STW*, 25 March 1989, 3 November 1990).

On the other hand the PAP cannot go too far down this path. It is sacrificing a higher general standard of English in order to undermine middle-class political influence. In the long term it must maintain the standard of English or change its economic policies.

Consigning Malays to the Reserve Army of Labour
The implication of the Mandarin–English policy for Malays is that the inferior status of the Malay–English combination will be permanent. Despite the assurance that special schools will be established for them if they want them, the argument has been advanced that, since Malays already speak their mother tongue, such schools are not necessary. Hence, Mandarin–English Chinese-only schools will be the elite of all schools and Malays will be shut out on ethnic grounds.

This writing off of Malay education is extremely provocative and has been accompanied by other initiatives. To lower the cost to the state of Malay tertiary education (a paltry $1.4 million per year because few Malays make it that far) and to remove it from direct political responsibility, the PAP-state has privatised the scheme and introduced means-testing (*STW*, 9 June 1990).

Racial slurs against Malays in the education system have also been intensified. Malays have been told they should work harder on learning English and that, according to Lee Kuan Yew, the answer to Malay boys' underachievement is more parental discipline (*STW*, 25 August, 13 October 1990). Examination results have been publicly analysed according to racial composition by the Education Minister who noted that Chinese achieve three times better than Malays in A-levels. This was put down to 'socio-economic factors, the importance placed on education by parents of various races, the different make-ups and aptitudes of the various racial groups' (*STW*, 17 November 1990).

The number and frequency of PAP-state direct attacks on the Malay minority since 1985 indicate a new twist in the communalist strategy. The state visit of President Herzog of Israel in late 1985 seemed calculated to heighten communal tension in the region, with objections coming from Malaysia, Indonesia, Brunei and Malays in Singapore. However, the PAP smoothed over its regional government-to-government relationships with vague statements of regret, somewhat unconvincingly apportioning responsibility for the invitation to a civil servant who acted without authority from the cabinet. The event provided an opportunity to question local Malays' loyalty to the nation. Said Lee Kuan Yew of the Singapore Malays' negative reaction:

> Are we sure that in a moment of crisis, when the heat is on, we are all together, heart to heart? I hope so. But we ought to have a fallback position and quickly fill up all the missing hearts if some go missing. (*Asia Yearbook*, 1988, p. 222)

Subsequently, the government openly raised the sensitive question of low Malay involvement in the Singapore Armed Forces (there are no Malay fighter pilots, for example) because it did not trust them to fight other Malays on behalf of Chinese (*ST*, 23 February, 6 April, 18 May 1987). After the 1988 elections, Goh Chok Tong and other PAP leaders attacked the Malays for not voting for the PAP and said that various educational schemes to assist Malays would need to be reconsidered (*STW*, 1, 22 October 1988).

Since then the issues of preventing racial enclaves (i.e. Malay concentrations) in public housing estates, the SAP schools, the Speak Mandarin campaigns and the recruitment of Chinese migrants from Hong Kong have added to Malay grievances. The long-standing Malay resentment of PAP-co-opted Malay leaders has also surfaced publicly (*STW*, 9 February 1991). Most recently Malay loyalty has again been questioned by a *Straits Times* survey showing that most Malays did not support the war against Iraq whereas most Chinese did (*STW*, 27 January, 9 February 1991). Despite Malay outrage at being singled out for criticism, the PAP has persisted in stating that the Malays are wrong and are not yet thinking like Singaporeans.

The PAP has no interest in permitting the cohesive Malay community to organise politically or advance educationally and economically, except on PAP terms, terms it has not accepted. Previously the PAP-state strategy has been one of containment.

> If we were less skilful, [a Malay opposition party] would have emerged. Because there was, even today, even in the last election... I know we didn't win more than fifty per cent of the Malay votes; we never did.... But had there been a Malay group that emerged, and they would have emerged easily if we had pro-

portional representation and not first-past-the-post in each constituency, you consider the polarisation that would take place as they expound Malay rights and Malay language, and the policies which they think should prevail seeing what goes on around us. (Lee Kuan Yew at National University of Singapore, reported in *ST*, 16 December 1986)

Now the PAP has decided simply to consign the Malay community permanently to the bottom of the working class. However, to ensure the continuing credibility of its claims to multi-racialism, it has also suggested that the brightest top ten per cent of Malay pupils should be 'nurtured' through the education system by special subsidies (*STW*, 9 February 1991). This modest expenditure will guarantee a token Malay presence in the capitalist class.

The Malay minority can now be written off in this way because of the shift in the global economy and the alliances which underlie it. With the United States being unable to sustain its high level of military dominance in the region and the new importance of Japanese capital in Asia, the PAP-state has had to reconsider its long term security guarantees. It has therefore attempted an accommodation with the capitalist classes of Malaysia and Indonesia by ensuring they have an increasing interest in Singapore's economic growth. Hence, the 'growth triangle' agreement between the three states jointly to develop Johor state and Riau province (especially Batam island) as an industrial hinterland for Singapore to soak up cheap labour and highly polluting industries.

The Singapore government also sought to minimise its past political conflict with the Malaysian state leadership by collaborating in internal security operations in 1987 to suppress liberal democratic and anti-communalist dissent in both countries, using the stigma of alleged Marxist conspiracies and communalism. A common interest was thus reaffirmed in exploiting communalist and red-scare tactics to suppress legal, democratic dissent at a time that both governments faced a crisis of legitimacy (Jomo, 1988; European Committee for Human Rights in Malaysia and Singapore, 1990). Also the PAP-state began military exercises with the Malaysian and Indonesian armed forces for the first time since independence (*STW*, 27 May 1989).

The new relationship between Singapore, Malaysia and Indonesia has undermined the geopolitical potency of local Malay dissent. The PAP-state's communalist strategy in the past has been aimed both at heightening tension in the region to divert attention from nationalist movements against foreign investment and control and at suppressing domestic dissent among the Chinese working class. The current strategy moderates the regional thrust while intensifying domestic contradictions to prevent the emergence of local inter-racial working class solidarity.

The intensified attack on the Malays is therefore related to the process of breaking up the liberal democratic political consensus emerging among the English-educated Chinese and Indians which would become a powerful political force if linked with entrenched Malay dissent. The schooling of Chinese in separate schools in Mandarin and the even greater class separation of Malays through educational deprivation is a concerted attempt to block the long-term development of such political solidarity.

This readjustment of communalist strategy together with the adjustment of population policy and the lowering of state welfare were among the changes associated with the shift to a multilateral alliance with foreign capitals which produced new demands for ideological legitimation.

The Search for Ideological Hegemony

By 1988 the PAP-state decided that its introduction of religious education had been a mistake. Religious education had assisted in communicating to the young that there were higher authorities and allegiances than the state and had also given them, to varying degrees, an alternative ideological comprehension of society. The government realised that the values being taught somehow did not fit with life in a meritocratic, authoritarian society and were capable of being further developed in a manner outside its control.

Religious institutions had been among the last community organisations to remain comparatively autonomous in their own affairs and, with cultural and political life suppressed at all other levels, the young had been attracted to them and their ideologies. The spread of English made Christianity more accessible to young Chinese and, as a religion well-adjusted to capitalism, gave it an image as a modern religion. The number of Christians rose from 9.9 per cent of the total population over ten years of age in 1980 to 12.5 per cent in 1990 although some estimates of the increase are considerably higher (Kuo *et al.*, 1988, p. 9; Ling, 1989, p. 693; *STW*, 22 April 1989; GOS, 1994, p. 2). More significantly for the PAP, 40.6 per cent of Chinese university graduates are Christian (GOS, 1994, p. 6). An estimated 30-40 per cent of professionals, executives and managers along with a high percentage of the general population between 15 and 25 years of age are Christian. Four cabinet ministers, more than a third of members of parliament and many senior government officials are known to be Christian. With 39.4 per cent of Christians being university graduates (compared to 2.6 per cent of Muslims), it is the religion with the most highly educated following (GOS, 1994. p. 6). Christians are overwhelmingly English-educated Chinese middle- and upper-class members.

The rise in adherents was accompanied by the increasing influence both of progressive Christian social teaching in the Catholic church and of Protestant fundamentalist demands for evangelistic freedom. Both traditions were claiming the right to judge publicly the righteousness of government policies. The PAP-state realised its religious education policy was assisting the consolidation of autonomous institutional power bases which would threaten both its political and ideological hegemony (*FEER*, 19 October 1989). The government also had a continuing concern to contain the incipient Malay nationalism assisted by Muslim teaching, especially in view of the Islamic resurgence in Malaysia and the Middle East.

Therefore, on 6 October 1989, the government announced two measures to deal with the situation. First, the Education Minister announced that Religious Knowledge was to be phased out and replaced by a civics course. For the first time, voluntary religious education also would be forbidden within school hours. This prohibition was aimed at Catholic church schools.

Secondly, in parliament on the same day, the Home Affairs Minister announced that legislation would be introduced to restrict the involvement of religious groups in politics (*STW*, 7 October 1989). This was eventually passed in the form of the Maintenance of Religious Harmony Bill which enables the government by executive decision to suppress almost any activity of a religious institution or leader (*FEER*, 18 January 1990; GOS, *Maintenance of Religious Harmony Bill*, Bill No. 1/90 1990; *STW*, 24 February 1990; see also Chapter 7).

The government maintained it was taking these steps of abolishing religious education and criminalising religious dissent in the interests of racial and religious harmony. Yet ethnic minorities were the primary educational casualties of the abolition of religious education and the government knew it.

> A study done by the Education Ministry indicates that had there been no religion courses, there would have been 13 per cent fewer Malay students, 15 per cent fewer Indian students and 15 per cent fewer students from other minorities (including Eurasians) at pre-university institutions. The study also indicated that only four per cent of Chinese students used the religion courses to fulfil admission requirements. (*FEER*, 19 October 1989)

There could be no convincing argument that the initiatives were not politically motivated. The PAP belatedly saw the potential of religion as a unifying force against the state. Undoubtedly the role of the Catholic Church in the overthrow of President Marcos in the Philippines had precipitated the PAP-state's initial move against church community workers in 1987 and led to the realisation that religious education was not necessarily a passive instrument for shoring up the legitimacy of the state.

Unwittingly, by abolishing religious education, the PAP removed one of the educational practices which had exacerbated the conflict between meritocratic and patriarchal values. That it was unwitting can be seen by the reintroduction of this ideological tension in its newly formulated state ideology.

Ideology in Context

It appears that the PAP at least partially understood the reasons for the failure of its religious education policy. It saw that the formulation of ideological principles needed to be more closely related to the social and cultural context of the practices they were designed to legitimate, if not to the real ideological effects of the practices themselves. Religious ideology was too diffuse. People were able to think about their actions and their social context in ways which did not directly support capitalist social relations or which even opposed them.

Under the guise of formulating a national ideology suited to the religio-cultural context of Singapore, the PAP-state has proceeded to impose an ideology which it hoped would legitimate its political actions. Hence, the moves from October 1988 to develop a national ideology, leading to a Green Paper on National Ideology in 1989, a White Paper on Shared Values in 1991 (*STW*, 24 June 1989, 12 January 1991) and numerous government-sponsored academic papers (for example, Quah, 1990).

According to the White Paper, the National Ideology is intended to provide the ideological content of moral education, mother-tongue language learning and civics in the education system as well as the ideological parameters of the mass media. The National Ideology has been variously described as being composed of 'key', 'shared' or 'core' values which are common to the major ethnic and religious groups of Singapore and which are identifiably Asian rather than Western in nature (*ST*, 6 January 1991). These shared values are:

(1) nation before community and society above self;

(2) family as the basic unit of society;

(3) community support and respect for the individual;

(4) consensus not conflict; and

(5) racial and religious harmony (*ST*, 16 January 1991).

From the above it is clear that the PAP-state has elaborated a set of ideological principles far more closely related to the legitimation of its policies than derived and diffuse religious dogma. The 'values' have been carefully chosen to accord with the PAP's past and present political strategies to reproduce the division of labour amenable to its alliance with foreign capital.

Under the first principle, wages can be lowered, individual human rights restricted and the grievances of minority communities ignored. For many years the nation has been equated with the PAP-state. The interests of the PAP and foreign capital constitute the national interest. As the President of Singapore said to parliament regarding this value:

> Putting the interests of society as a whole ahead of individual interests has been a major factor in Singapore's success.... If Singaporeans had insisted on their individual rights and prerogatives, and refused to compromise these for the greater interests of the nation, they would have restricted the options available. (*ST*, 6 January 1991)

The second value has been explained in the following terms:

> The family is the best way to provide children with a secure environment to grow, and to look after the elderly. Singaporeans must not also uncritically

adopt the 'alternative lifestyles', such as casual sexual relationships and single parenthood. (*ST*, 6 January 1991)

This value seeks to legitimate the capitalist preference for the nuclear family because it is the social unit which can supply and reproduce the most labour power at least cost. It also reinforces patriarchal relations and, thus, male control of women's sexuality, specifically excluding the life patterns which would enable women to escape domination through parenting. The official denial of HDB flats to single people or single parents can continue on moral grounds while encouragements to breed can increasingly be given the moral tone of national duty.

The inclusion of grandparents has become especially important in avoiding higher welfare costs to the state in terms of child care as well as pensions and health (Table 5.2).

Table 5.2   *Proportion of Population Aged 65 and Over (per cent)*

	1989	2025
Philippines	3.0	7.5
Indonesia	4.0	8.7
Malaysia	4.0	9.1
Thailand	4.0	9.1
Singapore	6.0	17.0
Japan	12.0	23.8

Source: *STW* (24 November 1990).

The third value reinforces the responsibility of the 'community' rather than the state for the welfare of the poor and disadvantaged. As the White Paper states:

Community support for individuals will keep Singapore a humane society. At the same time, it helps us avoid the dependent mentality and severe social problems of a welfare state.   (*ST*, 6 January 1991)

The fourth value legitimates the labelling of political dissent or even parliamentary opposition as anti-national and entrenches the PAP's supremacy. It promotes a petitionary political process rather than a participatory one. Only the PAP-state has the political reach to organise national consensus.

The fifth value will be used to legitimate the PAP-state's communalist strategies and to suppress the grievances and political demands of the varying racial and religious groups.

It can therefore be expected that the PAP-state will attempt to consolidate its ideological hegemony through intensive educational initiatives based on the National Ideology. However, the PAP-state has not differentiated between the *actual* ideological effects of its educational practices (and other mechanisms of social control) and their *desired* ideological effects as represented by the National Ideology.

For example, common experience of meritocratic educational practices produces the shared ideological perception articulated by the Prime Minister's political secretary:

> Competition in school is the natural result of Singapore society becoming more and more classless. The son of a noodle-seller can become a top manager in a large company provided he works hard and earns his qualifications. (*STW*, 9 December 1990)

Whether the National Ideology value of 'society before self' will be perceived as consistent with this ideological effect is dependent on the educational practices. That is, personal success can only be seen as a contribution to society as long as personal success is perceived by everyone as a realistic possibility for everyone. However, with the communalist shift in educational practices, the ideological effect for an increasing minority will be that no matter what they do, they will not be permitted to succeed. The reality that people succeed by putting themselves first (or their race and class) will be a more widely shared perception in contradiction with the National Ideology. Similarly the changing patterns and perceptions of family life will continue to be shaped by the actual practices of the patriarchal family and patriarchal state, not by imposed values.

If the contradictions become too great, once again the government will undermine its own legitimacy by attempting to impose a set of beliefs which do not conform with people's perception of their own experience and which, because of possible alternative interpretations of the shared values, is susceptible to mobilisation against it. Already legal opposition parties (*ST*, 16 January 1991) and the remnants of suppressed Catholic community groups have been criticising the National Ideology as an ideological weapon for PAP supremacy.

> The national ideology is nothing more than a life-line for a party determined not to lose its hold over the electorate and fearful of the people's increasing demand for democracy and human rights. (*Voices from Singapore*, December 1990, p. 8)

The PAP-state may then regret this official attempt at a systematic ideological statement of the social relations conducive to its alliance with foreign capital.

EDUCATION AND SOCIAL CONTROL

In the development of the education system since 1959 educational practices have had the primary and related functions of countering political opposition and sorting agents into class positions for the reproduction of labour power. This sorting has been carried out by means of meritocratic educational policies integrated with state breeding and immigration programmes.

The working class has been fragmented into a labour hierarchy of a core of employed workers and a reserve army of unemployed workers, itself further stratified into a floating reserve (short-term unemployed) and a latent reserve (unemployed but able to subsist) (Hill, 1979, pp. 7–8; Steven, 1983, pp. 178–9). The core of mostly Chinese, mostly male workers has been created above a subsidiary floating reserve of Singaporean women who move in and out of the latent reserve. Their subsistence is usually guaranteed by means of another family member – a spouse, sibling or parent – being engaged in wage labour. Beneath them are the foreign workers who also move between the floating and latent reserve; when they float or they enter the latent reserve they do so by leaving the borders of Singapore.

At the same time meritocratic educational practices have maximised the advantages of the wealth and linguistic heritage of the upper class while also focusing on the reproduction of a skilled, obedient middle class. Legitimation of this process of social reconstruction has been achieved through the ideological effects of educational practices and by the formalisation of these effects into the ideology of meritocracy by politicians and institutions.

However, sharp contradictions have arisen. Working class non-cooperation has been evident in low educational achievement and non-conformity with government breeding programmes as well as a 37 and 38 per cent opposition vote in the 1984 and 1988 elections, respectively.

Using English-medium education to demolish Chinese education and destroy Chinese working-class political opposition has produced an English-educated middle class with a desire for liberal democracy. There has been a new phase of liberal democratic dissent through opposition parties, professional and Christian organisations. The use of Mandarin as a weapon against the middle class emphasises the historical irony of the English-educated becoming a threat to the PAP.

Middle-class women have become more organised and vocal as a result of linking government population policy to education. Government harassment of educated, single, women with its official dating and breeding programmes has fuelled resentment. The PAP-state's fostering of middle-class male political, business, professional and military leadership and a male core of the working class increasingly highlights its patriarchal power base. The middle class, both women and men, have responded to the increasingly competitive system of education and social stratification by emigrating in large numbers.

While the labour power of the Chinese working class has been reproduced, the geopolitically sensitive Malay underclass has been excluded not only from the capitalist class but from the core of the working class as well. The racism inherent in educational and population policies has both legitimated and undermined educational policies. The visibility of racial classification has functioned to consolidate the perception of the superiority of the dominant race and assisted its sense of unity. But at the same time the exclusion of the overwhelming majority of Malays and Indians from social advancement has led to the refusal to support the PAP electorally, the withholding of community support for Malay leaders chosen by the PAP and the attempt to retain a sense of community by means of geographical concentration in public housing estates. Continuing with communalist policies may repeatedly expose the class and race sorting functions of education thereby contributing to new crises. The recent emphasis on Mandarin may light the fuse of communalism to an extent that may prove to be beyond even PAP control.

As a means to produce submission through the imposition of ideology, the vacillation between civics, moral education, values education, mother-tongue learning, religious education and latterly the National Ideology, has also led to new tensions. The most serious disjunction to emerge may have been that between the ideological effect of highly individualistic, class-based and racist, meritocratic practices and the newly formulated axioms of collective loyalty to the state combined with the needs of patriarchal social relations.

Related to this structural problem is the conflict between tight authoritarian control and the aspiration to be a regional services and information centre. Unadaptable, inflexible technicians have been the product of an elitist, competitive, rigid system with a high drop-out rate. Many writers have noted that this contradiction is an extremely serious block to the PAP-state's aspirations (Linda Lim, 1989, p. 181; Rodan, 1989, p. 205; Sandhu and Wheatley, 1989, p. 1099; Tham, 1989, p. 492). Although government officials have often talked of the need for more creativity, the government appears to be seeking it by exacerbating the contradiction as it has done with its move towards elite independent schools.

The privatisation of education is partly an attempt to restore legitimacy in the face of many forms of non-compliance. It is also aimed at reducing government welfare expenditure while increasing control, at 'shifting the electorate's judgement of the PAP's performance away from its ability to provide ongoing and expanded social welfare programmes' (Rodan, 1989, p. 164). The PAP-state therefore is continuing to use the education system to regulate many social and political conflicts even as it draws back from direct political accountability.

The development of this institutional mechanism of social control has had two main features. The first characteristic is that noted above: as educational practices have dealt with manifestations of underlying structural pressures and conflicts, new forms of non-cooperation and opposition have arisen. The government itself has come to recognise this.

Prime Minister Goh Chok Tong expressed his concern that Singaporeans might vote against the government because they were unhappy about certain policies and were succumbing to envy when the 'talented' get special attention. He said, 'It is very dangerous. But it is already a trend. Can we reverse the trend?' He also said that minorities should not 'impose their views on the majority' as when Malays have objected to Speak Mandarin campaigns. He concluded, 'Education is the key to the future. This is assuming that the politics are right' (*STW*, 27 July 1991).

The second major characteristic of social control through the education system is that it has worked very effectively. The main form of political struggle has not been a form of dissent but a form of cooperation: the generalised struggle to rise out of one's class. People have been willingly involved in the education system because they recognise it is the only pathway to jobs and economic survival, the only means to increase their access to welfare. This ideological effect of educational practices has been achieved by the actual necessity of having to acquire an education to get better jobs and more money, the appearance of equality of opportunity and of social advancement on the basis of merit. The PAP-state's absolute control of the national education system has enabled it to define the ostensibly neutral criteria of merit and, thus, control the pathway to upward mobility.

The education system's success is all the more remarkable considering the fact that it is structurally impossible for all Singaporeans to attain their aspirations because the political goals of class stratification stand in direct contradiction to them. Yet the education system has made it appear as a real possibility for everyone. Education has put people in their class positions while giving them hope of bettering this position. Like a lottery, enough people have 'won' their way to the middle class to convince the majority that their efforts at upward mobility are not in vain. The real social relations between a tiny capitalist class and a mass of exploited workers has not only remained but has been reinforced by the aspiration to get out of one's class. The education system has enabled people to think that they are advancing their own interests while their cooperation ensures they are also doing what is necessary to support the PAP and to advance its economic strategy.

However, the strength of non-cooperation and opposition has compelled the government continually to give precedence to the repressive aspects of social control. This emphasis has prevented it from matching the educational levels of its main international competitors and presages further crises of accumulation and regulation.

6 Parliament, Elections and Parties

Elections have regularly played a vital role in social control ever since the PAP came to power by providing a universally accepted mechanism for converting submission into consent. The practice of voting has given the PAP its right to govern and to intervene in all aspects of people's lives. The procedures of parliament have then confirmed the legitimacy of PAP governance.

But parliament itself faded in public significance between 1966 and 1981 when the PAP held all the seats. In the early 1980s when education and other welfare mechanisms were failing sufficiently to suppress or divert disapproval, social conflict surfaced through the electoral process. Parliament once again became the site of genuine political contest and thereby more central to social regulation.

This chapter examines the role of parliament and parliamentary politics in social control. It also examines more broadly the historical origins of the forms of liberal democracy, especially elections and parties and their relationship to class and underdevelopment in Singapore. In this way it is intended to throw light on the conflicts which have emerged between the legitimating and governing functions of parliament.

There are several main phases in the history of the Singapore legislature and they reflect the phases of social and political conflict: the period of transition from colonial assembly to independent parliament from 1955 to 1965, the consolidation of the party-state from 1966 to 1980, and the resurgence of parliamentary competition from 1981. The first two periods will be referred to briefly, mainly in order to establish the new significance of parliament in the latter periods. From 1981 Singapore's political system has been transformed by renewed political opposition, creating a crisis of legitimacy to which the PAP has been forced to respond.

COLONIAL ASSEMBLY TO INDEPENDENT PARLIAMENT, 1955–65

The decade from 1955 was a period of genuine political contest between political forces within the Legislative Assembly. The British introduced a liberal democratic parliamentary system as a form of government congenial to their objective of consolidating a local capitalist class while bringing working-class politics into a forum they could control. They used the colonial legislature as a proving ground for local parties in order to test their support in the electorate, their administrative competence and, most importantly, their suitability as a future partner after independence. Although conducted within the parameters of imperial rule, the electoral contest for power was real. There was a plurality of legal political forces organising outside the legislature as well as within and decisions in the assembly, like electoral results, were by no means foregone conclusions (Table 6.1).

Table 6.1   Legislative Assembly Elections

Date	No. of Seats	Party Returned	No. of Seats Won
2 April 1955	25*	Labour Front	10
30 May 1959	51	PAP	43
21 September 1963	51	PAP	37

* The 1955 Legislative Assembly consisted of a speaker, 3 ex-officio, 25 elected and 4 nominated members.

Source: GOS (1989a), p. 232.

Along with this legislative system, the British and the PAP developed a range of measures to prevent political opponents getting elected to parliament. The PAP also used the state bureaucracy and government community organisations to mobilise votes.

The most obvious tactic was the detention without trial of left-wing leaders in 1959 and 1963 to obstruct the most popular independence leaders from standing for election. When the Lee faction had gained direct control of the electoral apparatus in 1963, this overt tactic of state terror was accompanied by a comprehensive subversion of the electoral process. The PAP enhanced its control of who would get elected to the assembly by the following methods:

(1) restricting the campaign period to the constitutional minimum of nine days, a restriction which effectively applied to the opposition only, since Lee, as prime minister, began a tour of all constituencies in November 1962, at least ten months before the campaign;

(2) ordering state festivities for the proclamation of Malaysia during the campaign, giving the government leadership maximum publicity from the festivities but effectively reducing the number of days for campaigning by the opposition to four and a half;

(3) blocking off all printing facilities with urgent government orders for Malaysia Day, making it impossible for the opposition to print in bulk in the short time available after the election date was announced (the PAP got their printing done in Hong Kong three months in advance);

(4) pressuring the printer of the official *Barisan* publication to cease publication;

(5) obstructing the booking of public places for opposition rallies and the granting of police permits for them to be held;

(6) freezing the bank accounts of the three largest *Barisan*-linked unions three days before nomination day;

(7) dissolving by government order two of the *Barisan's* biggest community organisations, the Singapore Rural Residents' Association and the Singapore Country People's Association;

(8) possibly starting and certainly not countering the rumour that a *Barisan* victory would bring in federal troops and Singapore would be ruled from Kuala Lumpur;

(9) arresting and detaining without trial under the ISA all the main *Barisan* leaders during the months before the election (throughout 1963 over 130 opposition organisers and community leaders were arrested) (George, 1984, pp. 66–8).

Such tactics were necessary because, after the split within the PAP and the loss of its mass base, the PAP could not be sure of winning a clean electoral competition with the *Barisan*. The PAP still lacked a strong electoral base even though the Lee faction had largely overcome *Barisan* organisation through mass arrests and the deregistration of trade unions and other supporting organisations.

Bellows claims that the 1959 elections were 'the last general elections in Singapore in which [either of] the two major competing parties would have been allowed to form a government' (Bellows, 1970, p. 5). However, the British commitment to the PAP was not necessarily unconditional in 1963 (Minchin, 1986, p. 115). Whatever the truth of these judgements, it is clear that by 1965 the PAP had been transformed from a mass party into an exclusive governing group which had yet to consolidate an electoral base it could depend on. Electoral victory and dominance of the legislature was essential to its legitimacy and to its political power because it governed through the Assembly not through a colonial governor or the military. The PAP's power could therefore still be circumscribed by a lost vote in the Assembly.

CONSOLIDATION OF THE PARTY-STATE, 1966–80

In December 1965 the 13 opposition *Barisan Sosialis* members quit parliament in protest at the obstruction and harassment of their party. They boycotted all proceedings and all but two of them formally resigned by October 1966 (Bellows, 1970, pp. 96–7). The two remained in hiding from late 1963 in fear of detention and were unable to present their resignations personally as required by law (Bellows, 1970, p. 195). For the next 15 years there was no opposition member in Singapore's parliament. The PAP had succeeded in acquiring not merely dominance but total supremacy in the legislature.

It was during these years of uncontested legislative power that the PAP consolidated its party-state apparatus of control and used it, along with criminal law and political detention, to suppress all forms of organised dissent outside parliamentary politics. These included the unions, educational institutions, student movements, the print media and professional societies (International Mission of Jurists, 1987; Asia Watch, 1989). This was also the period of large-scale public housing and educational initiatives to reconstitute the social formation in consonance with the EOI accumulation strategy.

In order to increase its control of the working class, the PAP-state suppressed the pluralism of liberal democratic politics. The legal channels for releasing popular pressures of dissent outside parliamentary politics were minimised because it could not allow any growth in working-class organisation. But to sustain the illusion of liberal democratic political contest within parliamentary politics, some opposition parties were permitted to exist. They were constantly harassed to keep them fractious and weak.

> Opposition parties have been badly bruised and mauled. The Prime Minister and Rajaratnam [PAP minister] have ridiculed their activists and candidates, labelling them 'jokers' and 'opportunists'. They have been infiltrated by security and intelligence agents; they have been charged with receiving foreign funds and engaging in 'black operations'; defamation suits have been filed or threatened by PAP ministers to avenge or discourage alleged excesses. (Minchin, 1986, p. 217)

In these circumstances elections became a ritual legitimation of PAP rule with the leadership claiming them as ratification for their most recently announced or implemented policies. For example, the 1968 elections, in which only seven out of 58 seats were contested, were claimed to be an endorsement of the new draconian labour laws depriving workers of many rights and conditions (Table 6.2). Over the next three elections (1972, 1976 and 1980), the total opposition vote declined from approximately 30 per cent to approximately 25 per cent. The number of uncontested seats rose from eight in 1972 to 37 in 1980 (GOS, 1989a, p. 232). The PAP won all the seats in every election.

Table 6.2   General Elections, 1968–80

Date	Seats	Parties Contesting	Party Returned	Seats Won	% Votes Won
1968 13 April	7+(51)*	2+5(I)	PAP	58	84.43
1972 2 September	57+(8)	6+2(I)	PAP	65	69.02
1976 23 December	53+(16)	7+2(I)	PAP	69	72.40
1980 23 December	38+(37)	8	PAP	75	75.55

*Uncontested seats in brackets.
(I), Independents.

Source: GOS (1989a), p. 232.

These figures reflect the intensified control and the climate of fear that had been generated. Voting for the PAP was an act of obedience to avoid any negative consequences since the party-state now directly controlled the housing, the schooling, the breeding habits, the local community organisations and the pensions of the working class.

Parliament became merely a forum for making announcements about what the government had done or was going to do. The PAP found parliament a most convenient governing mechanism when it had exclusive control of it. Whatever the PAP decided could be implemented with a full constitutional *imprimatur*. The centre of executive power was the small group of senior members in the PAP's Central Executive Committee who were also cabinet ministers (Pang, 1971; Chan, 1976). Parliament enabled the stamp of democratic legitimacy routinely to be given to their decisions.

> from 1966 to 1981, its legislation underwent little thorough scrutiny.... Sittings were kept to a minimum, the Prime Minister was often absent, and when he intervened he swamped the matter at hand. The quality of a member's contribution to debate suffered from the lurking thought that it made no difference to the outcome. PAP back-benchers were encouraged, sometimes orchestrated, to ask questions and even to play at being a loyal Opposition. But only a hardy soul would willingly risk the Prime Minister's or Dr Goh's [Deputy Prime Minister] wrath if he exceeded the bounds.   (Minchin, 1986, pp. 218–19)

Parliament was necessary to the legitimacy of democratic process but its proceedings were no longer a matter of public moment. Backbench members were engaged in other full-time employment. As an institution it functioned at a minimal level and faded from the public eye.

Rapid economic growth was seen by the PAP as sufficient justification for its extension of social control throughout the society and its evisceration of democratic institutions. The material achievements did indeed enhance their legitimacy. But by 1981 the sharp increase in inequality had spawned new political dissent which, because practically all other forms of legal expression of grievances had been proscribed, surfaced through renewed support for the enfeebled Workers' Party (WP).

The WP is a social democratic party with working class links and, not being a total creation of the security police, it had been constantly pilloried and harassed. Nevertheless it had been permitted to exist, presumably because the PAP had a low estimate of the political abilities of its leader, J. B. Jeyaretnam and of its political prospects. The declining opposition vote in the 1970s was misread by the PAP as growing approval for its policies rather than conditional acquiescence out of fear. With the resurgence of political opposition in the early 1980s in response to the Second Industrial Revolution, the disposition of parliamentary political forces changed rapidly.

Each new example of persecution or discrimination, each episode of the PAP pack baying at one or two isolated figures, each litany of actionable offences, draws more Singaporeans to join or sympathise with Opposition parties. (Minchin, 1986, p. 217)

The defeat of the PAP in the 1981 Anson by-election ushered in a new period in the development of Singapore's political system.

STRATEGY OF EXCLUSION, 1981–4

The PAP's general election victory in 1980 with 75 per cent of the vote, enough to take all the seats, proved to be false reassurance that all was well with the comprehensive system of social control they had put in place. In 1981 the WP's Jeyaretnam won Anson in a by-election precipitated by the PAP incumbent, Devan Nair, assuming the presidency. With 51.01 per cent of the vote in a three-way contest (GOS, 1989a, p. 232), Jeyaretnam entered parliament much to the venomous displeasure of the PAP leadership (Minchin, 1986, p. 219).

Behind the PAP's reaction lay its shock at having its governing preserve breached. Even with only one opposition member in the House, it again became a public forum for political accountability. The opposition victory loosened the grip of fear on the electorate. Although the majority might be scared by the numbering of the ballot papers in elections (*FEER*, 30 May 1985, p. 21) or by the official letter demanding an explanation if an elector abstained, an increasingly entrenched minority, loyal and obedient in every other respect in their outward behaviour, felt more and more able to risk dissenting in the one legal political activity still open to them, the act of casting a ballot.

This 1981 breach of PAP control marked the beginning of a decade when the PAP was forced to change its pattern of governing through parliament and the party-state structure. It brought a conflict between its method of governing and its means of acquiring legitimacy. Between Jeyaretnam's election and the 1984 general election the PAP's unsophisticated response was simply to crush the opposition and once again exclude it from parliament.

In early 1982 the government made a confidential study of voter opinion which showed most Singaporeans wanted to see more opposition members in parliament and that the government was 'seriously out of touch with voter sentiment' (*Asia Yearbook*, 1983, p. 239). The PAP's first reaction to this finding was to put off all pending by-elections indefinitely. Then it moved quickly to counteract the growing public desire for both an effective opposition and a PAP government. The PAP-state had difficulty portraying this objective as disloyal because the aim was not to unseat the government but to make it more accountable. Ministers consequently took the line of promulgating a new theory of parliamentarism: an opposition prevents good government. Second Deputy Prime Minister, S. Rajaratnam, part of Lee's 'Old Guard', stated to government unionists in 1982:

> The theory of democracy as opposition is founded, at least as far as Singapore is concerned, on intellectual dishonesty.... No opposition enters parliament to help a government govern well.... Put bluntly, the role of an opposition is to ensure bad government. (*Asia Yearbook*, 1983, p. 239)

In August 1982 Rajaratnam tried to frighten people away from the opposition. He warned that Jeyaretnam's Workers' Party would provide a cover for subversive elements (*Asia Yearbook*, 1983, p. 240). Parliamentary opposition in the eighties was tarred with the same brush of national disloyalty as in the sixties. Voting for the opposition was merely misguided but the opposition itself was disloyal by definition.

The PAP-state also tried to convince the electorate that an opposition was not only damaging but also unnecessary because of the quality of PAP government. This strategy had two thrusts, electoral and administrative. The electoral thrust was to claim that the PAP embodied all legitimate political forces in Singapore and was therefore above party politics. In 1982 this secretive, exclusive, cadre-based party declared itself 'a national movement dedicated to the service of Singapore and to the advancement of the people's well-being' (Minchin, 1986, p. 210). It later set about establishing peripheral PAP organisations without democratising its core structures (Chan, 1989, p. 83).

The second thrust was to show how the government had learned its lesson and would now be more responsive in its administration. In 1982 the government began its attempt to humanise the image of the party-state. Public relations officers were employed in ministries and concern for the individual was stressed in the media. Defence Minister Goh Chok Tong was quoted saying 'We do care' (*Asia Yearbook*, 1983, p. 239).

It would appear, however, that the PAP still saw Jeyaretnam's election as an exceptional event and not indicative of a trend. It therefore took only cosmetic measures to accommodate what it thought was a temporary phenomenon which could be removed by the full power of the PAP-state's electoral apparatus at the next election.

In 1984, the year of election, the PAP grudgingly allowed that an opposition might be desirable but it took another initiative to convince the public that actually voting for one was not necessary. It amended the constitution to establish the position of Non-Constituency Member of Parliament (NCMP). In the event that less than three opposition MPs were elected at a general election, this amendment made provision for the appointment of up to three NCMPs to make up the difference. The NCMP seats would be offered by the PAP-state to the losing opposition candidates who scored the highest percentage of votes. The government stated that it was legislating to guarantee that there would always be at least three opposition MPs in the House.

This new-found PAP commitment to an opposition presence in parliament was aimed at forestalling the electorate from casting a protest vote in the 1984 elections. The government's logic was that everyone could vote for the PAP and there would still be a parliamentary opposition. But an NCMP would not be permitted to vote on fiscal, constitutional and confidence matters and would therefore be very much a second-class MP. By this constitutional ruse the PAP was not only hoping to maintain control of all who entered parliament, including opposition members, it also aimed to protect matters central to its governing authority and legitimacy from direct political contestability by a credible opposition. In this way it could give the impression of political plurality that constitutional legitimacy required without granting the substance of it. Moreover, because it would be the opposition members who were not popularly elected, it would be their legitimacy that would be in doubt not the PAP's. The PAP would be seen as generously accommodating them.

This short period before the 1984 elections was therefore characterised initially by PAP-state resistance to any form of parliamentary opposition. Its main objective was to be rid of Jeyaretnam at the next polls and purify the chamber once again. But, at the last minute, it was forced by political dissent to accommodate opposition in the politically castrated form of NCMPs.

ACCOMMODATING POLITICAL PLURALISM, 1984-8

The 12.6 per cent swing against the PAP in the 1984 elections was a major blow to the government's exclusion strategy (Table 6.3). Although only two opposition members were elected as against 77 for the PAP, it meant that the PAP-state had not succeeded in keeping popularly elected oppositionists, including Jeyaretnam, out of parliament. As soon as the election results had been declared, a visibly angry Lee Kuan Yew went on television in the early hours of the morning and threatened that the universal franchise may have to be reconsidered. This outburst probably arose from the unexpected magnitude of anti-PAP feeling and the realisation that the NCMP tactic had been ineffective. This was further confirmed when the opposition later spurned the offer of an NCMP seat to make up the PAP's arbitrary minimum of three opposition MPs.

Table 6.3 General Elections, 1984 and 1988

Date	Seats	Parties Contesting	Party Returned	Seats Won	% Votes Won
1984 22 December	49+(30)*	9+3(I)	PAP	77	62.94
1988 3 September	70+(11)	8+4(I)	PAP	80	61.76

*Uncontested seats in brackets.
(I), Independents.

Source: GOS (1989a), p. 232.

By the following year the PAP had drawn back from Lee's threat. Deputy Prime Minister Goh Chok Tong said, 'I hope the day will never arrive when waiting for the general election result is like watching the flipping of a coin.' He implied that a strong protest vote might accidentally defeat the PAP. This would undermine the nation's stability and erode the confidence of foreign investors. The ideal he advocated for stability was a broad-based mainstream party, the PAP, with a few 'serious-minded' opposition parties. 'I would not apologise... if the PAP will be returned for the next 25 years, better still for the next 50 years. If we tell investors that, they can plan their future in Singapore' (*FEER*, 15 August 1985, p. 10). This explicit reference to the PAP as the only suitable local partner for foreign capital again reminded Singaporeans of the alliance which had produced economic growth and which would be destabilised by an opposition strong enough to become an alternative government.

The main point behind Goh's rhetoric was that although an opposition presence in the legislature could not be avoided, it was still as far as possible to be one of the PAP's choosing. The PAP's modified approach gradually emerged: a public impression of plurality and political accountability was to be sustained while any undesirable opposition especially any party with working-class links would be systematically blocked.

Petitionary Politics

After its 1984 setback the PAP-state institutionalised its previous public relations campaign in a highly controlled process of public consultation. It aimed yet again to convey the ideological message that a parliamentary opposition was unnecessary in the light of the government's responsiveness to public opinion. The government attempted to deflect public attention away from its political accountability in parliament to a paternalistic process of consultation which it completely controlled.

The government, stated one Singaporean academic, was moving towards 'a more consultative style of government, initiated by the younger PAP leaders after the 1984 general election' (Quah, 1989, p. 1). The government Feedback Unit, headed by a PAP MP, was established in March 1985 ostensibly to assist voters to convey their views to the government. But its real function was to gather political intelligence.

On 18 February 1987 Brigadier-General Lee Hsien Loong, Lee Kuan Yew's son, launched the National Agenda 'to enable all Singaporeans to participate in formulating the means of attaining the goals identified in the Government's Vision of 1999' (Quah, 1989, p. 2). The rest of the year was taken up with a government media blitz, Feedback Unit-sponsored seminars, forums, presentations and discussions on 'the goals which we wish to achieve together and the challenges which we have to overcome as a nation' (Goh Chok Tong in GOS, 1988b, p. 7).

In presenting the 'Agenda for Action: Goals and Challenges' to parliament as a green paper on February 15, 1988, Goh Chok Tong stated that 'the ties between elected leaders and the people ... must be constantly nurtured through continual discussion, feedback and explanation [so that the Government] will have a close feel of the mood of the people, and the people will understand thoroughly what is at stake and what needs to be done' (GOS, 1988b, p. 7).

When announcing the government's adoption of the Agenda for Action in parliament on 25 February 1988, Goh stated that the four goals it identified (nation-building, economic growth and progress, human resources and education and social and cultural development) could best be reached by the appointment of six advisory councils each headed by a cabinet minister. The councils were given carefully depoliticised areas: culture and the arts, sports and recreation, family and community life, youth, the handicapped and the aged. Each of these advisory councils then began its own process of public consultation throughout 1988. This plethora of quasi-governmental consultative bodies established a petitionary political dynamic whereby the government could say it had heard public opinion and then do anything or nothing about it. The PAP tried to take the focus off its political accountability in the forum of parliament where it had to deal with real political challenges on more equal terms.

In 1988 the government also began to use the same technique inside parliament through its parliamentary select committee system which had previously been in disuse except for occasional political show trials (see Parliament of Singapore, 1986). For example, it encouraged public submissions on a widely unpopular proposed electoral change. The legislation was introduced to the House on 30 November 1987 and read for a second time on 11 January 1988. Of 99 written representations received by the Select Committee, 12 representers were chosen to appear before the Committee for a nationally televised public hearing on 7–9 March, 1988 (*FEER*, 24 March 1988, p. 26; Quah, 1989, pp. 3–4). The legislation (amendments to the Constitution and to the Elections Act) was then passed without substantive changes in May 1988 with the government claiming that the voters had been consulted adequately.

Parliament had been televised from March 1985 by the state-controlled media. When parliament was in session, edited excerpts were screened on a special programme every evening. Proceedings were also extensively covered in the state-controlled newspapers. The government made the most of the opposition presence to show that parliament was a forum of real political contest between differing forces. It may have calculated that the uninspiring performances of the opposition members would be sufficient to dent public confidence in them. However, some observers have maintained that the televising of parliament 'backfired on the ruling party', because it increased the public perception of the two opposition members as besieged underdogs (*FEER*, 11 July 1985, p. 34). In fact it did both things. It did strengthen the illusion that the PAP would allow real political plurality. Through its media publicity the PAP-state made a virtue of its controlled public consultation both inside and outside of parliament by portraying itself as seeking consensus and national unity and depicting the opposition as contentious and divisive (*STW*, 14 January 1989, p. 6). It also reinforced the public desire for more opposition.

Government-approved Opposition

Although the PAP-state reverted to traditional liberal democratic parliamentarism and accepted that an opposition is supposed to help governance, it worked to provide that opposition from within its own ranks and from opposition candidates of its own choosing.

The government brought into play nine Government Parliamentary Committees (GPCs) in 1987 (Chan, 1989, p. 85) (increased to ten in 1989), consisting of all the backbench PAP MPs, except three who had 'distanced themselves from current PAP policy' (*FEER*, 26 March 1987, p. 23). These committees were encouraged to take on the role of a critical presence in parliament. The chairmen of the GPCs sat alongside opposition MP Chiam See Tong on the front bench opposite the PAP Cabinet 'to counter the impression that the chamber is merely a rubber stamp'. By this time Jeyaretnam had already been excluded from parliament on framed-up charges in the courts. Only the more pliable Chiam remained. The GPC chairmen stated they must not appear to 'collude' with the government if they were to be credible and might even abstain on some issues. Goh said that some of the chairmen might become 'a bit of a threat' to ministers (*FEER*, 26 March 1987, p. 23).

The public were not very convinced by this pretence. In 1989 Goh averred that GPCs faced the 'unfortunate misconception ... that they were not independent because their members came from the ruling party' (*STW*, 1 July 1989, p. 2). The *Straits Times* further reported his statement as follows:

> Asked if GPCs were meant to displace the Opposition and render it irrelevant to the political system, Mr Goh said it was his belief in the continued dominance

of the PAP that prompted him to set up GPCs as a way of ensuring that Government policies would always be scrutinised. (*STW*, 1 July 1989, p. 2)

The PAP was concentrating on supplying the forms of parliamentary plurality and accountability but not the substance. It was enhancing its ability to provide an opposition acceptable to itself and to exclude members of any independent strength if they nevertheless managed to get elected.

The persecution of Jeyaretnam continued unabated until he was criminalised by the courts and deprived of his seat (Asia Watch, 1989, p. 73). His strength derived not merely from his dogged concern for the poor, which somewhat overcame his lack of skill as a debater, but more importantly for the PAP, from his party's links to the working class. Scrutiny of PAP legislation was to be permitted by a fabricated and tame opposition chosen by the PAP, an opposition which would never dig too deep or have a popular base among the working class. But political accountability could quickly be transformed from illusion to reality if connected to autonomous working class political organisation outside the House. The middle class base of Chiam's SDP and his own lack of political fire and clarity, rendered him an acceptable opposition member. He was therefore chosen by the PAP in the sense that the harassment of his party was routine and the PAP decided not to eject him from parliament.

Lee Kuan Yew put the distinction more colourfully. In 1986 he differentiated between Chiam whom he likened to the English-educated liberals with a gentlemanly approach to politics and the 'riff-raff', the 'fly-by-night politicians' such as Jeyaretnam (*Asia Yearbook*, 1987, p. 64).

Undermining Opposition Members' Effectiveness

While the PAP-state allowed the public semblance of parliamentary opposition, it did not permit opposition MPs to perform their parliamentary and constituency functions unhindered. Obstacles placed in the way of these MPs included the following:

(1) Delaying the granting of office space in the government-administered housing estates where more than 86 per cent of the population lives. Jeyaretnam obtained an office eight months after his election in 1981. Chiam was elected on 22 December 1984 and obtained his office on 20 November 1985 (*FEER*, 30 May 1985, p. 21; *ST*, 30 November 1985). It was not possible to obtain offices prior to election as an MP.

(2) Ensuring that annual publication permits for party organs and police permits for holding rallies is usually an uncertain and lengthy process often resulting in rejection (Asia Watch, 1989, p. 80).

(3) Bringing politically motivated criminal charges for mismanagement of funds, illegal assembly and so on or charges for defamation and libel against opposition leaders who have little hope of defending themselves

successfully in front of a compliant judiciary (Asia Watch, 1989, pp. 71–81). These frequent prosecutions are aimed at keeping the opposition impoverished and criminalising the most effective leaders.

(4) Denying reliable information from the civil service to opposition MPs and parties, making it more difficult to criticise government policies from an informed position and to develop alternative policies (*ST*, 3 March 1984).

(5) Placing party officials under constant surveillance by the Internal Security Department and infiltrating the parties (Minchin, 1986, p. 217).

(6) Using the government-controlled mass media to report minimally and negatively on opposition party affairs.

(7) Excluding opposition MPs from government-controlled community organisations which monopolise local affairs in each constituency.

The latter exclusion is hardly surprising since these government bodies, a system of community centres, consultative committees and residents' committees in each area or housing estate, are a vital governing mechanism of the PAP. As mentioned in Chapter 3, they are all appointed by the Prime Minister's Office. The prime minister has been the chairman of the over-arching coordinating body, the People's Association, since its inception in 1960. PAP MPs head the local committees and PAP members hold the influential positions. Yet Lee, when faced with a complaint about this from Jeyaretnam, stated that these organisations must be insulated from 'interference by political parties or opposition MPs' (*ST*, 30 June 1985).

To protect this governing structure from also becoming a site of political competition as parliament had, the PAP-state refused the repeated applications of both Chiam and Jeyaretnam to join these bodies which PAP MPs routinely sit on in order to have access to local community affairs (*FEER*, 30 May 1985, p. 21; *ST*, 30 June 1985). In this case, liberal democratic ideology could be summoned, if ingenuously, to the PAP's support: the civil service is not supposed to be the place where political forces vie for supremacy whereas parliament is. The PAP upheld the public fiction of a separation of party and state in order to maintain the legitimacy of this governing mechanism and its exclusive grip on it.

Eliminating Opposition within Parliament

The PAP went beyond measures to contain opposition members. The unexpected re-election of Jeyaretnam kept this populist rival in the public eye and he had the added advantage after 1984 of another opposition member to second his motions. His increasing effectiveness and his symbolic importance made him a potential focus for the coalescence of a more competent political leadership. However haltingly, Jeyaretnam was beginning to develop a public critique of the PAP's use of the institutions of liberal democracy including parliament, the judiciary and the police.

The moves to criminalise Jeyaretnam in the courts and remove him from parliament took time (Asia Watch, 1989, pp. 71–81) and this gave him the opportunity to speak out in parliament and expose the PAP's tactics. He had to be silenced quickly. The PAP did this by removing the protection of parliamentary privilege. As Lee said on television, 'I think I am slowly convincing my colleagues that the only way to get a skunk is to skin him and nail his skin' (*Time*, 8 September 1986, p. 17).

During the debate on the privileges amendment, Foreign Minister Dhanabalan stated that 'the aim of the bill is not to stifle democracy but to enable it to work in our particular circumstances'. Explaining this later, he said, 'There are certain key institutions in Singapore that must be beyond reproach – parliament, courts and so on' (*FEER*, 8 January 1987, p. 55). Lee's accusation that Jeyaretnam's comments about the judiciary were 'totally treasonable' reveal the centrality of liberal democratic institutions to the PAP governing strategy and show that Lee recognised the crisis of legitimacy that was being precipitated (*Asia Yearbook*, 1987, p. 234).

The legislation increased the penalties that could be imposed by the parliamentary Privileges Committee. In six hours on 25 August 1986, amendments to the Parliament (Privileges, Immunities and Powers) Act were passed through three readings. These changes increased the possible fine from $1000 to $50,000 'if a member is found guilty of dishonourable conduct, abuse of privilege or contempt' and they gave parliament the right to imprison a member for the remainder of the session (*FEER*, 4 September 1986, pp. 12–13). The amendments maintained the penalties of suspension for the remainder of a session and of reprimand. A provision was added which gave parliament the right to remove a member's immunity from civil action for a specified period. Thus, a member could be silenced for fear of civil proceedings.

The power to deal with contempt cases summarily was extended from parliament as a whole to the Speaker and any chairman of any committee, that is, to the PAP exclusively. In the same session the government introduced constitutional amendments which denied the right to counsel for any member accused of contempt (*Time*, 8 September 1986, p. 17) and denied members the right to be brought before a magistrate within 48 hours of their arrest. Members could therefore be held incommunicado. Moreover, the seat of an expelled member would automatically fall vacant (*Asia Yearbook*, 1987, p. 234). The legislation gave the PAP the power to silence any member it disapproved of through the fear of heavy penalties and criminalisation in the courts and to expel them from parliament at its convenience.

The amendments were introduced hurriedly before a Privileges Committee hearing on Jeyaretnam's questioning of the independence of the judiciary. Noting the impending hearing in his introduction of the amendments, Dhanabalan stated that the hearing should not be allowed 'to become a forum for another debate, an opportunity for more smears or a platform for histrionics'. He continued, 'By all means take the government to task, scrutinise its actions. But don't resort to defamatory statements which cannot be proved and which only undermine our institutions' (*FEER*, 4 September 1986, p. 12). As a consequence Jeyaretnam could be cited for contempt if he repeated before the Privileges Committee his original comments in the House.

At the end of the televised Privileges Committee hearing in 1986, during which Lee fulminated against Jeyaretnam for several days, the opposition MP asked whether Lee hated him and thought he had to be destroyed. Speaking under privilege, Lee answered: 'Politically, yes. You have to be debunked, exposed as a charlatan, as basically dishonest, as immoral and utterly unscrupulous, that you make any allegation against anybody, so long as you are protected [by parliamentary privilege]. But the moment you bear the consequences, you flinch and you cringe, which is shameful' (*Asia Yearbook*, 1987, pp. 233–4).

Although this televised show trial may have earned sympathy for Jeyaretnam, it also demonstrated the limits to parliamentary opposition and the power of the PAP's continuing ability to exact revenge. Asked whether the government was making a political mistake in turning Jeyaretnam into a martyr, Dhanabalan replied, 'Even if Jeyaretnam is made a martyr in the eyes of his supporters, we have still made a point to the others, and that is what we are interested in' (*FEER*, 8 January 1987, p. 58). Fear was used to set the limits to parliamentary opposition. Criticism of specific policies of the government could be countenanced but the development of a political critique of the PAP's use of the institutions of liberal democracy in Singapore could not.

The Washington-based human rights organisation, Asia Watch, criticised these new measures:

> it is especially troubling because that Parliament's members come almost exclusively from the ruling party (and so control the disciplinary process); because there are no clear definitions of what constitutes behaviour that warrants disciplinary action: and because decisions of Parliamentary disciplinary bodies are not reviewable by the judiciary. Our concerns are only heightened by the fact that, at least in recent years, Parliamentary disciplinary actions seem to have been reserved exclusively for members of the miniscule opposition in Singapore. (Asia Watch, 1989, pp. 79–80)

These measures, for all practical purposes, removed parliamentary privilege for the opposition and meant that opposition MPs must be able to prove their every statement in parliament according to legal standards of proof if they are not to make themselves liable for action under the privilege provisions. The PAP thereby set in place the parliamentary mechanisms to deal with the *fait accompli* of an opposition politician who had won a seat despite the government's system of blocks.

The PAP-state also strengthened its ability to prevent a recurrence of the Jeyaretnam phenomenon and to select its own opposition with more success. It changed the electoral rules, heightened manipulation of electoral campaigns and made outright threats against voters.

Neutralising Opposition Votes

The PAP-state not only engaged in the time-honoured process of changing electoral boundaries to its own advantage but it also changed the whole voting system to this end. The Group Representation Constituencies (GRC) scheme, passed by parliament on 18 May 1988 by amendments to the Constitution and the Elections Act, was designed to raise the threshold of votes needed by the opposition to get members into parliament in the first-past-the-post electoral system. Its aim was to 'dilute opposition votes by combining constituencies with dominant opposition sympathies with neighbouring constituencies which strongly support the PAP' (Linda Lim, 1989, p. 184). The GRC scheme was designed to protect the PAP from a further swing to the opposition.

First mooted during the 1984 elections, the scheme created 13 GRCs from 39 constituencies, each group of three constituencies becoming a single voting block. To contest a GRC, a party was required to put forward a slate of three candidates all of whom become MPs if they jointly obtained the most votes.

When the scheme was implemented in the 1988 elections, eight of the ten most marginal PAP seats from 1984 were placed in the ten contested GRCs along with safe PAP seats.

In the boundary changes associated with its introduction, the solidly opposition Anson constituency of recently expelled MP Jeyaretnam was abolished even though he was still appealing his case. Two other constituencies were abolished (Rochore and Telok Ayer), which were the seats of increasingly critical PAP backbenchers and former senior ministers, Toh Chin Chye and Ong Pang Boon (*FEER*, 4 August 1988, p. 22; 1 September 1988, p. 20).

The government initially justified the scheme in terms of its proposal to set up Town Councils (see Chapter 3), but the punitive implications of the proposal for the opposition was immediately obvious and provoked a strong public reaction (*FEER*, 26 March 1987, p. 22). The government then switched its ground. It stated that the GRC scheme was actually to ensure minority race representation in parliament and that this had not been said initially for fear of stirring up racial tension. Each slate of candidates was then required to have at least one minority representative. The government went to considerable lengths to convince the electorate of its sincerity in this. It released cabinet papers dating back to 1982. Lee Kuan Yew staged another 'political TV spectacular to put his case over' (*FEER*, 24 March 1988, p. 26). The parliamentary select committee hearing on the legislation was televised each evening from 7 to 9 March 1988.

However, the Malay and Indian communities were prominent in opposing the proposal on the grounds that they did not want the PAP to define either who is a Malay or to choose their representatives (*FEER*, 4 August 1988, p. 22). In addition, as Jeyaretnam pointed out, in 1984 all the PAP's minority race candidates had won. The only two PAP candidates defeated were Chinese and one of them was defeated by himself, a member of a minority race (*FEER*, 10 December 1987, p. 14). The voting figures from the previous three elections (1976, 1980 and 1984) showed that PAP Malay candidates polled only marginally fewer votes than the average for all PAP candidates (*FEER*, 11 February 1988, pp. 32–33).

As Jeyaretnam implied, if the PAP's concern for minority representation was genuine it could easily have nominated more minority representatives to its own safe seats. Besides, the 1988 elections with the GRCs in operation produced exactly the same number of minority race representatives in parliament as before (16), and reduced the elected opposition members by 50 per cent, from two to one. The number of Malay MPs increased from nine to ten, Indian MPs stayed at six and a Eurasian MP did not stand.

The condition that each slate of candidates must include a minority representative made it harder for the opposition to put forward slates. Being the most politically insecure community in Singapore, Malays are reluctant to enter politics for either the PAP or for the opposition (*FEER*, 4 August 1988).

The GRC gerrymander achieved its real goal of neutralising the increasing opposition vote in 1988 as a survey of the closeness of some results shows. Without the GRC scheme, there would have been a sharp increase in opposition members (see Table 6.4).

Table 6.4   Marginal Results in 1988 Election

Seat	No. of MPs	% of valid votes			
		PAP	WP	SDP	Other
PAP vote below 55%					
Eunos GRC	3	50.9	49.1	–	–
Paya Lebar	1	52.4	–	47.6	–
Bukit Gombak	1	53.5	–	46.5	–
Bedok GRC	3	54.9	45.1	–	–
PAP vote 55–60%					
Aljunied GRC	3	56.3	–	43.6	–
Bukit Panjang	1	57.3	–	30.8	–
Nee Soon Central	1	57.6	–	38.4	–
Tiong Bahru GRC	3	57.8	42.1	–	–
Fengshan	1	57.9	42.1	–	–
Braddell Heights	1	58.8	–	41.2	–
Hougang	1	59.0	41.0	–	–
Chua Chu Kang	1	59.3	40.7	–	–
Changi	1	59.4	40.6	–	–
Whampoa	1	59.5	–	–	40.5*
Punggol	1	59.9	–	40.1	–

WP, Workers' Party; SDP, Singapore Democratic Party.
*National Solidarity Party (split from SDP).

Source: *FEER* (15 September 1988), p. 16.

The PAP secured all but one seat in parliament on the basis of 61.8 per cent of the total vote (GOS, 1989a, p. 232). The remaining 38 per cent secured a single seat. This extreme distortion of the plurality system of voting meant that it took an average of 12,290 votes to elect a PAP candidate while it took an average of 494,406 votes to elect an opposition candidate (election results, *STW*, 4 September 1988).

Through this manipulation of the electoral process, the government was able to exclude most opposition candidates and choose one of its preference. It was able to prevent the strongest and working-class-linked opposition party, the Workers' Party, from winning a seat and to permit the re-election of PAP-approved opposition member Chiam See Tong (Singapore Democratic Party). The PAP had decided not to include his single member constituency in a GRC.

In addition, the PAP seats could be protected from future anti-government by-election swings under the GRC legislative provision that by-elections need not be held in GRCs until the entire team of MPs ceases to hold office.

Threats and Imprisonment Precede Elections

The tying of welfare to political loyalty by linking housing values and services to the Town Councils scheme was not the only way voters were cajoled into supporting the government. There were more direct threats as well.

The detention of 22 young professionals and community workers in May–June 1987 was partly aimed at preventing the effective mobilisation of intellectuals and the working class behind the Workers' Party. Several of those detained had been legally and openly assisting the party (International Mission of Jurists, 1987). Their detention served as a warning to opposition party workers as well as supporters.

The subsequent detention without trial in 1988 of one of the detainees' lawyers, Mr Francis Seow, who had declared his interest in standing at the polls, was also aimed at discouraging him and other capable candidates from doing so. Seow was a former solicitor-general who had fallen out with Lee. As president of the Law Society in 1986, he had the best of Lee in a televised select committee hearing on legislation designed to force his resignation from the Society's presidency (Parliament of Singapore, 1986, B60–94). 'My arrest and detention under the ISA [Internal Security Act] has frightened many potential candidates away,' said Seow after his release shortly before the elections (*Asiaweek*, 2 September 1988, p. 34).

These threats and obstructions set the scene for the 1988 election campaign. On 17 August 1988, the President announced the election date as 3 September, 16 days hence and nomination day as 24 August, allowing a nine-day election campaign. The Electoral Act forbids campaigning outside of the campaign period. However, once again this effectively applied only to the opposition. The National Day celebrations were on 9 August. The Prime Minister's National Day Rally speech was on 14 August and he described, in the words of the *Straits Times* headline, 'How the Reds can hit us a second time' (*STW*, 20 August 1988, p. 13). Deputy Prime Minister Goh's National Day message included a warning about ensuring political stability or else 'economic growth would take a plunge and that extra [Christmas] bonus may disappear' (*STW*, 20 August 1988, p. 2). On 22 August the Prime Minister gave a highly publicised address to university students widely seen as a pitch to the new generation of voters. On 27 August, during the campaign and one week before the election, the government threw the 'Swing Singapore' Party in downtown Orchard Road. Sponsored by the government and planned by the US public relations firm Ogilvy and Mather to soften the stern image of the PAP, it was a free extravaganza to which 250,000 people turned up (*FEER*, 8 September 1988, p. 16).

On the announcement of the election, the deposit for candidates was raised from $1500 to $4000. During the campaign the Workers' Party and its star attraction, Seow (released from 72 days detention under the ISA on 16 July), regularly drew crowds of 15,000–18,000 at its rallies. The PAP rallies, even with the Prime Minister speaking, attracted crowds of only a few thousand. However, the *Straits Times* and the television gave considerable prominence to Lee and barely mentioned Seow (*FEER*, 8 September 1988, p. 18). On election eve, the media did suddenly give prominence to government allegations that Seow 'was financially untrustworthy, had criminal acquaintances, and might be disqualified from taking his seat should he be elected' (*The Economist*, 10 September 1988, p. 30).

With this kind of systematic crippling of opposition organisation, it was extremely difficult for the opposition to mobilise its supporters and to inform them of its policies. The opposition vote nevertheless increased by one per cent (GOS, 1989a, p. 232) although only Chiam was returned as a duly elected opposition member. (Jeyaretnam was banned from standing.)

To make up the quota of three opposition MPs, two NCMP seats were offered to the two highest polling losers: Francis Seow and Lee Siew Choh, both from the Workers' Party. They had narrowly failed to win the Eunos GRC where the PAP won by 50.9 per cent of the vote (*STW*, 4 September 1988). They accepted the seats. Dr Lee had been a leader of the *Barisan Sosialis* in the mid-1960s and his erratic leadership then had been a political gift to the PAP. He was permitted to enter parliament after the election. However, Seow was disqualified from his seat before he was able to take it up owing to tax charges brought against him after he was released from political detention. Seow escaped to the United States before the court proceedings began (*STW*, 24 December 1988). The PAP evidently recognised that, even as a second-class MP, a person of Seow's eloquence and skill would provide too serious a challenge. Both Jeyaretnam and Seow were excluded from parliament by a process of criminalisation.

In summary, from 1984 to 1988 the PAP-state moved decisively to protect its ability to govern through parliament. While of necessity acknowledging the place of an opposition in parliament, the government went to considerable lengths to undermine genuine opposition and to fabricate political pluralism. It used threats and fear to prevent opposition members being effective in parliament and to prevent the electorate voting for them. If they persisted in casting an opposition vote, this was structurally neutralised by the GRC electoral gerrymander.

The PAP-state ensured that no member of an opposition party with a strong personal following or working-class links was elected.

THE TRANSFER OF POWER

The question of the political succession to Lee Kuan Yew was a common topic of the 1980s. Although Lee has since handed over the Prime Ministership, the effective transfer of power, as opposed to administrative responsibility, has yet to take place. But an equally significant transfer of power has been accomplished. Substantive executive powers of government have been transferred to the Presidency. This is the main constitutional development since 1988. It has occurred within the context of continuing PAP efforts to construct an acceptable opposition in parliament.

The Non-elected MP

Despite the GRC gerrymander a five per cent swing against the PAP in subsequent elections may still bring into parliament some opposition members it regards as undesirable. It cannot manipulate the voting system much more without the electoral process losing all credibility. The PAP-state therefore created another category of MP outside the franchise, the non-elected MP (NMP).

On 6 October 1989 Deputy Prime Minister Goh introduced an constitutional amendment to provide for the appointment of up to six non-elected MPs (NMPs) for two-year terms and with the same restricted voting rights as NCMPs. It was proposed that the NMPs be chosen by a Special Parliamentary Select Committee headed by the Speaker and then be appointed by the President. That is, the PAP would choose the NMPs. The first NMPs would be appointed as soon as practicable after the passage of the legislation (*STW*, 14 October 1989, p. 8).

NMPs were first mooted in parliament in January 1989 by Brigadier-General Lee Hsien Loong who termed them 'non-partisan' MPs. He put the idea forward as a way of making Singapore's democracy 'as stable, as well supported and as feasible as we can contrive' (*STW*, 28 January 1989, p. 6). NMPs could make a contribution by representing the views of various sectors such as community leaders, university dons, workers and employers, noted Lee. In May Goh raised the issue again, stating that people who did not want to spend their whole career in politics could make a contribution through becoming short-term MPs (*STW*, 20 May 1989, p. 2).

This is a reversion to the British practice of appointed members of the colonial legislature. It is also a reversion to nineteenth century concepts of rule by the 'educated' rather than the 'ignorant'. Everyone should have a vote but some should have more votes than others (Macpherson, 1977, p. 57). The NMP scheme is a way of giving more votes to the upper class. This is an echo of John Stuart Mill's meritocratic political theory of more than a century ago which held that 'those who had already attained superior station in life must not be made to yield their power to the rest' through equal voting power (Macpherson, 1977, p. 60).

The junior Lee has put forward the view that the NMPs will mean that Singapore 'will not be the same as other people's democracy because the circumstances are different' (*STW*, 28 January 1989, p. 6). This statement seeks to avoid the criticism that the government has dispensed with universal suffrage. However, the PAP is on firm ground domestically because the opposition have already agreed to this truncation of fundamental liberal democratic principle through their acceptance of NCMP status in the House. The NMPs can henceforth be used against the opposition by claiming that they are neither government nor opposition and thereby neutral and non-partisan.

The benefit to the PAP will be considerable because the political effect of having yet a third category of MP in parliament will be to undermine the democratic concept of opposition. With the Government Parliamentary Committees also pretending to be in opposition, there will be a confusion of political accountability. The line between government and opposition, and between elected and appointed, will become blurred – presumably an intentional effect. Deputy Prime Minister Goh Chok Tong said that the 'GPCs, together with the non-constituency MP scheme and the recently proposed non-elected MP scheme, will make up for the small number of Opposition MPs' (*STW*, 1 July 1989, p. 2).

The number of NMPs can also be increased to counter any increase in popularly elected opposition members. The number of NCMPs has recently been raised to four (*STW*, 29 June 1991). In addition, changes to parliamentary privileges and procedures (for example, cutting down speaking times and requiring four members to support a call for a division) are also designed to hobble the opposition.

But there is also another possibility for the PAP to undermine genuine opposition by shifting the ground of political competition. It may be possible at some stage to move from interparty and intraparliament contests to intraparty struggles. The controlled opposition role allowed to the GPCs could be developed into one or more ostensibly opposing factions within the PAP, possibly using the Japanese Liberal Democratic Party or the Indian Congress Party as models. By focusing on these contrived political rivalries, the PAP government might add to the illusion of political contest and of PAP responsiveness to popular opinion. The contest would be mainly within the controlled environs of the party itself and parliament would be the showplace for exhibiting it. Such artificial political contest might provide a useful testing ground for rising PAP leadership just as the present GPCs do already.

The unprecedented statement by Lee Kuan Yew that the PAP could possibly lose power if there was 'a split in the leadership over policy, not a personality clash, but a real difference over economic or political policies' (*STW*. 28 October 1989, p. 13) may presage such a development or may simply be justification for an executive presidency.

Whatever form this strategy takes momentarily, the possibilities fit well with the government's view that it has to create an opposition in its own image which would wait on the sideline as a kind of emergency replacement team. 'In terms of the thinking of the first generation leadership, it essentially means the creation of a PAP "A Team" and a PAP "B Team"' (Vasil, 1984, p. 185). Because such an opposition 'must share the ruling party's philosophy and differ only in membership' (*Asia Yearbook*, 1989, p. 214), the policy debates between the PAP government and the PAP opposition are likely to be fake. The risk for the PAP is that after the final departure of Lee, they may not stay that way. However, it has created enough kinds of MPs and illusory opposition politics to have many options open to it as occasion demands.

Parliament and Presidency

The PAP has often contemplated what it has termed a 'freak' election result, an election which it actually loses (*FEER*, 8 September 1988, p. 18). The PAP's main concern has been to protect its governing powers over the long term against such an eventuality. Even a steadily rising opposition vote or a real split in its own ranks would restrict its ability to govern. It spent seven years effecting a transfer of power to insure itself against such eventualities.

In April 1984 Lee Kuan Yew stated that the government was 'seriously thinking about amending the Constitution to introduce a blocking mechanism so that foreign reserves could be spent only with the assent of the President and a special committee' (Quah, 1989, p. 17). This soon developed into a proposal for an elected presidency (*ST*, 20 August 1984).

After the December 1984 elections it was increasingly suggested that the elected president should also have the role of safeguarding the integrity of the civil service.

The White Paper presented to parliament on 29 July 1988, spelt out the government's rationale and intentions in detail.

> Any government, even a temporary coalition which comes into power by a majority of only one seat in parliament, has complete legal access to all the levers of power and decision-making.... It can do anything it wishes to the financial assets and reserves. It can also change any appointment in the civil service.... Overnight, everything can be dismantled.   (GOS, 1988c)

The White Paper proposed that the elected president would have a six-year tenure with the right to veto the spending of the country's assets and reserves which the government of the day had not itself accumulated, the right to make appointments to all senior positions in the civil service (including the judiciary), the military and statutory boards, the right to attend and make speeches in parliament and the right of access to all government offices (*Asia Yearbook*, 1989, p. 213; Quah, 1989, p. 17).

The financial assets entrusted to the president have generally been alluded to as the foreign reserves. On a per capita basis, Singapore's reserves are the highest in the world. Even then they are grossly understated (US$16.9 billion in 1988) because Singapore is said to value its instruments at purchase price rather than current value (for example, gold at US$35 an ounce rather than current value of approximately US$376) (*FEER*, 25 May 1989, p. 68). Thus, the amount to be guarded by the President is considerable.

However, the implication of the White Paper was that the assets to be so protected include even more:

> assets and reserves (including land and immovable property) of the government, the reserves and foreign exchange assets managed by the Government of Singapore Investment Corporation/the Monetary Authority of Singapore/the Board of Commissioners of Currency, Singapore, the capital assets and surpluses of the statutory boards, the capital assets and surpluses of government companies and those arising from any extraordinary measures which involve raising loans in the local and international markets and pledging the credit of Singapore. (Low and Toh, 1989, p. 21)

This proposal was clearly much more than 'an elected president without executive powers to perform a custodial role' (Quah, 1989, p. 17). It was a proposal 'to divest Parliament of its powers and reinvest the powers in one man' (Low and Toh, 1989, p. 25). Public reaction was very negative before the 1988 elections because the position appeared tailor-made for Lee Kuan Yew. This reaction forced Lee to say that he would not necessarily be the first elected president (*FEER*, 15 September 1988, p. 15). After the elections Goh announced that legislation on the proposal was a major priority but would not be rushed (Quah, 1989, p. 19).

When finally passed into law through a constitutional amendment (*STW*, 5 January 1991) and the Presidential Elections Act (*STW*, 6 July 1991), further provisions had been added. Among the powers of the president are the following.

- The right to veto government expenditure bills; this veto can be overturned by a two-thirds parliamentary majority only if a majority of the president's six-member Council of Advisers does not support the president;
- the right to veto budgets of the government and key statutory boards and government-owned companies and bills raising loans, incurring debts or providing guarantees on the part of the government; this and subsequent veto powers below may only be overturned by both a two-thirds majority in parliament and in a referendum;
- the right to veto any bill that changes the investment powers of the Central Provident Fund Board;
- the right to veto such key public service appointments as Supreme Court judges, the Attorney General, Public Service Commission members, the

Auditor General and Accountant General, members of the Armed Forces Council, the Chief of Defence Force, the Chiefs of the Air Force, Army and Navy, the Commissioner of Police and the Director of the Corrupt Practices Investigation Bureau;

- the right to refuse a recommendation from the government to declare a state of emergency, since this may enable the government to circumvent his powers;
- the right to veto bills he considers are circumventing his blocking powers;
- the final say over release of political detainees, the issuing of prohibition orders against religious leaders (under the new maintenance of religious harmony law) and the investigation of cabinet members for corruption (GOS, 1990; *STW*, 1 September 1990, p. 8; *Asia Yearbook*, 1991, p. 204).

These presidential powers are entrenched; changes require a two-thirds majority both in parliament and in a referendum if the president does not concur. The presidency has been bestowed with executive powers which give him the final say on all major financial and personnel matters. No party can govern without his cooperation.

The composition of the Council of Presidential Advisers ensures the perpetuation of PAP political dominance through the presidency in the unlikely event that another party attained a parliamentary majority. Of the six members, two will be chosen by the President (one of whom will be chairman), the Chairman of the Public Service Commission (who owes his job to the president) will nominate two members and the prime minister will nominate two (GOS, 1990).

The current head of state has become the first elected President and his term ends in 1993. Voting for the Presidency will be compulsory (*STW*, 6 July 1991, p. 1). Only those persons screened by a three-member Presidential Elections Committee and granted an eligibility certificate may stand for election (*STW*, 6 July 1991). The exceptions to these requirements are those who have already received government approval or are leading business figures.

> He is automatically qualified if he had served at least three years in one of the following positions: Minister, Chief Justice, Supreme Court Judge or Judicial Commissioner, Attorney-General, PSC [Public Service Commission] Chairman, Accountant-General, Permanent Secretary, Chairman/CEO [Chief Executive Officer] of one of nine major statutory boards, or Chairman/CEO of a company with paid-up capital of at least $100 million. (*STW*, 15 September 1990, p. 9)

The Workers' Party and the SDP have objected to the legislation mainly on the grounds of the stringent qualifications for candidacy (*STW*, 3 August 1991, p. 4). The qualifications for candidacy ensure that only a PAP-approved member of the capitalist class may stand for election.

The PAP-state has successfully transferred its core governing powers to a mechanism it completely controls and which cannot be breached by any number of opposition members in parliament – even a majority. The president will have the legitimacy of being popularly elected even though the circumstances of his election will be anything but democratic. This ideological effect is enhanced by the PAP's tactic of coining the title Elected President.

Whether or not Lee Kuan Yew takes the presidency is not of major significance. As he has noted, his control of the PAP as secretary-general is more crucial to his power (*Asiaweek*, 26 August 1988, p. 43) although, in the style of Deng Xiaoping, even this position is not essential to his continuing authority. Through his influence Lee can determine the membership of the Council of Presidential Advisers, the membership of the Presidential Elections Committee and, thus, the presidential candidate.

The PAP has set in place a presidential system whereby the levers of power remain in the hands of a democratically unaccountable capitalist class faction through their control of a president and his appointed advisors. The accountability of the executive in parliament has become a step removed. The PAP is now in the position to concede seats in parliament without any immediate risk to its political hegemony. The transfer of executive power to the presidency lessens the contradiction that had arisen between the PAP's practice of governing through parliament and the legitimating function of the legislature. This function can only be sustained if the opposition is perceived as having a real chance, even if a slim one, of becoming the government. The elected presidency reserves ultimate executive authority outside parliament against such a contingency.

PARLIAMENTARISM AND SOCIAL CONTROL

A common view among Singapore oppositionists and international human rights advocates is that the PAP has subverted parliamentary democracy, cynically using it as a facade for one-party rule. The litany of PAP political manoeuvres traversed so far in this chapter would appear to substantiate such a position. At the same time the international business media frequently opines that, while a measure of authoritarianism may have been necessary to set Singapore on the right economic path, the PAP can now afford a period of political liberalisation, to be more relaxed and open towards parliamentary opposition.

The moral condemnation which routinely accompanies such positions hides much deeper questions about the role of liberal democracy in Singapore, questions which relate to the underlying social relations which constrain the PAP to use parliamentarism in a certain way. Why, for example, does the PAP bother with the forms of liberal democracy when its failure to give them substance precipitates crises of legitimacy and undermines its social control? Why is the PAP so politically successful yet so politically insecure? Why does a majority of Singaporeans continue to vote for the PAP? Is it really out of fear alone?

These questions require attention to the historical particularity of liberal democracy as a form of government in order to lay bare the reasons its practice in Singapore faces contradictions not evident to such an extent in the advanced capitalist countries. The manner in which voting transforms submission into consent and becomes an act of obedience is also central.

Liberal Democracy and Class

Western liberal democracy developed out of the liberal state and capitalist society. Liberal democracy was a form of government adapted to a class-divided society from the beginning. It did not develop a new kind of society or inspire a vision of a new kind of humanity. It developed because the pressure for universalising the franchise became irresistible and because the ruling classes of Europe and America realised that it posed no threat to their property and, thus, their power. For them, democracy no longer meant rule by the wrong class, the working class.

> What the addition of democracy to the liberal state did was simply to provide constitutional channels for popular pressures, pressures to which governments would have had to yield in about the same measure anyway, merely to maintain public order and avoid revolution. By admitting the mass of the people into the competitive party system, the liberal state did not abandon its fundamental nature; it simply opened the competitive political system to all individuals who had been created by the competitive market society. The liberal state fulfilled its own logic. In so doing, it neither destroyed nor weakened itself; it strengthened both itself and the market society. It liberalised democracy while democratising liberalism. (Macpherson, 1965, p. 11)

From these beginnings grew the now-familiar 'pluralist, elitist, equilibrium model' of liberal democracy (Macpherson, 1977, p. 77). Macpherson draws an entrepreneurial market analogy to explain its dynamics. He sees liberal democracy as a market mechanism, with voters as consumers and politicians as entrepreneurs, which maintains an equilibrium between the demand and supply of political goods. It is elitist because groups of self-selected leaders take the main roles. It is pluralist because individuals are pulled in various directions by various group interests at different levels (in parliament and outside) and these interests compete for political power. It has thus become 'simply a mechanism for choosing and authorising governments, not a kind of society nor a set of moral ends' (Macpherson, 1977, p. 78). The choosing and authorising is done by the practice of voting under the universal franchise.

The type of liberal democracy bequeathed to Singapore by British colonialism fitted well with the ideology of the political economy and the increasing inequality in society. But there is a fundamental difference between Singapore and Western industrialised countries which has precluded the intraclass competition normally characteristic of liberal democracy. That difference is underdevelopment. The

Singapore capitalist class does not compare in strength to those of the West with their centuries of accumulation, technological advancement and class rule. The PAP's position within its own class has also been insecure, hence the constant attempts to shift the fault lines of linguistic and ethnic loyalty to the governing faction's advantage and to consolidate local capital behind its economic strategy.

This insecurity derives from the very specific historical development of class relations in Singapore. In the transition from colonialism in Singapore, the primary conflict which shaped the independent state was that between the anticolonial lower classes and the British ruling class and its state. The struggle for political independence forced the British to hand over state power to a fraction of the local capitalist class in cooperation with which it could continue to rule.

The local capitalist class in Singapore was not and has not become economically dominant. During the colonial period it was dependent on British trade and investment for its survival. Consequently, the Chinese-educated nationalists of this class did not have sufficient economic and political power to advance their own interests in the transition to independence or since and, thus, lost the opportunity for political leadership. An English-educated group, led by Lee Kuan Yew, was therefore able to consolidate an alliance with the British and acquire state power. Its main opposition was the anti-colonial mass movement of the lower classes with which it initially made an accommodation. Hence, when the Lee group came to power, it was relatively autonomous from the nationalist fraction of its own class but reliant on British imperial power as its main base from which to defeat the mass movement and then to entrench itself in government.

The economic policies of the PAP-state alliance with foreign capital in its subsequent phases of development have kept local capital peripheral to the main productive sectors of the economy even though some local capital accumulation has been encouraged. The PAP-state therefore has been characterised by its autonomy from local class forces, for example, in its ability to expropriate land, to finance industrial infrastructure, to organise the working class and to override the interests of local capital. In other words the PAP's weakness within its own class has had the advantage of greater autonomy of action domestically provided the PAP-state retained the partnership with foreign capital which provides its main power base.

When the core of the capitalist class is not a strong national bourgeoisie but a party organisation which governs mainly through the state and only indirectly through the foreign-owned means of production, it is not possible to talk of a Singapore ruling class. The distinction between 'ruling' and 'governing' becomes crucial. The PAP-state governs alone but it does not rule alone. It does not constitute a local ruling class or rule on behalf of one. It has always ruled in an alliance with foreign capital and could not have survived to rule at all without this partnership with the ruling classes of the advanced industrialised countries.

At this point the underdevelopment or the weakness of the capitalist class and, in this case, its governing faction, becomes relevant to the practice of liberal democracy in Singapore. Liberal democratic institutions legitimise one-class rule by giving political space for intraclass competition. The insecurity of the PAP has caused it to suppress all political challenges even those from within its own class. But this suppression of political pluralism did not shake the PAP-state's legitimacy too seriously as long as a genuine interclass challenge existed or could be claimed to exist.

During the 1960s and 1970s, in the name of anti-communism the PAP-state crushed opposition from outside and from inside its own class, from outside and inside parliament. Interclass conflict was characterised as a threat to the state rather than to the rule of a particular class alliance and the means of combatting it was a lesser version of the colonial tradition of military attack and emergency rule under which some temporary circumscription of civil rights is acceptable to the business and professional classes.

The failure of parliamentarism to legitimate PAP governance in moments of crisis came when the excuse of interclass conflict was less and less convincing and when opposition began emerging in the 1980s through a middle class committed to the substance of liberal democracy especially genuine intraclass political contest. At the same time the growth of a business class with vested interests in the alliance with foreign capital raised the possibility that the Singapore capitalist class had developed a sufficient unity of interests and depth of control at all levels of society to sustain a longer term self-confidence in its political hegemony.

The implication of such a development is that the PAP is no longer essential to secure this class hegemony. It means the local capitalist class is strong enough to field a number of parties which would continue the alliance with foreign capital. Should it lose an election, the PAP is aware that foreign capital would cooperate with any new government that had the same economic priorities and the same ability to control the working class. It therefore remains in the PAP's party rather than class interests to stifle political pluralism and intraclass rivalry. But it has not been able to do this without undermining the legitimating power of liberal democracy. The elected presidency therefore enables the PAP potentially to accommodate political alternatives from within its own class if it is constrained to do so by rising dissent and at the same time to preserve its grip on the state.

It has remained crucial for the PAP-state to maintain the ideological legitimation provided by parliament, parties and elections because such sanction extends beyond the administrative functions of the state to mask its joint rule with foreign capital and the weakness of its position in this partnership. The Singapore state has been one of the most cooperative in Asia in its relations with foreign capital. But this characteristic can only be publicly intimated in the economic form of investment incentives and not revealed in its political form of a collaboration which cedes sovereignty if the PAP-state's power of social control is not to be compromised.

A national parliament is an important nationalistic symbol of state sovereignty which is doubly important to a regime without a secure base in its own society. This tension between the PAP-state's necessity to be both cooperative with foreign partners and nationalistic for domestic consumption has been constantly present. These contradictory pressures were most obviously revealed in recent times when the government drove Francis Seow from parliament in a manner sufficiently aggressive to stimulate widespread cynicism about the electoral process and to expose the PAP's political selfishness. The government tried to whip up nationalistic feelings by then expelling a US diplomat for alleged interference in Singapore politics through his encouragement of Seow to stand for election (*Asia Yearbook* 1989, p. 215). This act might be seen as both a blind to cover the depth of the PAP–US relationship at a moment when local liberal democratic institutions were in crisis and also as a sign of PAP resentment that its necessity of collaborating with US capital also opens it to criticism over human rights abuses.

The above are the underlying social relations which have led to the common objections to the PAP's political tactics. The absence of an explicit interclass conflict and the rise of the middle class has brought the dissatisfaction with one-party dominance in a political system designed for multiparty intraclass competition. The consolidation of a business and professional class with an interest in the partnership with foreign capital has engendered the call for political liberalisation.

Liberal democratic practices have overall, however, been extraordinarily successful as mechanisms of social control through their legitimation of PAP governance despite the continual manifestation of social conflict through new forms of non-cooperation and resistance at each stage of economic development. This success is due in no small part to the practice of voting as a means of extracting consent.

Elections – Voting to Obey

The principle of individual choice as a pillar of parliamentarism has early origins. Before the capitalist state yielded to working-class pressure to extend the franchise, liberal principles and practices were already entrenched: 'both the society as a whole and the system of government were organised on a principle of freedom of choice' and on the politics of competition and the market (Macpherson, 1965, p. 6). Social inequality in a class-divided society meant some had more freedom of choice than others.

The concept of free and rational choice as both explanation and justification for human behaviour is predicated on the understanding of the human being as an atomised, self-interested individual, an ideology which preoccupies modern economists as much as it did the nineteenth century European upper class. The practice of voting in liberal democracies reinforces this ideology but also goes further; it converts individual choice into consent to the actions of others. On the basis of elections, governments are able to claim a mandate to govern. Voters can be said individually to have consented in advance to the decisions of the government. In this sense, voters do not directly decide political issues for themselves but they authorise others to do the deciding.

It has been argued that liberal democratic voting is therefore essentially a promise to obey. 'The essence of liberal social contract theory is that individuals ought to promise to, or enter an agreement to, obey representatives, to whom they have alienated their right to make political decisions.... liberal democratic voting is a series of renewals of the promise to obey' (Pateman, 1979, pp. 19–20).

Before elections in Singapore, voters are continually reminded not of the government's accountability to them but of their accountability to the government. The ideological effect of voting on Singaporean voters is that they have consented either to the government in power or to the whole system of governance or both. This consent is further internalised as obedience, a perception which is constantly reinforced by the formulations of liberal democratic principles articulated by those within the parliamentary system.

Elections have been the primary mechanism for establishing the PAP's constitutional legitimacy, for claiming that people have consented to its rule. To ensure this ideological effect, the government has to make sure that people do vote. Therefore voting is compulsory (GOS, 1989a, p. 56).

By holding elections, Lee Kuan Yew has been able to say, 'If I had been autocratic and authoritarian, I would not have won eight consecutive general elections over a period of thirty years' (*STW*, 11 November 1989). While the PAP won these elections precisely because it had been ruthlessly authoritarian in its reconstruction of Singapore society, the act of voting and the resulting electoral statistics have shored up the legitimacy of the regime.

Table 6.5 General Elections since 1955

Date	Seats	Parties Contesting	Party Returned	Seats Won	% Votes Won
Legislative Assembly					
1955 2 April	25*	5+11(I)	Labour Front	10	26.74
1959 30 May	51	10+39(I)	PAP	43	53.40
1963 21 September	51	8+16(I)	PAP	37	46.46
Parliament					
1968 13 April	7+(51)**	2+5(I)	PAP	58	84.43
1972 2 September	57+(8)	6+2(I)	PAP	65	69.02
1976 23 December	53+(16)	7+2(I)	PAP	69	72.40
1980 23 December	38+(37)	8	PAP	75	75.55
1984 22 December	49+(30)	9+3(I)	PAP	77	62.94
1988 3 September	70+(11)	8+4(I)	PAP	80	61.76

* 1955 Legislative Assembly consisted of one Speaker, 3 ex-officio members, 25 elected and 4 nominated members.
** Uncontested seats in brackets.
(I), Independents

Source: GOS (1989a) p. 232.

The ideological effect of Table 6.5 from the Ministry of Communications and Information is extremely useful to the PAP because it highlights the fact that there was a plurality of parties contesting each election and that the PAP won a high proportion of votes and, therefore, of seats. Citing the 1988 result, Brigadier-General Lee Hsien Loong stated, 'What we do is with the consent of the majority', an echo of PAP functionaries since 1959 (*The Bulletin*, 21 March 1989, p. 132).

But the table plays down the fact that, in the first four elections of the independent parliament, the PAP won all the seats. It provides no explanation for the result in 1968, when the highest percentage vote was gained, but only seven seats were contested. The analysis also blurs the fact that in 1988 nearly 40 per cent of the vote translated into just one opposition seat. However, the number of seats uncontested in each election is a major anomaly in a liberal democracy. The inclusion of these statistics presumably derives from the PAP's assumption that readers will understand the failure to contest as a mark of contentment with its rule.

But, overall, such a statistical presentation assists PAP legitimacy by avoiding the necessity to inform the reader of the most vital information of all. Electoral statistics fail to take account of the circumstances in which votes are cast. Not only the statistics do this. The system of voting ideologically represents each individual's vote as equal without regard to the unequal power of different classes to organise electoral support.

Table 6.6, which is derived from Table 6.5, demonstrates how much is left unexplained. It shows the control exerted by the PAP over the electoral process. The results suggest submission rather than consent, acquiescence rather than authorisation. From this perspective, voting in Singapore is an act which attests to the accountability of the individual citizen to the PAP and not of the government to its electors. To understand this relationship, the function of parties and specifically of the PAP must be examined more closely.

Table 6.6   General Election Results, 1968–88

Date	% Vote Against PAP	Opposition Seats	PAP Seats	Total Seats
1968	15.57*	0	58	58
1972	30.98	0	65	65
1976	27.6	0	69	69
1980	24.45	0	75	75
1984	37.06	2	77	79
1988	38.24	1	80	81

* Opposition boycott; only 7 seats contested.

Parties and Circumstances

The success of the PAP in the regular electoral vote counts accurately reflects the number of ballots cast in its favour. Because the PAP-state has the power to control the circumstances of voters at many levels, it has no need to resort to the ballot-stuffing or election violence of weaker governments. This power to control is partly due to the miniscule geographical size of Singapore but previous chapters have also outlined the PAP-state's ability to extract political loyalty through welfare provision, notably housing and education. Control of the media and of labour in the workplace are other major ways that voters' circumstances are regulated. In addition to these areas, there are more specific functions of political parties in general and the PAP in particular which impinge directly on the electoral circumstances and, thus, the electoral choice of voters.

The party system of liberal democracy has been a major factor in securing the dominance of one class. One reason that the democratic franchise did not bring about working-class government in Western democracies was that the chief function of the party system has been to diffuse and disguise class conflicts to prevent direct confrontation. Political parties have maintained upper-class rule by blurring social divisions and by standing between governments and their direct responsibility to the electorate. The PAP's self-advertisement as a national movement is just such a blurring of its social origins.

The other feature common to political parties is the ideological effect of candidate selection. In elections, voters believe they are choosing who will represent them in parliament. But parties actually make this choice and the voters are merely given the opportunity to confirm the choice of one or other of the parties. Singapore is slightly different because the PAP plays a part in choosing not only its own candidates but those of the opposition as well. It tried to do this first by keeping all opposition members out of parliament and then, when it failed, by using its apparatus of political repression to choose which opposition candidates it would let through.

Another special feature of the PAP is that it is not simply an electoral organisation. Its leadership also governs through the party and the state apparatus is an adjunct to the party apparatus. Chapter 1 mentioned how, in 1957, Lee amended the PAP's rules to establish a cadre system completely under the control of the Central Executive Committee. By this action he created a central ruling authority entirely under his control. Only cadres could attend the party conference and vote for the Central Executive Committee. Only the Central Executive Committee could choose the cadres and the list was and is secret (Bellows, 1970, p. 24). As Secretary-General of the PAP, Lee has retained central and undisputed authority over the ruling body. He has overseen who is admitted and who is expelled as well as the entire system of party patronage. The operation of the PAP is largely secret and therefore without open annual conferences to elect new party leadership. There is no mass base of party members since membership is by invitation only. In other words, the PAP is not so much an electoral party in the liberal democratic tradition as a governing clique secure from any democratic challenge. This structure was necessary for the survival of the English-educated faction of the capitalist class when faced with the threat of an internal takeover by the left. It is still necessary to prevent the PAP from factionalising and to exclude other class interests. Thus, the Central Executive Committee of the PAP, not the cabinet or a ruling majority in parliament, is the core of its power.

As Lee has admitted during a debate on introducing an elected presidency, it is not the official titles of state which are fundamental to his power, but his control of the PAP:

> Given me and my links with so many people, all I have to do is stay secretary-general of the PAP. I don't have to be president. (*Asiaweek*, 26 August 1988, p. 43)

He reiterated the point shortly afterwards but rather less directly:

> I belong to that exclusive club of founder members of new countries; first prime ministers or presidents of a new independent country. And even from my sick bed, even if you are going to lower me into the grave and I feel that something is going wrong, I'll get up. Those who believe that when I have left the government as prime minister, that I have gone into permanent retirement, really should have their heads examined. (*Asia Yearbook*, 1989, p. 212)

In Chapter 3 it was noted how the PAP extended its party organisation in the form of branch offices and state-sponsored People's Associations, Community Centres, Residents' Committees and so on, into the housing estates. The entire working class and much of the middle class have the party-state apparatus directly imposed on them in their own localities. This governing function is common in some other political systems but not in liberal democratic ones.

> it is crucial to recognise that the long years of partnership between the PAP and the civil servants have undoubtedly accelerated the fusion of the party and Government identity, a development which quite clearly can lead to the institutionalisation of the party as synonymous with State. (Chan, 1976, pp. 224–5)

The fusion of the 'identity' of the party and the state is a euphemism for the governing function of the party and the auxiliary function of the civil service. This fusion has provided the political context for the electoral process. It is the party-state with its secretive, unaccountable party core under a dominating, often threatening personality which administers Singaporeans' housing, property values, pensions, breeding, health, media, schooling and also the electoral process itself. It is this reality which is only too well-known to Singaporeans and which introduces a substantial element of fear into the circumstances of voting.

This complete control of civil society has also had a negative side for the PAP especially after 1981. The legitimating function of elections has come into contradiction with the PAP's governing functions by undermining those important ideological illusions of liberal democracy, the neutrality of the state and the apolitical character of the civil service. In addition, as noted earlier, one of the circumstances of voting that is essential to its legitimating function is the existence of a plurality of political forces in order that the possibility of the government being voted out is perceived as a real one. The PAP's difficulty with this political principle lies not just in the close relationship between party and state in the process of getting elected to govern. It also lies in the PAP's very success in this endeavour: the fact that it never stops getting elected to govern. It has therefore had to make some concessions to the middle class in terms of contrived debates on peripheral issues in parliament and the media while still keeping an absolute hold on working class political organisation.

But the PAP's problems with legitimising its roles as both an electoral vehicle and a governing institution can also be traced to a historical weakness of the party. Unlike the governments of Malaysia and Indonesia, the PAP cannot claim the historical legitimacy of a party which led the nationalist struggle for independence. The PAP was deprived of this mantle in 1961 when the working class and left-wing intellectuals deserted it to form the *Barisan Sosialis*. The PAP finally lost any residual claim to the ideological legitimacy of the nationalist struggle when, in 1976, it withdrew from the Socialist International shortly before its impending expulsion (Minchin, 1986, p. 187) and could no longer convincingly claim the success of Singapore-style 'socialism'.

> [The PAP] did not have to its credit a long history of a nationalist struggle for independence and of personal sacrifices by many of its leaders. Furthermore, it was not viewed by the populace as the unchallenged leader of Singapore nationalism.... None of them [the Lee faction] had a special charismatic appeal and a mass base. (Vasil, 1984, pp. 9–10)

Making a virtue out of necessity, the PAP has eschewed the popularity and emotional commitment attracted by political liberators in favour of justifying itself on its record: a party willing to take the tough decisions in the interests of the people even if they do not like it. The PAP's academic supporters have similarly resorted to extolling its material achievements and the wisdom of its leaders over the past 30 years as the historical basis for its legitimacy and its right to govern in perpetuity:

> Prime Minister Lee Kuan Yew, along with his two advisers belonging to the first generation leadership, Goh Keng Swee and S. Rajaratnam, has presided over the government. A unique personalised system of government has been built up around the personalities of these three, Confucian, wise and dedicated rulers who are viewed as the repositories of the national will and the custodians of the nation and its interests. The Prime Minister is acknowledged as the embodiment of the party and the government and the person who provides and sustains the

credibility of the government as a performer. He is the creator of modern Singapore. He is seen to enjoy a special, higher and overriding mandate from the people of Singapore.   (Vasil, 1984, p. 154)

Slightly more soberly, Vasil notes the PAP's 'spectacular achievements in the social and economic spheres' (Vasil, 1984, p. 48). Chan, in a more rigorous study, refers to this source of legitimacy as the 'performance variable' (Chan, 1976, p. 14) or the successful management of 'important political issues in the process of governance' (Chan, 1976, p. 165).

This stance of political pragmatism coupled with authoritarian paternalism consistently provides the PAP's electoral platform. But it leaves the PAP vulnerable to the vicissitudes of economic growth as it discovered in the mid-1980s and as most governing parties in advanced industrialised countries know to their cost. This uncertainty along with the PAP's continuing insecurity within its own class has caused the PAP to sustain high levels of threat and fear in the electoral process.

This analysis of the political system has shown the functioning of the process by which Singaporeans have democratically agreed to obey the government. Just as public housing and education have put people in their physical and social places, the political system has ensured they stay in their political places. But there is another institution of social control which supplements these. The law focuses the repressive power of the state on the working class to force its members not only to stay where they are put, but to cooperate with the accumulation strategy.

7 The Law, Coercion and Terror

The ordering of society is most effectively achieved by consent. However, when consent is not forthcoming or the ordering process requires the rapid breakdown of existing social relations, then various degrees of coercion become necessary.

The PAP-state's priority has been the reordering of Singapore society in consonance with the economic strategy of its partnership with foreign capital. This has involved the sudden reconstitution of the relations of production. These changes have required increasing state control both to initiate them and to secure them. With its unbroken control of the legislature, the PAP-state has been able to place the force of law behind its restructuring of the social formation. Even its most violent methods of engendering fear to force submission and obedience have been legitimated by the law.

A general understanding of the relationship between the law and the state in a class-divided society is fundamental to comprehending how the law and its administration have developed in Singapore.

THE STATE AND THE LAW

In a class-divided society the relations between the classes need to be regulated and the working class not only put in its place, but forced to cooperate with the mode of production. This may take the form of general social discipline or more extreme forms of coercion. Thus, consent is backed up by force.

> In a system based on capitalist reproduction, labour has, if necessary, to be *disciplined* labour; ... in a society of 'free individuals', men and women have to be disciplined to respect and obey the over-arching framework of the nation-state itself. Coercion is one necessary face or aspect of 'the order of the state'. The law and the legal institutions are the clearest institutional expression of this 'reserve army' of enforced social discipline. (Hall *et al.*, 1978, p. 202)

The law functions to produce conformity to the new social structures that capitalism requires. It does this by administering the key relations of capital (private property and contracts), defining and upholding the public order necessary for the steady reproduction of capital, defending the state against its enemies and sanctioning dominant social mores as universal (Hall *et al.*, 1978, p. 208).

Accordingly the law legitimates the state's use of force in regulating the social relations of capitalism. This is achieved on one level by the state itself appearing to be organised in the common interest and independent of any class interest. This appearance enables the state to define rights and obligations which it labels universal but which guarantee particular class interests. The relationship between the state and the law in liberal democracies is not that of the state openly using the law to impose the will of one class against the interests of another. Rather the state serves the supremacy of the ruling class and the development of productive forces while maintaining the appearance of neutrality, of standing above politics and society in order to act as an impartial moderator of conflict.

The previous chapter provided the example of the appearance of control by one class being avoided by the separation between the state and the legislature and through the competition of political parties in parliament. The ideological effect is of a state above class politics.

In the case of the law, this effect is reinforced by the separation of the making of law from its administration; the separation of the executive of the state and the legislature from the judiciary. The state appears to make laws in the common interest. It has the power to define what is legal and illegal and what is a crime. This ideological power is legitimated by its apparent lack of class interest and its separation from the process of administering the law. It is the judiciary which imposes sentences and subjects people to state violence in order to force their compliance with the social norms set by the state. Thus, the independence of the judiciary from the state is a crucial ideological effect which is produced by the actual functioning of the law and covers up the real relation.

Furthermore, the law does apply to everyone, rich and poor alike. The fact that some members of the upper class are criminalised along with large numbers of the working class is a concrete practice which covers up the law's class interest and attests to the state's neutrality.

> If the law is evidently partial and unjust, then it will mask nothing, legitimise nothing, contribute nothing to any class's hegemony. The essential precondition for the effectiveness of law, in its function as ideology, is that it shall display an independence from gross manipulation and shall seem to be just.   (Thompson, 1975, p. 263)

Again, at another level, the way the administration of the law is organised produces this effect of equality of justice. The legal apparatus is divided into three main areas of law: administrative, civil and criminal. Administrative law is that law administered directly by the government to ensure that executive decisions are obeyed and to protect the direct interests of the state. The ideological effect of this practice is that, since every citizen has an interest in the smooth operation of the 'neutral' state, these powers of regulation are normal and uncontroversial.

The civil law mainly regulates capitalist exchange. The distinction between civil and criminal law avoids the criminalisation of normal capitalist competition allowing it simply to be regulated for the efficient operation of business.

The criminal law criminalises forms of appropriation outside the control of the state and the capitalist class, along with other forms of social behaviour which threaten the existing social order. As the state has the power to define the common good and the law focuses on an individual's actions (taking individual circumstances into account only to a limited extent), the operation of the criminal law generates an ideological consensus that it is combatting social ills on behalf of society. The criminal law produces the ideological effect that crime is the fault of those who are punished for it. The particular class interest behind this imposition of social discipline is thereby obfuscated. The 'illegal' activities of the working class are heavily criminalised; an ideological sanction which legitimates the use of state violence against the poor.

> By operating strictly within judicial logic... [the law] constantly brackets out those aspects of class relations which destroy its equilibrium and impartiality *in practice*. It equalises... things which cannot be equal. In the famous words of Anatole France: 'in its majestic impartiality it forbids the rich and the poor alike to sleep under the bridges of Paris'. It addresses 'class subjects' as individual persons. (Hall *et al.*, 1978, p. 208)

Thus, these practices of the law and their ideological effects enable the state to criminalise the activities of a group or class that it wishes to control while at the same time disguising its class interest.

Class Conflict and Singapore's Legal Inheritance

From this analysis of the state and the law in liberal democracies it would appear that Singapore has a legal inheritance ideally suited to the PAP-state's political objectives. However, the British colonial government left behind a system of law and a body of statutes which contained contradictory influences from a long history of social conflict both in England and in Singapore. The continuing connections with all jurisdictions applying British common law with its convention of precedent also meant Singapore law would continue to be shaped by external as well as domestic influences.

The nineteenth-century victories of British working-class resistance to the new set of class alliances established by the transition from landed to industrial capital came to be formalised as concessions within the legal system. The distancing of routine legal practice from the direct intervention of the executive secured a greater measure of justice for the poor, while at the same time giving the law greater power to regulate on behalf of capital (Hall *et al.*, 1978, p. 193). Real concessions were won in the administration of the criminal law, such as the right to be tried by one's peers (the jury system), the rules of evidence, the right not to incriminate oneself, the right to legal representation and restrictions on the powers of the police. The extension of the rule of law, the freedoms of speech and assembly, the right to strike and organise in the workplace were also gains of the working class which were raised to social norms by the law. More recently the abolition of the ultimate terror of capital punishment and the trend towards judicial review of executive decisions in administrative law reflect further concessions to political challenges.

But in Malaya and Singapore the British colonial state confronted a different social formation and mode of production. Chapter 1 alluded to colonial emergency laws by which the state 'temporarily' negated many of the above legal developments in order to suppress class conflict. The state gave itself arbitrary powers to suppress dissent: it was able to act without the normal processes of judicial criminalisation which were slow, individualised and uncertain of successful conclusion – conviction – in all cases. The powers of the state under administrative law were vastly increased through granting itself such rights as the right to detain without trial and to kill on sight. These extreme powers of administrative law were used to crush the anti-colonial movement's attack on the British ruling class. This entailed destroying class organisation, not just disciplining individuals of a certain class, which is the function of the criminal law.

The contradictory influences of the criminal law and the administrative law, each shaped by social conflict, were part of the legal inheritance of the PAP-state. This inheritance reflected the historical mix of consent, accommodation and coercion within two different societies. In deciding the weight to give to these various influences, the PAP-state was right to claim it had little choice if it was to follow the EOI strategy. The Singapore government could not allow the victories of the British working class to prevent it from exploiting its own.

> Parliamentary system, parliamentary procedures, sophisticated election systems, bill of rights, rights to counsel – do you find these in our histories?.... all these are alien concepts. But overnight, they've been put in a constitution, drafted, bound and given to us at the birth of our nation. And we're supposed to use that constitution and work it and run the nation without any departures from these Western notions.
>
> But can it work? Will it always work? Will it be the recipe for our growth? Not necessarily. In Western societies, they may be able to work it, they may be able to harbour some of these communist, Marxist or other tendencies. But we have seen, as I have shown, our short history since independence has been replete with all sorts of special problems, special circumstances. So, in the ultimate analysis, we will have to devise our own solutions to deal effectively with our own peculiar threats and problems. (Home Affairs Minister Jayakumar justifying the detention without trial of 22 professionals and community workers to a PAP Youth Wing Seminar, 5 July 1987, GOS Press Release)

Lee Kuan Yew has made the point more concisely on many occasions, although sometimes more personally.

> Certain liberties in a developing nation sometimes have to be sacrificed for the sake of economic development and security and to prevent communist oppression. (*The Times*, London, 25 May 1977)

I spent a whole life-time building this and as long as I am in charge nobody is going to knock it down. (*FEER*, 26 December 1980)

To reconstitute the social formation and discipline the labour force to suit its economic policy, the PAP-state not only had to move in the direction of greater coercion and, thus, greater executive power, but it had also to use the judicial terror reminiscent of eighteenth-century England. Therefore, Singapore law has regressed through the removal of many of the gains made by the British working class which had been incorporated into the law.

This study of the development of Singapore's legal system will focus on two areas: administrative law and criminal law. This division, as pointed out earlier, is essentially one of function. Politically, administrative law enables the state to criminalise and suppress class politics. The individuals involved are not targeted primarily for individual criminal actions which could be dealt with under the criminal law. Many victims of executive law have not committed any such offence and cannot be criminalised in this way. The state therefore uses this kind of law primarily to suppress political organisation.

Criminal law enables the state to criminalise a whole class by criminalising individuals. This area of law essentially imposes social discipline by punishing individuals for actions which disrupt the social relations imposed by the state. These transgressions are overwhelmingly by the working class. In this sense, if administrative law is the criminalisation of politics, then criminal law is the politicisation of crime. The criminal law is aimed mainly at the discipline of one class.

This distinction between administrative and criminal is not an absolute one but a matter of emphasis when seen in the context of suppressing class conflict. Both areas of law come into play in some cases, while both commonly use coercion and fear as an integral part of their imposition of social control.

This examination will not be periodised in the manner of earlier chapters as it will be obvious that, within in each area of law, there has been intensification of executive control and continuous removal of working class protections as the PAP-state required more and more control to implement its economic strategy. In addition, as political dissent resurfaced in the 1980s, the legal system became part of the crisis of legitimacy which the PAP attempted to solve by even greater repression.

The following overview of the specific relationship between the PAP-state and the law sets the context for this detailed examination of administrative and criminal law in the city-state.

Rule by Decree: The PAP-State and the Law

In liberal democracies the state's constitution is usually held to entrench the fundamental liberties of the individual citizen and can be appealed to for redress against abuses of executive power. Appeal is normally through judicial review of executive decisions. Singapore has removed these checks on executive power and has thereby extended the reach of administrative law.

Law and order is another basic goal for both political and economic transformation, and the Constitution was adapted to provide for the smooth passing of legislation which would facilitate the implementation of government policies. The removal of the two-thirds majority requirement for constitutional amendments in 1965 was crucial in this scheme of things. The government needed also to expedite the passing of legislation without being unduly hampered by procedural delays by the Opposition. (Pillai and Tan, 1989, p. 658)

The PAP-state may also have been concerned that, despite its best efforts, the *Barisan Sosialis* might increase its members at the next elections. In 1965 the PAP had only three more members than a two-thirds majority (57 to the *Barisan's* 13). As it happened, with the *Barisan* boycott of parliament, the removal of this provision proved unnecessary. The government has changed the constitution numerous times since then (Pillai and Tan, 1989, pp. 660–3).

The existence of a constitution, even if it can be changed at will, appears to provide an ultimate guarantee for liberal democratic rights in Singapore. The PAP-state is deemed to operate within the procedural and substantive limitations of Singapore's written constitution. 'It is commonly assumed that in Singapore the Constitution is the supreme law and that Parliament... can only enact legislation which is consistent with the Constitution; legislation which is inconsistent with the Constitution is liable to be struck down by the Courts. This view is held, as far as I know, universally' (Harding, 1983, p. 351).

However, it has been argued by Harding that 'the accepted notion of constitutional supremacy as the guiding principle in Singapore's Constitution is an illusion which rests on a fundamental misunderstanding of Singapore's constitutional history' (Harding, 1983, p. 367). He holds that Singapore is an example of 'legislative supremacy' and has been so since 1965, from which date 'the Constitution could be amended simply by a law enacted by the legislature' (Harding, 1983, p. 354). Therefore, the PAP-state has not been at all confined by the entrenched provisions of the constitution because it could change the constitution at will. However, it continues to derive legitimacy from its appearance as a constitutional democracy.

In 1979 when the PAP was confident of its continuing legislative supremacy, the two-thirds provision was restored (Pillai and Tan, 1989, p. 661). Nevertheless, this did not mark a democratic advance, not only because of the PAP's overwhelming parliamentary majority but also because the PAP-state had other reasons to be confident of the safety of its executive decisions from judicial review.

While administrative actions in many states with a British common law tradition are becoming subject to judicial review, no such trend exists in Singapore. Its administrative law remains undeveloped in this respect in comparison with other Commonwealth states such as Zimbabwe, India, the United Kingdom and

Australia (Goldring, 1988, p. 489). This is partly because Singapore judges are kept directly accountable to the executive.

The Singapore judiciary has retained much of the pomp and ceremony of the British colonial courts. This gives the impression of a powerful, independent arm of the state, an impression very much at odds with reality. Whereas it may be claimed that the judiciaries in other jurisdictions administer the law in favour of a particular class owing to their unconscious class interest and the bias of the law itself, the PAP-state's insecurity within its own class has meant it could not rely on such subtlety.

> The Singapore judiciary's lack of independence begins with its structure.... By granting short-term appointments that may or may not be renewed at government discretion, Prime Minister Lee Kuan Yew has ensured that fully half of the twelve judges on Singapore's Supreme Court are kept on a short leash.
>
> Three of these have been named so-called 'judicial commissioners', a designation which amounts to a one- or two-year probationary term during which the government can review a new judge's rulings before entrusting him with full tenure.... The necessity [for this] seems to evaporate when loyalty is not at issue. In July, Yong Pung How, a long-time crony of Lee, gave up his highly successful business career to be appointed not a judicial commissioner but a fully tenured judge. The preferential treatment was not due to his legal prowess, since Yong has not practised law for eighteen years.
>
> The three other judges with limited tenure – including the chief justice – who has the all-important power to select which judges hear sensitive cases – have all passed the retirement age of 65. They continue to serve as judges, and to receive full judicial salaries rather than their smaller pensions, solely at the discretion of the government, which decides whether to renew these appointments every three years.
>
> Matters only get worse at the lower-court levels, where judges enjoy no tenure and are routinely shuttled back and forth between the judiciary and government service. (Sidney Jones, Asia Watch in *FEER*, 21 September 1989)

A year later Yong was appointed chief justice (*FEER*, 13 September 1990), becoming only the second to hold the post since independence.

The independence of the judiciary became a political issue in 1986 when it was raised in parliament by opposition member Jeyaretnam. The government tried to quash the debate by disciplining Jeyaretnam and by holding a commission of inquiry into his allegations. The sole commissioner was a Supreme Court judge, Mr Justice Sinnathuray. The propriety of a judge enquiring into his own independence could not be a matter of public comment as the alacrity with which the government serves defamation writs is well known. Sinnathuray was reputedly one of the most politically reliable on the bench. He had convicted student leaders of rioting on framed-up charges in 1974 (Tan Wah Piow, 1987b) and had since presided over internal security act procedural reviews of detainees' cases. He concluded that Jeyaretnam's allegations were 'wholly unfounded and scandalous' (International Mission of Jurists, 1987, p. 5). The parliamentary Privileges Committee then convicted and fined Jeyaretnam for breach of privilege. This had the effect of criminalising any discussion of the issue.

In short, judicial review of executive decisions is unlikely either to be initiated or to succeed if initiated. First, judges are directly controlled by the PAP-state. Secondly, in the rare event that they do allow appeals (probably in the knowledge of the executive's political strategy), the government can immediately change the constitution and the relevant law, retrospectively if necessary (for example, see Asia Watch, 1989, p. 27). Thirdly, recent legislation enacting administrative law aimed at political suppression has contained clauses which explicitly exclude judicial review (for example, the Maintenance of Religious Harmony Act 1990).

The PAP-state is too insecure to yield any ground in its discretionary powers by allowing a second opinion on its decisions. The ideological effect of the separation of the two arms of the PAP-state would also break down if political conflict was able to force the judiciary to encounter the executive directly on constitutional issues. The judiciary's lack of independence would become too obvious.

The creation of the Elected Presidency takes increased control by the executive a stage further. The president's executive actions are immune from judicial review (with minor exceptions) (Constitution of the Republic of Singapore (Amendment No. 3) Bill 1990, Clause 22J). His constitutional powers are entrenched. Therefore, the two-thirds majority provision for amending the constitution, originally intended to safeguard individual liberty and to restrain the executive, is now safeguarding the executive powers of the PAP against the rise of democratic opposition. The latter has to get not a simple majority but two-thirds of the seats in the House to rescind those powers.

Although the formal separation of state and judiciary continues to have an ideological effect in Singapore, in reality the PAP-state has few checks on its lawmaking and law-administering powers. In fact the situation amounts to thinly disguised rule by decree.

ADMINISTRATIVE LAW: THE CRIMINALISATION OF POLITICS

The criminalisation of politics through the administrative law is an attractive option for the PAP-state since executive discretion is the basis for all decisions and, as just noted, there is no effective legal redress for victims. Criminalisation through administrative law is primarily aimed at destroying political organisation through denying freedom of association. It takes place on two levels. The first level is that of sorting out legal from illegal politics and criminalising the latter. The second level is suppression of illegal politics by the imposition of state terror. The ideological effect of terror – fear – also permeates the first level as it is intended to do.

Legal and Illegal Politics

Liberal democracy usually functions in a political environment where there are many sectoral organisations and pressure groups attempting to influence public opinion. A citizen therefore has many ways to participate politically. The administration of political discipline in Singapore suppresses this political pluralism by declaring what is legal and illegal politics. It prevents the growth of any autonomous political association in the community. It defines all non-PAP political action outside of political parties as illegal and subversive. It steers all political activity into parliamentary politics, preferably the PAP, or proscribes it. One of the legal mechanisms for doing this sorting between legal and illegal politics is the Societies Act.

Any group or association of ten or more persons must be registered under the Societies Act if it is not registered under another law such as the Companies Act. In applying for registration, information must be supplied concerning the aims, the constitution and rules of the society and the names and background of office holders. The Registrar of Societies will often request more information or require that aspects of the proposed constitution be amended to suit government criteria.

A society will be refused registration if the Registrar is satisfied that 'the rules of the society are insufficient for its proper management and control' or 'it would be contrary to the national interest for the society to be registered'. Registration may be refused if 'a dispute exists among members of the society as to the persons who are to be officers' or 'it appears to him [the Registrar] that the name of the society to be registered is likely to mislead members of the public as to the true character or purpose... or is in [his] opinion... undesirable' (Section 4, Societies Act). The Registrar is not required to give reasons when he rejects an application. The UK-based development organisation, Oxfam, had an application for the registration of a local section rejected without explanation after a two-year wait (Asia Watch, 1989, p. 39).

If an organisation succeeds in becoming registered, it also requires the Registrar's permission to establish branches, change its name or place of business, amend any rules or use a flag, symbol, emblem or badge or other insignia (Sections 9, 11 and 13, Societies Act). By this means the PAP-state controls the organisational strength and the ideological impact of the organisation.

The Minister of Home Affairs may deregister and dissolve any registered society if he is satisfied that it is being used for unlawful purposes or purposes incompatible with its objects and rules or it is a political organisation with 'such an affiliation or connection with any organisation outside Singapore as is considered by the Registrar to be contrary to the national interest'. Without written permission from the Minister, officers of a dissolved society may not hold office in any other society for 3 years after its dissolution (Section 24, Societies Act). The Registrar also has the power to require any society to give him any information he requests, such as documents, accounts or books. The Minister of Home Affairs may declare someone unfit to serve as an officer of a society because of a criminal conviction. The Act provides for summoning individuals to give information about societies and for entering and searching premises. Penalties for contravention of the Act include large fines and imprisonment (Sections 10, 12 and 26–29, Societies Act).

In 1988, 176 societies were registered, four applications for registration were rejected, 45 societies were voluntarily dissolved and five societies were declared to have ceased to exist. There were 3873 societies on the register as at December, 31 1988. (GOS, 1989a, p. 185).

The above figures do not give an accurate picture of the deterrent effect of the Societies Act as they show that the vast majority of applications succeed. The inclusion of 'Registration of Societies' in the Information Ministry's 1989 yearbook under the heading 'Internal Security' points to the Act's real function. The investigation of applicants by the Internal Security Department is widely known (Asia Watch, 1989, p. 38). The successful applicants are therefore recreational, charitable or professional societies, not public interest groups.

One conclusion which might be drawn from the government's registration figures is that citizens rarely attempt to establish organisations which in liberal democracies would be regarded as public interest groups or pressure groups on particular issues. The legislation forces any such group to register as a political association or to be classified as subversive and illegal. Those that do register as a political party then draw the full weight of the PAP-state's security surveillance system onto themselves. In addition, the Societies Act legally enables the PAP to monitor the internal affairs of any rival party.

The Societies Act criminalises all political organisation which is not subject to direct government control or which is not criminalised by other legislation. Inherited from the British colonial administration, it was most used to sort out and criminalise existing political organisations during the 1960s and early 1970s when the PAP was securing its political hegemony and launching the EOI strategy. However, it continues in force as a preventive measure even though the sea of political pluralism was drained during that period.

Criminalising New Forms of Opposition
In the 1980s at the height of resistance to the policies of the Second Industrial Revolution and when Jeyaretnam was becoming a nationally popular figure in parliament, political dissent surfaced through organisations which the government had previously seen no need to criminalise: the Law Society and the Catholic Church. As institutions already controlled by the English-educated upper class and with a traditional role in the ruling structure, neither of these bodies was susceptible to proscription under the Societies Act. Therefore, specific legislative measures were taken to suppress the organisation of political challenges from within these institutions without proscribing the institutions themselves. The PAP-

state imposed its own definitions of the legitimate and illegitimate actions and concerns of these bodies. It then used legislation to impose these definitions. By this means the boundary line between parliamentary politics and pluralistic community politics was drawn across the organisational life of these bodies. Certain actions and concerns could thereby be separated out as subversive, as the pursuit of parliamentary political objectives by clandestine means.

> what the Government will not tolerate is sympathizers and political activists working their way into professional organizations and other bona fide organizations, establishing themselves in positions of influence, concealing their sympathies and activism from others, and using the umbrella of the organization for political purposes. (Home Affairs Minister Jayakumar, Parliament of Singapore, 1986, B105)

In 1986 the Law Society, the body established in law for the self-regulation of the legal profession, dared to offer a dissenting opinion on a government legislative proposal – the Newspaper and Printing Presses (Amendment) Act – to restrict the circulation of foreign publications carrying critical analysis of Singapore politics. The government retaliated by introducing the Legal Profession (Amendment) Bill to force a change in the leadership and in the disciplinary procedures of the Law Society. This bill also restricted the Law Society to commenting on legislation only when requested by the government. A line was drawn between legitimate professional concerns and 'politics' in order to prevent this upper-class organisation becoming a vehicle for public criticism of government policy.

In October 1986 the government subpoenaed the entire Law Society Council to appear before the parliamentary select committee considering the bill. They were interrogated by ministers, especially the Prime Minister, as if personally on trial.

> If I come to the conclusion that... some activists, through the indifference of the majority of members, have misled the Society to wilful ways unconnected with the profession, then I will find an answer to it. Because it is my job as Prime Minister in charge of the Government to put a stop to politicking in professional bodies. If you want to politick, come out.... You want to politick, you form your own party or join Mr Jeyaretnam. But if you stay in the Law Society Council and politick, and at the same time you consciously or sub-consciously ally these activities to those of the Workers' Party, then inevitably damage must be done.... Because I am not taking flak from the lawyers without giving them as good a response as they would expect from me if I were a counter party in an action. Whether you are communist, Workers' Party or whatever, if you want a scrap with the Government, sure you will get one.... You think you can be smarter than the Government and outsmart it, well, if you win, you form the

Government. If I win, we have got a new Law Society. It is as simple as that. (Lee Kuan Yew, Parliament of Singapore, 1986, B114–15)

Within 2 years of the hearing the government established the Academy of Law headed by the Chief Justice to which all members of the judiciary, the law faculty of the university and members of the legal profession must belong (*STW*, 13 August 1988, p. 4). It is poised to take over the regulatory functions of the Law Society. Having removed the Law Society's leadership the PAP-state established a parallel government-controlled organisation to replace it. By this use of administrative law, the government imposed political discipline on the legal profession. Uninvited professional comment was criminalised because an active, independent bar would soon expose the lack of judicial independence in Singapore and would provide a platform for the emergence of an alternative class leadership.

Criminalising Religion
The emergence of dissent within the Catholic Church was also a threat because it provided organisational links between upper class organisation and working-class grievances. It further provided both a religious ideological rationale for political action and an organised group of adherents who were not interested in the middle-class struggle to make more money and become members of the capitalist class.

In 1987 the government confronted the Catholic Church and forced it, by threats and intimidation, to close down its Justice and Peace Commission and its welfare centre for foreign workers, alleging they were bases for a 'Marxist conspiracy' (International Mission of Jurists, 1987, p. 13). Organisations within the church do not need to be registered under the Societies Act and the PAP-state threatened to change this policy if the archbishop 'could not put his own house in order' (Lee Kuan Yew in *FEER*, 17 December 1987).

The PAP-state confronted the problem that the demarcation between legal and illegal kinds of politics was insufficient to prevent religious organisations from being politically active within the community. The church could claim its activities to be religious rather than political. The government therefore redefined legal religious activity as the direct institutional concerns of religious bodies in their own organisational affairs. Religious activities concerned with changing Singapore society according to religious understandings of the nature and destiny of human beings were categorised as political and proscribed. On 6 October 1989 Home Affairs Minister Jayakumar announced that legislation would be introduced in the next sitting of parliament 'to ensure that religion is kept out of the political arena' (*STW*, 7 October 1989, p. 10).

To blur the issue the PAP-state entitled its legislation the Maintenance of Religious Harmony Act to create the impression that it was responsibly moderating the relations between Singapore's religions. The provisions of the Act, however, focus on the relationship between religious bodies and the state and give the government the power to suppress by executive decision almost any activity of a religious group or leader.

The Minister of Home Affairs is given the power to issue a prohibition order against any religious office-bearer to prevent that person from 'addressing orally or in writing any congregation, parish or group of worshipers or members of any religious group', from 'printing, publishing, editing, distributing or contributing to any publication produced by that religious group' and from 'holding office in an editorial board or a committee of a publication of that religious group'. A prohibition order may be issued on the basis of such catch-all provisions as 'carrying out activities to promote a political cause', 'exciting disaffection against the President or the Government of Singapore' and 'carrying out subversive activities under the guise of propagating or practising any religious belief'. The maximum penalty for contravening a prohibition order is a fine of $10,000 and/or two years imprisonment. Second or subsequent offences incur a fine of up to $20,000 and/or three years in prison. The decisions of the minister are not subject to judicial review (*FEER*, 18 January 1990; GOS, *Maintenance of Religious Harmony Bill*, Bill No. 1/90 1990; *STW*, 24 February 1990). This legislation was enacted on 9 November 1990 (*STW*, 10 November 1990).

In the late 1980s the PAP-state therefore began using administrative law to discipline upper-class organisations which sought to exercise liberal democratic rights and which had the potential to provide leadership to the wave of dissatisfaction. Because it could not proscribe the organisation as a whole, the government criminalised certain activities. The suppression of these organisations, as with working-class organisations in the past, was also accomplished with the aid of state terror which is another level on which administrative law operates.

Executive Terror and Illegal Politics

Under certain laws the PAP-state may arrest and detain without trial anyone it chooses for as long as it chooses. This power has two main functions. First, it physically removes from society those citizens who have refused to conform to PAP-state social and political organisation and who have established or have the potential to establish, alternative forms of organisation. Secondly, it has a profound ideological effect on others who may have contemplated similar dissenting behaviour or have been actively associated with such actions. By arresting a few, fear can be struck into the hearts of many.

Detention without trial at the discretion of the executive is possible under several laws, most of which derive from the colonial administration's attempt to suppress nationalist struggle and some forms of autonomous social organisation among the lower classes.

Suppressing Working-Class Social Organisation

In its quest for survival, the working class organises in ways which are classified as either legal or illegal by the state. Some of these forms of organisation, such as secret societies, are rooted in pre-capitalist traditions. Their activities are often not socially benign but this issue must be distinguished from the fundamental reason for their criminalisation. For example, the line of legality between right and proper exploitation, which is what capitalists do and extortion, which is what gangsters do, is not adequately explained in terms of the social worth of each activity.

Section 30 of the Criminal Law (Temporary Provisions) Act provides that the relevant minister, if satisfied that some person is associated with activities of a criminal nature, may with the consent of the Public Prosecutor, detain the person for a maximum (but renewable) period of one year. Section 33 of the Misuse of Drugs Act empowers the Director of the Central Narcotics Board to detain a person where it appears to him necessary to do so for the purpose of treatment or rehabilitation. There are also executive detention provisions in Section 4(1) of the Emergency (Public Order and Prevention of Crime) Ordinance 1969 (Tan Yock Lin, 1987, pp. 237–8, 243).

This body of legislation is justified as necessary to suppress Chinese secret societies and drug trafficking as it is claimed there is often insufficient evidence for criminal convictions and prosecution witnesses sometimes refuse to testify because of intimidation. In other words the power of the state to control through the normal operation of the criminal law can be partially resisted by this level of social organisation. Secret societies are a form of autonomous social organisation which, like the state, enforce discipline through violence. Drug trafficking is one of their economic strategies to accumulate capital. These alternatives have to be eliminated if the PAP-state is to ensure the distribution of the surplus on a class basis and to direct social control to the needs of industrialisation, namely wage labour.

By raising capitalist class social norms to the level of universal norms through the law, an ideological consensus has been generated behind the summary suppression of such organisations. The PAP-state has successfully criminalised this form of working class social organisation.

> As at 15 August 1989, 1,228 persons were being detained in prisons without trial, of whom 740 were said to be drug traffickers and the rest said to be involved in secret society and criminal activities.... [These are] figures disclosed in parliament by the Minister for Home Affairs.   (Seow, 1990, p. 7)

Since only 73 persons were detained under this legislation in 1988 and 31 in 1987 (*STW*, 5 August 1989, p. 3), it must be assumed that most are kept for several years.

This category of prisoner was useful in the government's international public relations campaign after detaining 24 middle-class professionals under a different act (see next section) in 1987 and 1988. In order to legitimise the practice of arbitrary executive detention, Criminal Law detainees were purposely confused with those who had been detained for liberal democratic political activities. In a speech to the Asia Society in Washington on 17 May 1989, the Minister of Trade and Industry, Brigadier-General Lee Hsien Loong, attested to the beneficial effect of detention without trial:

> Lee said when Americans talked about so-called repressive measures in Singapore, they were referring to 'a couple of people' who had been arrested because of political problems.
>
> 'You may not be aware of it, but one reason why our streets are safe and joggers are not subject to mugging [a reference to a recent violent 'wilding' of a woman jogger in Central Park, NY] is because we have a substantial number of people who are detained under criminal law provisions without trial,' he said.
>
> He said those detained without trial included gangsters, drug traffickers, murderers and those who had committed heinous crimes 'against whom charges cannot stick in court'. (*ST*, 18 May 1989)

Arbitrary detention of people on the basis of suspicion under the Criminal Law (Temporary Provisions) Act can also be seen, in political terms, as a way of suppressing traditional Chinese social organisation in favour of the colonial institutions of capitalism inherited by the Chinese upper class.

Hostage-Taking

The Internal Security Act (ISA) is the administrative law targeted at political organisation which could directly undermine the PAP's political hegemony. The provisions of the ISA include the following.

Section 8.
(1) If the President is satisfied with respect to any person that, with a view to preventing that person from acting in any manner prejudicial to the security of Singapore or any part thereof or to the maintenance of public order or essential services therein, it is necessary to do so, the Minister shall make an order
    (a) directing that such person be detained for any period not exceeding two years; ...

Section 74:
(1) Any police officer may without warrant arrest and detain pending inquiries any person in respect of whom he has reason to believe

    (a) that there are grounds which would justify his detention under Section 8; and

    (b) that he has acted or is about to act or is likely to act in any way prejudicial to the security of Singapore or part thereof.

The definition of the security of Singapore is a matter of executive discretion. Once detained under these provisions, a person may be:

- held up to 30 days for interrogation by the Internal Security Department who have no obligations to inform family members of the detainee's whereabouts;
- issued with a detention order for up to two years which is renewable *ad infinitum*;
- issued with restriction orders so that even after release from detention, a detainee may be restricted to living in internal exile (an offshore island) or, even if permitted to reside at home, may have restrictions placed on their movements, employment, freedom of association and other civil liberties (Amnesty International, 1980; Asia Watch, 1989).

The terror lies in the constant threat of indefinite detention and the immediate threat of maltreatment, torture and public humiliation. The pattern of treatment of ISA detainees during the period immediately after their arrest has been systematically documented by international human rights organisations. It has usually involved:

- sudden arrest in the early hours of the morning;
- no access to legal counsel or family for several weeks;
- being held in solitary confinement underground;
- being interrogated in freezing underground rooms under jets of refrigerated air, lightly clothed in prison clothes or naked, cold water may be poured over them at frequent intervals and they may be forced to drink quantities before being beaten;
- being questioned by rotating teams of Internal Security Department (ISD) officers for 72 hour periods without breaks, given a 30 minute respite and then interrogated for a similar period;
- physical beating which may be alternated with contrived concern for their welfare;
- interrogators concentrating on psychological blackmail techniques to make detainees feel guilty for getting their friends into trouble, saying that their families will be harassed if they do not confess or inducing detainees to implicate their friends;
- the threat of indefinite detention being frequently raised as a possibility;

- the continuation of this routine for as many days as it takes for the detainee to confess to whatever the ISD wants (Amnesty International, 1980; International Mission of Jurists, 1987).

After several days of continuous physical and psychological abuse, many detainees have admitted to the web of lies and insinuations put before them for their signature. Others have held out through punitive living conditions and repeated torture for many years. Lee Kuan Yew has described the interrogation process in a way which shows the results required:

> All interrogations must wear down resistance of [detainees] by sustained psychological pressure, including physical fatigue, to get them to give leads to the next links in a well-established underground movement. (*FEER*, 24 February 1978)

> It is not a practice, nor will I allow subversives to get away, by insisting that I got to prove everything against them in a court of law, or [obtain] evidence that will stand up to the strict rules of evidence in a court of law. (*ST*, 3 June 1987)

When the ISD has assembled the confessions, the government may announce, as it did in 1987 and many times before, that a Marxist conspiracy has been uncovered which was threatening the stability of Singapore. The confessions have then been published in the media and the detainees have been forced to incriminate themselves and others on television. After this the ISD has usually permitted lawyers and families to have brief but regular access under surveillance. Ultimate release is predicated on the willingness of a detainee to confess and incriminate others, on the amount of revenge the PAP wants to exact on a particular individual and on its political timetable. Detainees are utterly at the mercy of the government, a fact they are continually reminded of by their jailers.

> We were threatened with more physical abuse during interrogation. We were threatened with the arrests, assault and battery of our spouses, loved ones and friends. We were threatened with INDEFINITE detention without trial. Chia Thye Poh, who is still in detention after twenty-two years, was cited as an example. We were told that no one could help us unless we 'co-operated' with the ISD. (From statement of 18 April 1988 made by ex-detainees of the 1987 Operation Spectrum upon their release. They were immediately rearrested and forced to recant the above.)

Former Solicitor-General Francis Seow recalled one of his interrogators saying:

> Look, cut out all your court English. This is not a court of law. The rules of evidence do not apply here. We make the rules here. This is a kangaroo court. No one can help you. All the human rights organisations can do is to make noise but how long can they do so? After a while, you will be forgotten. (Asia Watch, 1989, p. 64)

Attempts at judicial review of detentions have consistently been blocked. Defence lawyers who persisted have been imprisoned under the ISA themselves in order to intimidate the legal profession as a whole (Amnesty International, 1980, p. 43; Asia Watch, 1989, p. 51). An English barrister, Mr Anthony Lester QC, forced the government to amend the constitution in order to avoid judicial review and was subsequently barred from practising in Singapore (Asia Watch, 1989, p. 51). In 1976 one lawyer who sought judicial review of detainees held under the Criminal Law (Temporary Provisions) Act was also detained under that act himself. Detainees who have initiated legal action have been imprisoned for longer periods as retribution.

The ISA is essentially a terror tactic of taking hostages. It removes from their organisational base in society those individuals who are a political threat and incarcerates them as political hostages, held against continuing organised dissent.

Historical Pattern of ISA Repression
Derived from the British colonial government's Preservation of Public Security Ordinance (1955), the ISA and its use reflect the history of political conflict in Singapore. The British used executive detention against the anti-colonial movement. The PAP-state used it before the 1963 elections to eliminate the top leadership of the *Barisan Sosialis*. Since the arrest of 133 persons in that year, many others have been detained under the ISA. However, no accurate statistics are available since it is not known whether the PAP-state necessarily announces all detentions.

> The PAP government has rigorously harassed all dissent and any potential opposition grouping in Singapore.... From 1963 to the early 1970s the number of political prisoners in Singapore fluctuated between a maximum of 250 and a minimum of 70. In the years 1963–1965, arrests far exceeded releases, whereas in the late 1960s this pattern was reversed. New waves of arrests occurred in 1970 and in the period 1974–76. (Amnesty International, 1980, pp. 15–16)

This pattern of detentions accords with the PAP-state's consolidation of its political position as it launched the EOI strategy. A sweep of opposition MPs, journalists and trade unionists in 1966 cleared the path for the 1968 elections and the passage of anti-labour legislation. The last of those detained in 1966, Chia Thye Poh, a *Barisan* MP, was released into internal exile only in May 1989. He was kept as a constant reminder that the PAP-state could hold a person as long as it wished.

In 1970 more trade unionists were arrested as a final clean-up of independent union leaders. In 1971, in preparation for the 1972 general elections, the main editorial staff of the Chinese newspaper *Nanyang Siang Pau* were detained under the ISA and two other newspapers were closed down. This was to prevent media support for Chinese education (International Mission of Jurists, 1987, pp. 3–7).

A similar pattern occurred prior to the 1976, 1980 and 1988 general elections to eliminate pockets of resistance which had emerged since the last sweep. The significance of the 1987 ISA arrests has been mentioned in terms of suppressing activism by young English-educated professionals within the legal profession (notably Ms Teo Soh Lung) and the Catholic Church. This multi-functional security operation was directed not only at the institutions involved but also at new social sectors: professional, single or childless women and both professional men and women who had no desire to join the capitalist class. The government press statement noted as much.

> With major changes in our education system since the 1970s as a result of parents opting for English-stream schools for their children, recruits to communism are no longer mainly the Chinese-educated. The younger generation of Singaporean Chinese are bilingual and bi-cultural. This has enabled the disaffected, the disgruntled and the misled amongst them to draw concepts and methods from both the Chinese-based CPM and West European Marxist groups. (Ministry of Home Affairs Press Release, 26 May 1987, p. 9)

The charges against these detainees included references to forsaking 'well-paid careers to take up lowly-paid jobs of $300–$400 per month which would allow them to influence others' (MHA Press Release, 26 May 1987, p. 9). One of the main reasons they were detained was their focus on the relationship between the PAP-state and foreign capital.

> The Marxist conspirators also targeted their attacks against Singapore's economic system and industrial policies. In their articles, they adopted familiar communist arguments to denounce the existing capitalist system as 'unjust', 'exploitative' and 'repressive', distort the working and living conditions of workers, and exaggerate the disparities between upper- and lower-income groups. In the 15 Sep 85 issue of the 'Catholic News', Vincent Cheng [a detainee] alleged 'wrongful beating up of workers by the police' and went on to suggest that the 'poor are never born poor, they are made poor' by the existing system... . [Other] articles attacked the role of MNCs [multinational corporations] in our economic prosperity... . No mention was made of the MNCs providing employment and bringing new ideas and technology. Instead, the articles, adopting the communist line, denounced MNCs for allegedly exploiting the people and bringing misery to the country. With such distortions, it is only a matter of time before industrial strife will resurface. (MHA, Press Release, Addendum 4, 28 May 1987, pp. 2, 3)

Through this exercise of executive terror, institutions had their autonomy restricted, the political idealism of a new generation of young professionals was extinguished and public discussion of the social effects of the PAP-state's alliance with foreign capital was proscribed.

In the 1980s there was also an important shift in the strategy for stifling legal opposition within the boundaries of parliamentary politics. Political leaders from legally registered political parties were no longer detained under the ISA as they were in the 1960s. The government began to criminalise such people under the criminal law as professionally negligent or as thieves, perjurers and bankrupts. An analysis of Jeyaretnam's convoluted battle against a series of trumped-up criminal charges illustrates this change of strategy.

The Criminalisation of Joshua Benjamin Jeyaretnam: A Chronology

1972	Workers' Party (WP) sues PAP MP Tay for libel.
1974	WP loses case.
1975	WP loses appeal. Ordered to pay costs but requests for payment lapse owing to WP poor financial position.
1981	Jeyaretnam (JBJ) wins by-election in Anson constituency.
1982 (January)	Tay demands full payment of costs within a week. Tay applies to court to seize WP assets but only $18.47 in account.
1982 (June)	Consequent to Tay's application, receiver appointed for WP.
1982 (August)	JBJ and Wong (WP Chairman) signed that materials submitted to receiver were fair and accurate.
1982	JBJ found guilty of two breaches of parliamentary privilege but the government, recognising that its pursuit of JBJ was generating public sympathy for him, waived the penalties.
1983 (August)	JBJ and Wong charged with making false statement about WP accounts and fraudulently transferring WP funds to avoid creditors. Case involved three donations totalling $1600.
1984 (January)	Senior District Judge Khoo acquits both of false statement charge and two defrauding charges. Convicts them on one defrauding charge involving $400 and fines each $1000.
	Khoo transferred from Bench to Attorney-General's department seven months after acquittals.
1984 (May)	Chief Justice Wee heard state's appeal.

1984 (December)	JBJ re-elected in general elections.
1985 (April)	Wee's verdict reversed defrauding acquittals and imposed $1000 fines. Ordered retrial on false statement charge.
1985 (May)	Application to appeal verdict to Court of Criminal Appeal is rejected. (This would have opened the way for appeal to the Privy Council in London.)
1985 (July)	JBJ fails in application to get retrial in High Court rather than District Court. (There is no appeal to the Privy Council from the District Court.)
1985 (September)	At retrial Senior District Judge Foenander finds both guilty and gives each a three-month prison sentence. Appealed.
1986	During parliamentary debate on amendments affecting jurisdiction of subordinate courts (January) and on the budget, JBJ stated more measures were required to ensure judicial independence and suggested transfer of Judge Khoo might be seen as politically motivated.
1986 (April)	Presidential Commission of Inquiry appointed to investigate charges of executive interference in the judiciary. The commission consisted only of Justice Sinnathuray, a judge notorious for his pro-government political decisions on the bench. JBJ refused to appear before the Commission. Sinnathuray found there was no executive interference and that the 'wholly unfounded allegations of Jeyaretnam were scandalous statements that should never have been made' (*FEER*, 31 July 1986, pp. 13–14).
1986 (August)	Just before Privileges Committee sits to consider disciplinary action against JBJ for his purported allegations against the judiciary, amendments to the Parliament (Privileges, Immunities and Powers) Act are quickly passed greatly enhancing the powers of the Committee and the penalties it may impose.
1986 (September)	For 5 days Prime Minister Lee conducted the Privileges Committee hearing as a trial of JBJ and called his questions on the independence of the judiciary 'totally treasonable' (*Asia Yearbook*, 1987, p. 234). Proceedings were televised.
1986 (November)	Justice Lai upheld convictions on appeal but changed sentence to 1 month's imprisonment and $5000 fine each, thus

disqualifying JBJ from parliament. A fine of more than $2000 disqualifies an MP from parliament for five years.

JBJ serves prison sentence.

1986 (December) On 9 December the Speaker announced that JBJ ceased to be an MP on 10 November, the date of Lai's verdict.

1987 (January) Parliamentary Privileges Committee announces decision to fine JBJ $1000 for his purported allegations about the judiciary. JBJ refused permit for opening ceremony of new WP offices on morning of ceremony. Opening proceeds. JBJ receives summons and is eventually fined $3500 under Public Entertainments Act. Fine is sufficient to bar him from parliament for another five years.

Soon after this JBJ was also fined $5000 by parliament for each of five newsletters he issued criticising the parliamentary disciplinary proceedings. Then he was again fined $1000 on each of two counts for alleging in parliament in March 1986 that a person had been wrongfully arrested when they had not and for, in the same month, failing to declare his alleged pecuniary interest in a question he raised in parliament.

1987 (29 July) JBJ's application to appeal his case to the Privy Council is rejected by the court.

1987 (19 October) JBJ disbarred after a three judge court chaired by the Chief Justice declare him unfit.

1988 (26 October) Judicial Committee of Privy Council (UK) grants JBJ's appeal against disbarment. The opinion harshly criticised the conduct of the legal proceedings against JBJ and Wong, concluding:

> They have been fined, imprisoned and publicly disgraced for offences of which they were not guilty. The appellant, in addition, has been deprived of his seat in Parliament and disqualified for a year from practising his profession. Their Lordships' order restores him to the roll of advocates and solicitors of the Supreme Court of Singapore, but, because of the course taken by the criminal proceedings, their Lordships have no power to right the other wrongs which the appellant and Wong have suffered. Their only prospect of redress, their Lordships understand, will be by way of petition for pardon to the President of the Republic of

	Singapore'. (Privy Council Appeal No. 10 of 1988, p. 22)
	Privy Council thereby reinstates JBJ to the Singapore Bar.
1989	Parliament amends relevant law and the constitution to abolish appeals to the Privy Council for disciplinary matters and for matters under the Internal Security Act.
1989 (April)	JBJ petitioned President of Singapore for pardon.
1989 (May)	President declines pardon citing reason that JBJ had not 'expressed any sense of remorse, contrition or repentance in respect of the offences' and that, according to the Attorney-General, 'there has been no miscarriage of justice and no injustice has been done to the petitioner'.

Sources: *FEER* (1984–89), Asia Watch (1989), *Straits Times*.

This criminalisation is a process of declassing middle- and upper-class politicians to the working-class level of the 'common criminal'. It is a strategy which enables PAP leaders to claim that legal parliamentary opposition politics is not suppressed by obviously political laws such as the ISA (see Jayakumar, 5 July 1987, Ministry of Home Affairs Press Release). It also makes it harder for opposition politicians to claim martyrdom.

Exclusion from the Nation
Provisions for executive detention are also included in the Banishment Act which enables the PAP-state to revoke the citizenship of Singaporeans who are citizens by registration and naturalisation and to hold them 'until he can be placed on board ship or other means of transport' (Section 6/4, Banishment Act). Since a large proportion of Singaporeans were recent migrants from Malaysia, India or China, this legislation was used very regularly in the 1950s and 1960s to deport political activists. Banishment frequently rendered them stateless. Those who refused to be banished, languished in jail. In 1978 Amnesty International estimated at least five people remained in this category, while at least 30 had been deported since 1965. It was common for ISA detainees who were not citizens by birth to accept release on the condition of deportation. According to Singapore government statistics, 90 persons were 'released and proceeded to other countries' in the years 1960–76 (Amnesty International, 1980, p. 23).

In the early years of its administration it seems the PAP frequently resorted to this power physically to remove people from the nation in a more complete way than that achieved by the ISA. However, having sorted and graded the population by means of the education system and the immigration laws, the PAP-state has found less need for these banishment provisions. Instead it has required a means not to expel citizens from Singapore but to prevent political exiles from remaining politically active abroad because they have the possibility of coming back. Against international law, it has therefore legislated to exclude locally born Singaporeans from the nation. The Constitution of the Republic of Singapore (Amendment) Act 1985 empowers the government by executive order to deprive any Singaporean of their citizenship if they have stayed away from the country for more than ten years. Those who have escaped or are wanted under the ISA cannot contemplate participating in Singapore's political life ever again. Political exiles such as 1974 student leader Tan Wah Piow, a charismatic political organiser and orator, now a London lawyer, have been deprived of their citizenship and cannot ever return to participate in Singapore political life. This is a summary punishment which in a way combines the old penalties of transportation and excommunication. While not carrying the physical terror of ISA detention, the deprivation of citizenship forcibly takes away a citizen's home for ever.

In the above ways the PAP-state has used administrative law to restrict freedom of association and suppress political pluralism. The process was aptly described by Lee Kuan Yew in 1956 when speaking in the Legislative Assembly against the arbitrary executive powers of the colonial state:

> First...you attack only those whom your Special Branch can definitely say are communists. They have no proof except that X told Z who told Alpha who told Beta who told the Special Branch. Then you attack those whom your Special Branch say are actively sympathising with and helping the communists, although they are not communists themselves. Then you attack those whom your Special Branch say, although they are not communists or fellow travellers, yet, by their intransigent opposition to any collaboration with colonialism, they encourage the spirit of revolt and weaken constituted authority and thereby, according to the Special Branch, they are aiding the communists. Then finally, since you have gone that far, you attack all those who oppose you....
>
> All you have to do is to dissolve organisations and societies and banish or detain the key political workers in these societies. Then miraculously everything is tranquil and quiet on the surface. Then an intimidated press... and the government-controlled radio together can regularly sing your praises and slowly and steadily the people are made to forget the evil things that have already been done. Or if these things are referred to again, they are conveniently distorted, and distorted with impunity, because there will be no opposition to contradict. (George, 1984, p. 111)

Administrative law gives maximum discretion to the executive arm of government and is legitimated by the ideology of the defence of the nation. Offenders against the state are thereby placed ideologically outside the law and physically outside the society (in prison) or even the nation (in permanent exile). Released detainees have been disqualified from political participation through continuing restrictions on their civil rights because of the indelible taint of their 'disloyalty' to the nation.

In this way, a challenge to the PAP is transformed into a subversive act against the nation.

The suppression of class politics has been achieved by distinguishing between legal and illegal politics and by the selective terror of removing political organisers from society. This is the criminalisation of politics. But the disciplining of a whole class has required coercion and violence on a much larger scale. The government has made official torture part of the daily administration of the law. It has also increased its power to kill so that fear permeates all aspects of working-class life. This is the function of the criminal law and it is the politicisation of crime.

CRIMINAL LAW: THE POLITICISATION OF CRIME

The introduction to this chapter noted that the criminal law enables the state to criminalise a whole class by criminalising individuals. This may be seen as part of tutoring the labour force to observe 'the rules of morality, civic and professional conscience, which actually means rules of respect for the socio-technical division of labour and ultimately the rules of the order established by class domination' (Althusser, 1984, p. 6). The working class is induced to conform to a pattern of life which involves continuous wage labour.

The criminal law in Singapore controls the working class by imposing social discipline. The harshness of this imposition has been partly due to the rapidity of the social changes required by industrialisation policies. Tensions of class, racial and linguistic affiliation have had to be addressed quickly. The high levels of coercion and state violence have also been partly due to the fact that other sections of the capitalist class did not always have a substantial vested interest in PAP governance. Therefore, while other institutions of social control have achieved much in the period of restructuring, a violent final sanction has been needed to secure these changes, the sanction of judicial terror.

The PAP-state cannot be seen to torture and kill on a mass scale. But the judiciary can. Combined with the individualisation of the criminal law, the system of judicial administration has the ideological effect of ensuring that members of the working class blame themselves for the crimes they commit. This is not to suggest that they do not commit them or that their crimes are morally acceptable. Rather the point is that the system of conviction and punishment for individual offences legitimises, by covering it up, a system of social discipline which mainly operates in the interests on one class and against the interests of another.

Legal Protections Against State Power Removed

The EOI policy and then the Second Industrial Revolution involved a process of increasing exploitation of labour necessitating an increasingly tight regime of class discipline. The PAP-state has been able to exert more direct control over the outcome of criminal cases by the progressive removal of legal protections won by the British working-class over many decades. There are many examples of this process but there are some important landmarks.

Juries, Hearsay and Self-Incrimination
In 1960, a year after the PAP took power, jury trial was restricted to capital offences only. In 1959 during the parliamentary debate on the matter, Lee Kuan Yew criticised jury trials for the premium they placed on a lawyer's 'skill and agility'. He held that 'Judges could make up their minds on facts as well as jurymen could, and the amendment would bring our system into line with Malaya's' (Phang, 1983, p. 53).

In 1969, arguing against the jury system even for capital offences, Lee used the partial removal of an obstacle to state control as the rationale for its complete removal:

> He was of the view that if judges could not decide questions of fact better than jurymen, then 'grievous harm' was being done every day when single judges and magistrates were sitting alone deciding questions of fact in civil and criminal cases. Further, the jury seemed 'overwhelmed with the responsibility of having to find a man guilty' when they knew that the death sentence was to follow. (Phang, 1983, p. 58)

The Minister of Law, Mr E.W.Barker (who retired from this position only in 1988), spoke of 'the *unreliability* of the system of trial by jury' (my emphasis). He said the chief justice and other judges supported the abolition and he stressed that it was inconceivable for the government to 'stoop so low' as to influence the judges in the absence of a jury system. Ten years earlier Mr Barker had assured parliament during consideration of the restriction of the jury system that it was not the government's intention that the jury system be abolished (Phang, 1983, pp. 57–8). In 1970 the jury system was completely abolished.

By 1983 a legal academic from the National University of Singapore was able to state that 'the criminal process, slightly over a decade after the abolition of the jury system, appears to be functioning extremely smoothly' (Phang, 1983, p. 86). This assessment reflects the fact that the removal of the 'unreliable' public from the judicial process, except as victims, increased the power of the government to secure convictions in criminal cases. More members of the working class could be criminalised and punished as examples to their class.

> Singapore's non-jury juridical system also may work against the poor. Low-income groups typically come before the court more frequently than do high-income groups, while judges themselves are governmentally appointed from the population's elite. Juries, which might include members of the lower class, have been discontinued. (Austin, 1989, p. 924)

In 1977 further protections were removed:

> The traditional caution given to a person charged with an offence was abolished. The courts were enabled, with certain exceptions, to accept hearsay evidence. Silence on the part of the accused, either when charged or in court, can give rise to adverse inferences. (Josey, 1980, p. 57)

In a study of lower court criminal cases in 1979 and 1980 it was found that defendants with legal representation who pleaded not guilty were acquitted in approximately 50 per cent of cases. Of those unrepresented, only 20 per cent were acquitted. Most of those who pleaded guilty to start with were unrepresented and received, on average, more severe sentences than those who were represented (Yeo, 1981, pp. 41, 43, 48). Since class generally determines the ability to pay for legal representation, it is likely that a higher proportion of working-class people are not only arrested for criminal offences but also plead guilty and, thus, are punished most severely.

However, the removal of many legal protections renders representation a far less potent factor than otherwise might be the case. One example is the removal of judicial discretion in sentencing, a step which cleared the way for the government to inflict a higher level of punishment on the working class.

Removal of Judicial Discretion

From 1973 the government began to restrict the discretionary powers of judges by legislating for mandatory, minimum sentences. The first major legislation was the Misuse of Drugs Act which provided minimum sentences for drug trafficking and possession. The nature of the offence meant that the legislation was not controversial. However mandatory, minimum sentences have since been extended to a great number of offences from car theft and letting off fireworks to rape, armed robbery and murder. The mandatory penalties involved in the sentences are mainly fines, imprisonment, corporal and capital punishment, with increasing emphasis on the latter two.

By removing judicial discretion in sentencing, individual circumstances cannot be taken into account. Individual cases cannot be treated individually: differences of background, personality, intention, intellect and other circumstances are irrelevant.

> A young adult who, on request, passes a 'joint' of cannabis to his host at a dinner party will receive the same minimum sentence of three years' imprisonment and caning as one who peddles small amounts of the drug to school children. A youth who steals a car hub-cap out of mischief will face the same minimum sentence of one year's imprisonment as a member of an organised syndicate of car thieves. A rejected lover who steals an involuntary kiss from his former girlfriend in a lift will be punished in the same way as a stranger performing the same act. (Yeo, 1985, pp. clxxxix–cxc).

In arguing for mandatory minimum sentences, the Home Affairs Minister Jayakumar, a professor of law, stated that 'the sentences meted out by our courts today appear neither to hurt the criminal nor are proportionate to the gravity of the offence' (*Parliamentary Debates*, 43/1984, 1864–5). The justifications of deterrence and community protection have been advanced by government spokespeople for this kind of legislation. Undoubtedly the effect of mandatory minimum sentences is to insert the power to punish more deeply into society. But it is increased power primarily to criminalise and punish the working class because, while individual circumstances related to the offence are not taken into account, class circumstances are. The offences to which mandatory minimum sentences are applied are overwhelmingly crimes committed by the working class or, because of policing policy, more likely to be detected if committed by a working-class person.

Examples of offences punishable by minimum terms of imprisonment and lashes of the cane are as follows.

Penal Code (with effect from 31 October 1984)

Robbery	Minimum 2 years, maximum 10 years; *and* minimum 6 strokes.
– if committed between 7 pm and 7 am	Minimum 3 years, maximum 14 years; *and* minimum 12 strokes.
– attempted	Minimum 2 years, maximum 7 years; *and* minimum 6 strokes.
Assault or using criminal force during snatch theft	Minimum 1 year, maximum 7 years; *and* caning
Theft of motor car or any part (including tyre, accessory or equipment)	Minimum 1 year, maximum 7 years; *and* fine *and* disqualified from driving for minimum 3 years after release.
Assisting in concealing or receiving stolen car (or component)	Minimum 6 months, maximum 5 years *and* fine.
Extortion	Minimum 2 years, maximum 7 years *and* caning.
Outraging modesty, voluntarily causing or attempting to cause death, hurt, wrongful restraint	Minimum 2 years, maximum 10 years *and* caning.

– in a lift or against any person under 14 years	Minimum 3 years, maximum 10 years *and* caning
Voluntarily causing hurt or putting fear of death or hurt in order to commit rape with a woman under 14 years	Minimum 8 years, maximum 20 years; minimum 12 strokes.

Dangerous Fireworks Act (with effect from 1 May 1988)

Letting off dangerous fireworks	Minimum $2000, maximum $10,000 or maximum 2 years or both.
– subsequent offence	Maximum 2 years (no fine) *and* maximum 6 strokes.

Vandalism Act

Act (or attempt) of vandalism	Maximum $2000 or maximum 3 years *and* minimum 3 strokes, maximum 8 strokes.

Immigration Act (with effect from 31 May 1989)

No valid entry/re-entry permit	Minimum 3 months, maximum 2 years *and* minimum 3 strokes.
Over-staying more than 90 days	As above.

Minor Offences Act (with effect from 9 June 1989)

Touting for business in public place	Minimum $1000, maximum $5000 or maximum 6 months or both.
– subsequent offence	Minimum $2000, maximum $10,000 or maximum 1 year or both.

For drug trafficking and possession (for example possession of over 15 grams of heroin regardless of circumstances), murder (regardless of circumstances) and some firearms offences, the mandatory minimum sentence is death by hanging.

Mandatory sentences give far greater power to the prosecution and the police to extract pleas of guilty and confessions or to induce defendants to implicate others. They 'provide prosecutors with too much bargaining power with which to influence or even coerce defendants into pleading guilty to other [lesser] offences', even if there is a good chance of acquittal on the original charge (Yeo, 1985, p. cxc). In this way mandatory sentences increase state control through the criminal law.

Some legal specialists recognise that 'mandatory minima are regressive, replacing emphasis on individualisation and rehabilitation with punitiveness, incapacitation and deterrence – sentencing objectives that were common in the late 19th century but have proved to be ephemeral' (Yeo, 1985, p. cxci). Perhaps what is not so widely recognised is that the political effect (in the short term at least) of such legislation is entirely desirable from the point of view of the PAP-state.

By the simple mechanism of passing laws setting mandatory minimum sentences for any offence, the PAP-state can now be confident that the level of legal repression of the working class will be instantaneously increased. Furthermore, the inability of judges to take individual circumstances into account increases the level of fear because of the arbitrary nature of punishment.

Crime as Politics

Previous chapters have shown that non-cooperation with government policy took many forms. Crime can also be seen as a form of non-cooperation and, in this sense, a political response. The need for the added repressive capacity of the PAP-state to discipline workers during the Second Industrial Revolution is indicated by the higher incidence of this kind of non-cooperation: an increased crime rate from the mid-1970s until 1980 (Austin, 1989, p. 919). The limiting of this tendency can be attributed, not to better community cohesion, but to increased control (Austin, 1989, p. 923). By 1988 Singapore had achieved a comparatively low crime rate (see Table 7.1).

Table 7.1   Comparative Crime Rate, 1987–88

	Serious Crimes per 100,000 People
Japan	2.70
South Korea	9.10
Thailand	18.88
Malaysia	45.26
Australia	57.88
Singapore	65.72
Hongkong	139.20
USA	225.15

Source: Interpol figures, *Asiaweek* (10 August 1990) p. 11.

The removal of legal protections for defendants in criminal cases accompanied the process of regulating more of the activities of daily life in order to discipline the labour force. With fewer defences against conviction, it was more open to control.

> the assumption that a government's use of law and control may benefit the middle classes and elite and yet be a detriment or misfortune to the lower classes, suggests that a conflict-theory approach may yield some worthwhile insights.... Our findings reveal several features of formal justice which hint that Singapore's law and control may be understood from such a perspective. For example, a number of the minor laws may tend to discriminate against the lower classes. It is true that laws against littering may benefit society, but the street worker, for instance, labouring under the equatorial sun may find it more difficult to avoid tossing a cigarette or spitting than would the white-collar worker in an air-conditioned office. The laws against picking fruit from trees in public parks may work against those lower-income street people who frequent parks and who may also suffer more from hunger than do higher-income groups.   (Austin, 1989, p. 924)

These minor laws were multiplied in the 1980s in order to discipline the working class to 'a regime of steady, regular, regulated, unbroken wage labour' (Hall *et al.*, 1978, p. 210) and the social behaviour conducive thereto.

The petty laws and regulations carrying heavy fines or other penalties to enforce the officially approved life-style eventually encompassed such matters as littering, smoking, spitting, hair-length, jay-walking, colour of front door, keeping of pets and type of TV aerial. The maximum fine for urinating in a lift was made $1000. On 23 June 1988 the *Straits Times* reported that a man appeared in court for this offence. A 'urine sensor' activated a jamming mechanism which sealed the man in the lift until the police arrived. A video camera in the lift 'automatically captured the activity inside... . The videotape recording of the camera confirmed that [the accused] was the culprit.'

The same day the newspaper announced: 'Failure to flush the water-closet and urinal after use is considered a public nuisance under the Penal Code, Chapter 224. The penalty for committing a public nuisance is a fine of up to $200.' The photographs of six men who had been booked by undercover environmental health officials for failing to flush a public toilet, appeared along with a story on their detection. (From 1 July 1989 the maximum fine for repeated offending became $1000.)

The publication of photographs in the *Straits Times* of people convicted on minor morals charges became a feature of daily life. In June 1991 the newspaper carried the picture of a man who was convicted for masturbating in a public swimming-pool (*STW*, 15 June 1991) and of another who stole women's underwear from a clothes-line (*STW*, 22 June 1991). Exemplary justice was extended to cover the most personal details of life, criminalising even those with psychological disabilities.

In 1986 legislative changes gave the HDB the right to acquire compulsorily an apartment if any authorised occupant was convicted of throwing heavy objects out of high-rise blocks or of harbouring illegal immigrants (*FEER* 14 August 1986, p. 18). This gave the government the power to punish twice: a criminal penalty in the courts and a penalty by executive order.

On 21 June 1989 a 32 year-old woman who threw three flower pots over the balcony of her flat when having a fight with her husband, was jailed for 3 weeks. The same day a 24-year-old man was fined $14,400 for selling fruit without a licence on 111 occasions in 1987 and failing to turn up in court on 33 occasions. If he could not pay, he would serve 8 months in jail. Between January and 21 May 1989, 243 persons were arrested for touting their wares on the street (*STW*, 24 June 1989, p. 5).

> [The government] is bringing in a law under which any person who's caught begging twice will be produced before the courts, and if he's found guilty – and of course what defence can he have, he was begging – he'll be fined $3000 and, if he can't pay that fine, and how do you expect a beggar who's begging on the road to pay a fine of $3000, he can go to prison for 6 months. (Opposition leader and lawyer J. B. Jeyaretnam speaking on 'The Law Report', no. 7, *Radio Australia*, 21 February 1989)

Control of all aspects of daily life was thereby extended and criminalisation made more likely by the parallel removal of defendants' protections in legal procedure.

Simultaneously the PAP-state moved to ensure that disobedience of administrative regulations restricting freedom of association could be dealt with as criminal offences along with burglary and soliciting. For example, 1989 amendments to the Miscellaneous Offences (Public Order and Nuisance) Act, previously the Minor Offences Act, set out substantial penalties for anyone who organises or assists in organising any assembly or procession which proceeds without a police permit or any person who participates in the same. The rules of the Act apply to any assembly or procession of more than five people in a public place intended:

(1) to demonstrate support for or opposition to the views of any person;

(2) to publicise a cause or campaign; or

(3) to mark or commemorate any event (Ministry of Home Affairs, S250/89, p. 887).

If a permit for such an assembly is not obtained from the police, then guilt is assumed and a fine of up to $5000 or imprisonment of up to 3 months or both is imposed.

This legislation covers such other 'public order and nuisance' matters as parliamentary election meetings (similar rules apply), being on private premises without lawful excuse, touting and prostitution. Increased control of daily life was clearly related to the suppression of organised political resistance during the 1980s as well as to unorganised non-cooperation arising from social alienation and dislocation.

Judicial Terror

The above laws regulating daily social behaviour have been additionally secured by the judicial terror of lashes with a cane and hanging. The fear of these penalties (and of executive detention) permeates the whole of society, strongly reinforcing political obedience and social conformity.

Official Torture

The Singapore Government is not reticent about the details of 'caning', a term which connotes schoolboy woes but is, in reality, a severe form of torture. In 1974 the Director of Prisons was interviewed in the local press.

> [He] gave a blow-by-blow account of how criminals are caned so that they will walk with scarred bottoms for the rest of their lives... . 'As executors of this punishment, we would be failing in our duty if we did not administer it in the spirit in which it was designed,' he told a press conference.   (*ST*, 13 September 1974)

He recounted how warders skilled in martial arts are trained for the task, how the cane is prepared and wielded, how each stroke splits the buttocks open and they become covered in blood and how the trussed, naked prisoners struggle in agony.

> Most of the prisoners put up a violent struggle after each of the first three strokes. Mr Quek said: 'After that, their struggles lessen as they become weaker. At the end of the caning, those who receive more than three strokes will be in a state of shock. Many will collapse... . Many will pretend to faint [in order to get a temporary respite from the half-minute interval strokes] but they cannot fool the prison medical officer'.   (*ST*, 13 September 1974)

This punishment has been frequently described as an exemplary and appropriate treatment by a no-nonsense government:

> Flogging is mandatory for nearly thirty crimes. According to the police, caning helps to restrain the vicious thug from committing physical violence and imposes a stigma on those who have been caned. The law exempts women, and men over fifty. Children taking part in armed robbery can also be caned, up to ten strokes with a light *rotan*. For adults, the limit is twenty-four strokes with a *rotan* no more than half an inch thick.   (Josey, 1980, p. 56)

When legislation was passed imposing caning on foreign overstayers, Thai officials, concerned about Thai migrant workers in Singapore, said such a practice was 'barbaric' and unacceptable in civilised countries (*FEER*, 6 July 1989, p. 14).

A PAP backbencher, Heng Chiang Meng, showing unusual fortitude for any PAP member, also called caning a 'barbaric act'. But Trade and Industry Minister, Brigadier-General Lee Hsien Loong, denounced this sentiment as 'mush' (*Time*, 13 March 1989).

In 1989 an amendment was passed to the Misuse of Drugs Act which permitted caning as a disciplinary measure within drug rehabilitation centres subject to the discretion of the superintendent. In 1991 a man convicted of armed robbery stated that he had received 48 strokes of the cane in one session on 8 April 1988, double the legal maximum (*STW*, 8 June 1991). Also in 1991 a young, working-class man (Chinese-speaking only), who pleaded guilty to 20 charges relating to two cases of robbery and rape, requested that his sentence of 20 years jail and 24 strokes be reduced in return for voluntary castration (*STW*, 13 July 1991). His request was refused. Such constant publicity in the media about this form of torture maintains the level of fear among the population, as does the extension of the penalty to more and more offences.

A common justification for caning was to give criminals 'a taste of the violence they have inflicted on their victims' (*ST*, 13 September 1974). But since the penalty has been extended to letting off fireworks, vandalism, immigration offences and drug rehabilitation, this rationale fails. Rather caning has been and is a form of mass torture to secure social discipline.

Death

Death is not the *maximum* but the *mandatory* penalty for murder (Section 302, Penal Code), trafficking in certain types and quantities of drugs (Misuse of Drugs Act) or using firearms in the commission of an offence (Section 4, Arms Offences Act). If a person is convicted of one of these offences, regardless of the circumstances, the judge must impose the death penalty.

Death sentences may be imposed under other provisions of the above acts as well as under the Internal Security Act, for treason, for hurting or imprisoning the President and for perjury which results in the execution of another person.

As with caning, the number of capital offences is constantly on the increase. On 27 March 1989 Home Affairs Minister Jayakumar stated in parliament that the government was considering making cannabis trafficking a hanging offence. Trafficking includes 'to give without any connotation of monetary benefit' under the Misuse of Drugs Act. In December that year, death was made the mandatory penalty for possession of more than 30 grams of cocaine, 200 grams of hashish, 500 grams of cannabis and 1.2 kilograms of opium. The capital sentence previously applied only to 15 grams of heroin and 30 grams of morphine (*STW*, 2 December 1989).

Executions by hanging are carried out at the Changi Prison across the runway from Singapore International Airport.

Hangings are often announced in the newspapers. Accurate statistics on executions are hard to obtain as those provided by the government may be incomplete. However, according to the PAP-state, 45 people have been convicted of capital drugs charges since 1975, of whom 28 have already been hanged (*STW* 19 May 1990). There must be considerably more awaiting trial or under appeal, judging from the regular arrests for trafficking announced in the media. Total figures for executions on other capital charges, such as murder, have not been obtainable.

Politics is Crime, Crime is Politics

The pattern of the law's development in Singapore is closely related to the PAP-state's phases of industrialisation. The social alienation and political dissent arising from increasing exploitation of workers have required intensified social control. The government's response has been to create a climate of escalating coercion and fear by constantly increasing its powers to punish through both administrative and criminal law. The administrative law has given the government discretionary power to act according to its own timing and political strategy in destroying political organisation. It has sheltered under the ideological pretext of the national interest.

The removal of judicial discretion and of defendants' legal protections has enabled the government to increase the severity of punishments and to assert discipline more directly. The ideological effect of the independence of the judiciary has preserved the legitimacy of the civil law for foreign investors and of the state for the working class. Permeating the whole system of administration of the law is the terror of indefinite detention without trial, state torture and state killing.

The result of this process is that crime and politics are now almost indistinguishable. Both have become offences against the government. Crime is not an offence against society but against the state. Politics is feared like a crime because it also attracts the penalty of state terror.

MILITARY FORCE: THE ULTIMATE COERCIVE GUARANTEE

The military can also legally kill in the name of the state. Military violence is the ultimate guarantee of the PAP-state's accumulation strategy and the final sanction of its system of social control. The maintenance of a standing military force is justified as protecting the state from external attack and internal subversion.

Internally, the constant threat of overwhelming state violence reinforces less coercive mechanisms of social control such as public housing, education and parliamentarism. Furthermore, in preparing for the use of military force externally, civilian life in Singapore can be militarised and workers placed under permanent military-type discipline.

Secondly, strong armed forces linked to the military power of foreign capital provide a guarantee regionally for their joint accumulation strategy. The military form of the alliance reflects its economic form.

Militarisation of Singapore Society

The working class assists in enforcing its own submission through its conscription into the military. As indicated already, all males must enter National Service on reaching the age of 18 years for a period of two to two and a half years. Most are conscripted into the armed forces and the rest into the police, fire brigade and construction brigade (GOS, 1989a, p. 172). After completion of training, they remain in the reserves until the age of 40 years (or 50 years for officers) and serve in the military (or the police) for up to 40 days per year.

Approximately 80 per cent of the Singapore Armed Forces are reservists. They are liable for call-up at any time and have to keep the Ministry of Defence informed of their whereabouts should they go overseas. Reservists can obtain passports with a maximum validity of two years compared to the normal ten year validity and exit permits have to be obtained from the Ministry if reservists intend leaving for longer than six months. A closer watch has been kept on the movements of reservists since the computerisation of immigration records (*STW*, 17 March 1990).

The active armed forces now number approximately 55,000 plus reserves of 200,000 and a People's Defence Force of 30,000. The Civil Defence Force of 100,000 includes regulars, conscripts, volunteers and 34,000 former army reservists (*Asia Yearbook*, 1989, p. 214; GOS, 1989a, pp. 171–6, 179, 228–9). Between 1967 and 1985 more than a quarter of a million males received intensive military training (Seah, 1989, p. 954). Most of the male population between 18 years and 40 years is therefore under military discipline and most of the remainder is under paramilitary discipline.

National Service is primarily a method of domestic regulation. The external defence capabilities of the Singapore Armed Forces depend more on technical ability than on size and on its willingness to collaborate with the forces of the major powers. A state of overt military preparedness gives greater confidence to foreign investors that the PAP-state is ready to meet both internal and external threats while generating a crisis atmosphere which legitimises the mass training of Singapore workers for factory discipline. The government's opposition to shortening the training period for National Service has emphasised these factors.

A shorter period of NS may erode confidence in Singapore and affect economic growth, Brig Gen (Reservist) Lee Hsien Loong has said. This is because the reduced security resulting from this could cause the manufacturing and financial sectors to shrink as investors turn elsewhere. (*STW*, 17 March 1990).

The Working-class Barracks
The militarisation of the public housing estates, from their architecture and physical position to community organisation and methods of surveillance within them were highlighted in Chapter 3. It was observed that housing estates are the barracks of worker–soldiers who live under military discipline, making Singapore into both a vast military base and a labour camp.

There are also military or paramilitary activities within the estates which residents have to participate in. For example, community exercises are held regularly to prepare for emergencies, from street demonstrations to the outbreak of war. In 1989 a civil defence exercise was held involving 236,000 households in water cuts and food rationing (*STW*, 13 May 1989). Military exercises intruding on civilian life are regularly held for such purposes as the requisitioning of civilian vehicles, the immediate mobilisation of reservists or the use of public expressways for landing jet-fighters (Seah, 1989, p. 957). To maintain the atmosphere of crisis which justifies such a scale of military activity, large underground bomb shelters are constructed under housing blocks (*STW*, 7 July 1990) and air raid sirens are to be installed in all areas by 1992 (*STW*, 21 January 1989).

The Militarisation of Education and Ideology
Secondary schools students receive military or paramilitary training through the National Cadet Corps or other uniformed services between the ages of 13 and 16 years. Such training may be chosen as one of three extra-curricular options, the others being sport and cultural activities (GOS, 1989a, p. 187). Military training has to be taken seriously. It is counted towards final marks in school.

Eligibility for officer training in National Service is related to scholastic record and ensures that the structure of the armed forces reflects the class structure of society as a whole. Military training reinforces the power relation that the working class must obey the capitalist class.

As National Service comes between school and employment, the PAP-state has also instructed civilian employers to take into account NS performance (such as rank attained) in recruitment and evaluation (Seah, 1989, p. 952), thereby further entrenching the results of the education system's sorting of class agents into their appropriate positions.

The PAP-state's ideology of 'total defence' is propagandised throughout the school system as well as in National Service training. It provides the formal ideological basis for the militarisation of civilian life and consists of five elements, each the responsibility of a particular ministry (see Table 7.2).

Table 7.2 The Elements of Total Defence and Implementing Ministries

Element	Ministry
Psychological Defence	Communications and Information
Social Defence	Community Development (includes social welfare, People's Association, political feedback unit)
Economic Defence	Trade and Industry
Civil Defence	Home Affairs (includes police and Internal Security Department)
Military Defence	Defence

Source: GOS (1989a), pp. 171, 234–7.

This ideology integrates all aspects of civilian life into a military strategy which politicises all behaviour as either for or against the PAP-state.

The patriarchal exclusion of women from National Service, from the habits of unquestioning obedience and from the high level of exposure to total defence propaganda has occasionally been raised as a reason for their prominence in political dissent in the 1980s. It has also been said that childbearing and rearing constitutes their National Service. This is another way of saying that control of women can be satisfactorily achieved through control of their reproductive labour.

The Militarisation of Governance

In the unlikely event that parliamentary challenges should threaten the political hegemony of the capitalist class, a final option is military rule. The systematic preparation which appears to be under way for this eventuality may be to reassure foreign investors or it may simply be that the armed forces are the best source of obedient technocrats. Whatever the reasons, military officers are being trained in civilian administration and politics.

This development is presented by Vasil as a way of ensuring that 'the military did not feel left out' and therefore did not simply take over as in other Third World countries. This explanation is derived from Rajaratnam's statement to Vasil in 1983:

> We definitely intend to introduce the military element into the Cabinet and Parliament.... The intention is to give them direct participation in Parliament and the Cabinet. If they are directly represented in the highest levels of decision-making, they can't blame the politicians for the mess. They would form part of the ruling class.   (Vasil, 1984, p. 188)

Vasil also relates this policy to 'one of the key overall objectives of obtaining a dispersal of power' into a variety of institutions in order to protect Singapore in the future. He further quotes Rajaratnam as saying, 'Anybody who wants to seize power now has not only to just set up a political party. Jeyaretnam, after the by-election, has been finding it out' (Vasil, 1984, pp. 188–9).

Brigadier-General Lee Hsien Loong, Deputy Prime Minister and the son of Lee Kuan Yew, has become the main link between the PAP and the military. Observers have noted the militarisation of Singapore's politics and bureaucracy as a consolidation of Brigadier-General Lee's political and administrative base. It has been noted that

> this trend could have fundamental long-term consequences for politics in the republic and that the ascendancy of [the junior] Lee – linchpin for the Mindef/ ex-army officer group – to the heights of power may be quicker than expected. (*FEER*, 20 April 1989, p. 33)

By 1989 military officers or former defence officials, many of them contemporaries of Brigadier-General Lee, occupied posts in the Cabinet as well as such positions as Permanent Secretary of Home Affairs (controlling the police and the Internal Security Dept), chief of the Central Provident Fund (administering the compulsory pension fund for employees of $32 billion), the Director of the ISD and the Chairman of the Economic Development Board. The government was also continuing its policy of placing military officers throughout the civil service for two-year assignments, of giving the armed forces higher pay rises than the civil service and almost as many scholarships as the entire civil service (*FEER*, 20 April 1989, p. 33).

Whether this mixing of military and civilian administration is to implicate the military in current governance or to prepare for military government or both, it remains a last option. If taken, this path involves no conflict between legitimacy and governance, since the right to rule is bestowed by supreme military force. It would also be difficult for the military to improve on the rigorous system of social control already in force in Singapore.

Securing Singapore's Regional Role

The military alliance between the PAP-state and the US has enabled the Singapore Armed Forces to obtain a technical ability in advance of its neighbours. It has upgraded its 'poison shrimp' military strategy (that is, swallow at your peril) to the 'porcupine' strategy (think twice about the cost of attack) with its purchase of early warning aircraft and the latest US combat aircraft. By the end of 1986, Singapore already had more combat aircraft than Malaysia and Indonesia combined (*Asia Yearbook*, 1988, p. 224). It is constantly upgrading its defence capability; for example, in 1990 it acquired Hawk surface-to-air missiles (*STW*, 19 May 1990).

The PAP-state's defence expenditure as a percentage of GDP is similar to that of the other Asian NICs, with the exception of Hong Kong which still has the direct backing of the British armed forces (Table 7.3). PAP leaders state that defence spending will stay at approximately six per cent of GDP. However, even one of its own backbenchers has pointed out that this is a nominal figure which leaves out 'hidden' items (*STW*, 17 March 1990). Singapore's defence spending has been rising rapidly as a proportion of government spending (Table 7.4).

Table 7.3   Comparative Defence Expenditure, 1990

	Singapore	Taiwan	S. Korea	Hong Kong
% GDP	5.1	5.2	4.7	1.6
% budget	36.7	20.1	27.9	12.5

Source: *Asia Yearbook* (1991), p. 9.

Table 7.4   Singapore Defence Expenditure, 1985–90

	% GDP	% Budget
1985	6.25	12.7
1986	6.25	15.4
1987	–	12.6
1988	5.7	21.00
1989	4.8	27.00
1990	5.1	36.7

Source: *Asia Yearbook* (1986–91).

Table 7.4 shows that the PAP-state began to spend much more on defence once the 1985 recession had been overcome and high growth rates returned. The reason for this lies in the ambiguity surrounding US strategic intentions in the region. Singapore sought to boost its capabilities to compensate for these uncertainties. Hence, also its attempt to improve regional military relationships through exercises with Malaysia and Indonesia (*STW*, 27 May 1989) and its more positive statements about a future role for Japan (*STW*, 4 May 1991).

> If the US significantly cuts back its military forces in the region, this will not be a signal for Singapore also to reduce our forces. It will be reason for concern over a potentially destabilising change in the regional balance of power, one which may lead to other significant powers playing a more active role in the

region.... No other ASEAN country is slashing its defence expenditures, demobilising its armed forces or acting on the assumption that it no longer faces any external security threats. It would be foolhardy for Singapore alone to do so. (Brigadier-General Lee in *STW*, 24 February 1990)

The PAP-state now faces another transition. It began its EOI accumulation strategy with British security guarantees.

This soon moved to a reliance on US military power. Now the PAP-state finds the more complex situation of multipolar global economy may require a multilateral approach to securing the military support of foreign capital. Its agreement to have a US military presence in Singapore on a regular basis following the announced closure of US bases in the Philippines (*STW*, 17 November 1990) can be seen as a transitional measure.

The regional political implications of this invitation to the US and the constant references by PAP leaders to threats from irrational leaders and irrational forces from other countries have been well understood by Singapore's neighbours.

'Many Malaysians cannot help but feel that the Singapore leadership may be referring to Malaysia, perhaps Indonesia too, and what it sees as a threat from the forces of Islam or Malay nationalism,' the UMNO vice-president and former defence minister [of Malaysia] said. Describing Singapore as the 'most densely defended country in the world', Datuk Abdullah... said, 'When you want to host US facilities here and when we perceive that you see us as a threat to your existence and your stability, then of course we see that the offer is directed as a deterrence against us. You are telling us: What you see is this sea of hostile Malays surrounding you and you are saying: "Hey, don't meddle with us, we have the Americans behind us". We feel a little hurt, a little suspicious of your intentions and motives, a little doubtful of your sense of commitment to ASEAN and the concept of the Zone of Peace, Freedom and Neutrality (Zopfan) and your sense of good neighbourliness'. (*STW*, 2 September 1989)

This tension arises from the PAP-state's regional military role of securing a regional accumulation strategy facilitating foreign capital's penetration of its neighbours. Singaporean capital also has interests in low-wage production in neighbouring countries.

Therefore, the ultimate sanction of military force functions at both the local and regional levels. Locally, militarisation is mainly a means of enforcing worker discipline and state violence is ordinarily mediated on a mass scale through the law. Regionally, Singapore's arms build-up not only acts as a military deterrent but heightens communalism thereby diverting attention from the social consequences of Singapore's role in facilitating foreign capital's penetration of Southeast Asia.

Conclusion

The political economy of social control in Singapore has been approached by examining central institutions of the system of social control and the political and economic relationships behind them. The relationships between the PAP-state, local capital, the working class and foreign capital have been the underlying social relations at issue. The arrangement whereby Singapore's productive sector is overwhelmingly dominated by foreign transnational corporations while the Singapore state is mainly responsible for controlling workers has been understood as representing a political alliance. It is a partnership – albeit an unequal one – between the PAP-state and the ruling classes of a small number of advanced capitalist countries.

Social control has been focused on pressuring Singaporeans to conform to the needs of this alliance expressed mainly in the economic form of the EOI strategy. The detailed periodisations of public housing, state education, parliament and the law have shown how social relations have been regulated in many ways with different institutions predominating at different times. The emphasis of each institution has also shifted in mediating particular kinds of social control, for example, sometimes mediating mainly violence, at other times inducing cooperation chiefly through extending the consumption of welfare. Other major institutions such as health, the media and the factory, have also played important roles.

Social control has not simply involved the imposition of an economic strategy on an unsuspecting population by a state bureaucracy. Attention to questions of class, ethnicity, gender and language has revealed a complex picture of a volatile, politically aware society constantly throwing up new challenges to the PAP-state's policies. The forms of social control can therefore be seen as representing institutionalised forms of political contest, significant for the indications they give of the nature and historical particularity of underlying social conflicts. The Singapore state can be seen as the product of social conflicts as well as the site of them.

Changes in the forms of non-compliance and dissent on the one hand and of social regulation on the other therefore reflect stages in a political contest, not merely qualitatively new phases of economic development. This contest has not only determined the nature of social control but also has placed limits on economic strategy, determining the feasibility of policies, how they have been implemented and whether they were successful. The stages of this conflict in each period can now be clearly identified.

THE STAGES OF CONFLICT

Anti-Colonial Movement and Military Violence (1945–59)

The first stage was the anti-colonial movement's opposition to British rule which met the regulatory response of military violence and police-state tactics to preserve an accumulation strategy of direct colonial plunder. But the partnership between the anti-colonial forces in Singapore and the Lee faction of the capitalist class, together with the general decline of British rule in the face of opposition elsewhere in the empire, precipitated changes in both accumulation and regulation strategies in order to defeat the left and to protect the profitability of British investment. The nationalist struggle had developed to the point where British capital and Western strategic interests could be preserved only by an accommodation with local political forces and by supporting the import substitution industrialisation policy designed to strengthen the local capitalist class. Thus, political challenges in Singapore and in other colonies undermined existing strategies and led to the 1959–65 period of transition.

Parliamentary Opposition and the Law (1960–5)

State regulatory power was therefore transferred to the Lee faction which, while allied to the anti-colonial movement, had manoeuvred to establish an alliance with British capital. After 1961 the PAP-state faced a strong and legal mass-based political opposition against which it used the repressive legislative measures bequeathed by the British colonial state. Violence was mediated mainly through legal coercion during this period of the PAP-state consolidating its political hegemony. The law was used to declare legal organisations illegal and to render their leadership vulnerable to attack by the security police. Parliamentary opposition members, trade unions leaders, journalists and other community leaders were politically neutralised by means of detention without trial in order to secure the PAP's parliamentary dominance and, thus, the legitimacy of its grip on state power. Welfare institutions were also used to suppress organised political opposition and to destroy working-class organisation in a violent way under the sanction of law. For example, public housing was implemented by forced resettlement and education was restructured by coercive measures against Chinese educational institutions as people were put in their physical and social places.

The continued high level of violence and coercion was related to the Lee faction's lack of a reliable base in the weak local capitalist class. However, as organised working-class opposition was increasingly neutralised and local capital gained a greater interest in PAP hegemony over the ensuing decades, state violence became directed more towards disciplining workers to regular wage labour than to breaking up their political organisations.

Worker Militancy and Welfare (1966–78)

The suppression of left-wing political organisation enabled the PAP to monopolise control of parliament, a development which caused it virtually to disappear from public view for 15 years because it was no longer the main site of political contest. However, a lower class remained with a tradition of militancy, with social cohesiveness stemming from linguistic and ethnic affiliations and with a degree of economic independence derived from alternative means of subsistence. These characteristics gave it some ability to resist the export-oriented industrialisation strategy. Singapore had become attractive to foreign investment because the combination of reasonably advanced technology, well-developed infrastructure and comparatively cheap, obedient labour was becoming an unbeatable one which enabled high levels of surplus value to be generated.

During the period between 1966 and 1978 the institutions of public housing and education occupied centre stage. They forced a new degree of social stratification by cutting away social roots and by ensuring that access to welfare depended on working for transnational corporations. Alternative means of livelihood to wage labour were progressively denied. It became increasingly difficult to find any house except an HDB flat and this could only be paid for by wage labour. Without educational qualifications, it became more difficult to find a job which paid enough to buy the essentials of life. Access to housing and education was controlled by the PAP-state and depended upon selling one's labour power to foreign capital. Women were exploited for their cheap labour as well as for their breeding capacity and their unpaid domestic labour.

The rapid sorting of the population into a rigid class system which was achieved during this phase, helped to consolidate the PAP-state's alliance with foreign capital and to bring a period of sustained economic growth. The law continued to be used to crush the remnants of political opposition especially in the press and educational institutions.

Non-cooperation and Parliamentarism (1978–85)

But the many contradictions created by the fragmentation of the working class gave rise to new tensions when the Second Industrial Revolution was launched in the late 1970s. There was a sudden increase in exploitation and, despite the PAP-state's pervasive system of social control, people increasingly refused to cooperate. This non-cooperation took various forms and included elements of the rising middle class. Workers did not reach the new productivity goals. Women widely refused to follow the state-breeding policy. Students did not perform to the required levels educationally. Malays attempted to rebuild their communities. People resented the control exerted by the HDB over their lives. This general resistance surfaced through increased electoral dissent and the election of opposition

Conclusion

members to parliament. The new accumulation strategy failed and the PAP-state faced a crisis of legitimacy in the mid-1980s.

The 1980s were characterised by parliament once again becoming an important site of political contest. While strengthening its control elsewhere, the PAP-state attempted to domesticate and control this dissent by giving it vent within parliamentary politics. It tied access to welfare more tightly to political loyalty. To discipline the working class into higher productivity, the PAP-state raised the level of mass violence administered through the law, increasing the offences which drew sentences of official torture and execution. It built up its military training.

Middle-Class Dissent and the Privatisation of Politics (1985–90)

Since 1985, with the reversion to the export-oriented industrialisation policy, the PAP-state has largely been able to reassert its authority over the working class. However, the urban middle class now wants the substance as well as the forms of liberal democratic political rights. The rise of local capital and the growth of a middle class concentrated in the service sector has confronted the PAP-state with a challenge from within its own class.

The PAP-state faces the danger of a democratically-inclined fraction of the capitalist class building an electoral alliance with elements of a resentful working class, just as the Lee group did in the 1950s. The development of capitalism in Singapore may come into conflict with the rights of the individual increasingly proclaimed by the meritocracy.

To date the PAP-state has moved to counter this potential threat to its control and to shore up its legitimacy through shifting public political accountability away from the PAP. Partly to address this threat, an elected presidency has been created to take the central powers of governance away from an executive accountable to parliament. The PAP's Central Executive Committee could now govern through the presidency in the unlikely event that it is forced to permit another party to win a parliamentary majority.

One response to the problem of entrenched working-class disaffection has been the privatisation of education which is the pathway to jobs and housing. This shift removes the PAP-state from direct responsibility for forcing the working class into wage labour by failing their children at school.

Multipolar Global Economy and Militarisation (from 1985)

The end of superpower rivalry has precipitated a shift in the PAP-state's strategy of regional social control. Although still reliant on its military alliance with the US, it has had to conclude a more complex multilateral alliance with Japan and the EC as well. Also, the end of the Cold War has laid bare the main source of international conflict: the exploitation of the underdeveloped countries by the advanced capitalist countries. Singapore's role as a facilitator of this exploitation in its own region is in danger of being further exposed. Even while strengthening its military capability, it has therefore sought economic and military accommodations with Malaysia and Indonesia.

STRENGTHS AND WEAKNESSES OF SOCIAL CONTROL

Social control in Singapore is conspicuous for its success. PAP-state regulation has:

(1) fragmented the working class and minority races in order to integrate them into capitalist social relations;

(2) guaranteed working-class subsistence on the condition of political loyalty;

(3) reproduced labour power by means of education and public housing, state-breeding programmes and migrant workers;

(4) made middle-class social advancement conditional on political conformity;

(5) extracted the semblance of popular consent, especially through providing social welfare and through parliamentarism;

(6) compelled compliance by constructing a powerful apparatus of state violence mediated through the law and the military;

(7) secured Singapore's regional role by aggressive militarisation and manipulation of communalism.

These are substantial achievements accomplished to a considerable degree by the combination of a high consumption of welfare services and a high level of state violence. One without the other would not have been so effective. The increased consumption of services and consumer goods has had the ideological effect of Singaporeans believing that they have more control over their lives rather than less. It has integrated them into an industrial lifestyle, giving them the same objectives in life and the same methods of reaching them.

This integration of the working class into the disciplined routine, the economic dependence and the ideological framework of capitalist social relations occurred rapidly enough for the export-oriented industrialisation accumulation strategy to succeed over more than two decades.

Furthermore the idiosyncratic leadership of Lee Kuan Yew must be counted as a success. The authority he wielded and the fear of disobedience that he generated have been widely recognised locally and internationally as well as by the man himself. Expressing his displeasure with the 1984 election results, Lee stated: 'They [the people] know they are unlikely to make any dent on me. Singaporeans know by now what kind of person I am' (*Asia Yearbook*, 1986, p. 226).

Conclusion

His personal presence has mainly been significant in setting up a system of social control which may survive without him. As a bourgeois nationalist who rode to power on the backs of popular forces only to take control of the state for his own class, Lee is unexceptional in the history of decolonisation. As an opportunist who failed to gain control of the larger Malaysian political stage, he can be considered a failure. However, as leader of a faction which held on to power through its alliance with foreign capital, he was the successful architect and builder of a comprehensive system of social control which will probably outlast him. But, at this point of strength, even he is plagued by a weakness. The insecurity of the PAP has spawned a dynastic tendency which is likely to undermine the legitimacy of PAP governance in the long term.

But the most obvious failure of the PAP-state's system of social control is that repression has always led to new forms of resistance, especially when the level of exploitation has been suddenly increased. Working-class organisation in the form of trade unions was demolished in the 1960s but working-class non-compliance re-emerged through non-cooperation both in the workplace (job-hopping) and outside it (refusal to learn technical and linguistic skills, electoral dissent and crime). Chinese education was suppressed in order to fragment working-class identity but English-medium education has given greater access to liberal democratic ideas and to the international media. Working-class women were pressured to stop breeding but so did middle-class women and Chinese women more than other races. Middle-class women began to organise against sexism and patriarchy. Other struggles have been only temporarily contained but not overcome. Malay alienation and resentment remains at a high level.

This failure stems partly from the PAP-state's attempt to use particular institutions to combat a wide variety of struggles all at once. The education system was used to change the linguistic habits of the entire population, to alter breeding patterns, to dissipate ethnic loyalties and to enforce moral discipline – all while sorting people into their appropriate class positions. Contradictions arose between these regulatory goals and as a consequence the education system failed to produce the skilled labour force necessary for the accumulation strategy of the Second Industrial Revolution. PAP legitimacy was undermined in the process and the privatisation of education was pursued to restore it. But this step may raise new contradictions as privatisation in one area undermines government influence in others.

Social control has created both new divisions and new forms of unity. The increasing levels of exploitation required by capital continue to demand greater and different regulatory efforts. With Singapore's highly centralised system of social control, each new crisis threatens to unravel the entire system of regulation. Decentralisation of the system is not really an alternative since the PAP-state would lose its ability to direct the labour force in ways which have given capital in Singapore its competitive edge.

CONTINUING INSECURITY

The PAP-state has been pressured to adapt to the resurgence of electoral dissent by permitting a degree of genuine political contest in parliament. But it is simultaneously strengthening its control in other areas. It is keeping a firm hold on the provision of welfare, especially housing and education (despite the 'privatisation' of the elite sector). It is ensuring continued Chinese racial dominance and it is sustaining a hierarchy within the fragmented working class through the importation of a revolving force of 200,000 foreign workers. Through the build-up of its military capacity and the increasing links between the military and civilian administrations, the final guarantee of PAP supremacy remains available. The unnecessary killing at Changi Airport of hijackers armed only with in-flight cutlery is a sign that the PAP-state does not hesitate to use ultimate force (*STW*, 30 March 1991). These trends reveal continuing insecurity rather than a government confident of its political base.

The reservation of its central constitutional powers of governance in the office of the Presidency may encourage other parties to believe their electoral objectives are more realistic than before. The PAP will not easily give way but it may calculate that it is better to do so to prevent a party with real working-class links emerging from a crisis precipitated by middle-class cynicism with the electoral process. The middle-class in Singapore may therefore have a possibility of attaining enhanced liberal democratic rights for itself.

But the working class is not likely to be permitted by any prospective government to organise autonomously, either within the workplace or outside it, as this would threaten the EOI strategy in which the capitalist class now has a considerable investment. There may continue to be room, however, to grant more concessions in terms of wage levels and working conditions at the expense of foreign migrant workers.

Working-class non-compliance in Singapore shows no sign of weakening. This resistance guarantees the persistence of high levels of state violence. But it is unlikely to alter the fundamental nature of capitalist social relations in the city-state until there is a much deeper political and economic crisis within the major advanced industrialised countries. Such a prospect is both a reflection on the PAP-state's weakness in the partnership with foreign capital and a tribute to its power of social control.

References

Aglietta, Michel (1979) *A Theory of Capitalist Regulation* (London: NLB).
Althusser, Louis (1984) *Essays on Ideology* (London: Verso).
Amin, Samir (1974) *Accumulation on a World Scale: A Critique of the Theory of Underdevelopment* (New York: Monthly Review Press).
Amnesty International (1980) *Report of an Amnesty International Mission to Singapore 30 November to 5 December 1978* (London: Amnesty International).
Andersen, Robert Allan (1974) *The Separation of Singapore from Malaysia: A Study in Political Involution* (Ann Arbor, Mich.: University Microfilms).
Anderson, Perry (1974) *Lineages of the Absolutist State* (London: New Left Books).
Andreff, Wladimir (1984) 'The International Centralization of Capital and the Re-ordering of World Capitalism', *Capital and Class*, 22, pp. 58–80.
Applebaum, Richard P. and Henderson, Jeffrey (eds) (1992) *States and Development in the Asian Pacific Rim* (London: Sage).
Ariff, Mohamed and Hill, Hal (1985) *Export-oriented Industrialisation: The ASEAN Experience* (Sydney: Allen & Unwin).
Arotcarena, G., Tan, Thomas T. W. and Fong, Hoe Fang (1986) *The Maid Tangle* (Singapore: Katong Catholic Book Centre).
Arumugam, Raja Segaran (1975) 'Education and Integration in Singapore', in Wu, Teh-yao (ed.) *Political and Social Change in Singapore* (Singapore: Institute of Southeast Asian Studies) pp. 55–69.
Asia Watch (1989) *Silencing All Critics: Human Rights Violations in Singapore* (Washington: Asia Watch).
Austin, W. Timothy (1989) 'Crime and Control', in Sandhu, K. S. and Wheatley, Paul (eds), *Management of Success: The Moulding of Modern Singapore* (Singapore: Institute of Southeast Asian Studies) pp. 913–27.
Barker, Colin (1978) 'A Note on the Theory of Capitalist States', *Capital and Class*, 4, pp. 118–26.
Barrett, M., Corrigan, P., Kuhn, A. and Wolff, J. (1979) *Ideology and Cultural Production* (London: Croom Helm).
Barrett, Richard E. and Chin, Soomi (1987) 'Export-oriented Industrializing States in the Capitalist World System: Similarities and Differences', in Deyo, Frederic C. (ed.) *The Political Economy of the New Asian Industrialism* (Ithaca, NY: Cornell University Press) pp. 23–43.
Bedlington, Stanley S. (1974) *The Singapore Malay Community: The Politics of State Integration*, doctoral dissertation, Cornell University.
Bedlington, Stanley S. (1978) *Malaysia and Singapore: The Building of New States* (Ithaca, NY: Cornell University Press).
Bello, Walden and Rosenfeld, Stephanie (1990) *Dragons in Distress: Asia's Miracle Economies in Crisis* (San Francisco: Food First).
Bellows, T. J. (1970) *The People's Action Party of Singapore: Emergence of a Dominant Party System* (New Haven, Conn.: Yale University Southeast Asia Studies).
Betts, Russell (1975) *Multiracialism, Meritocracy, and the Malays of Singapore*, doctoral dissertation, Massachusetts Institute of Technology.
Bloodworth, Dennis (1986) *The Tiger and the Trojan Horse* (Singapore: Times International).

Blum, Jeffrey M. (1978) *Pseudoscience and Mental Ability: The Origins and Fallacies of the IQ Controversy* (New York: Monthly Review Press).
Bonefield, Werner (1987) 'Reformulation of State Theory', *Capital and Class*, 33, pp. 96–127.
Brody, Reed (ed.) (1989) *The Harassment and Persecution of Judges and Lawyers, January 1988–June 1989* (Geneva: International Commission of Jurists).
Buchanan, Iain (1972) *Singapore in Southeast Asia* (London: G. Bell & Sons).
Burman, Sandra B. and Harrell-Bond, Barbara E. (eds) (1979) *The Imposition of Law* (London: Academic Press).
Busch, Peter A. (1974) *Legitimacy and Ethnicity: A Case Study of Singapore* (Lexington: Heath).
Business Environment Risk Information (1988a) *Singapore: Profit Opportunity Recommendation 1988* (Washington, DC: BERI).
Business Environment Risk Information (1988b) *Singapore: Recommended Lender Action 1988* (Washington, DC: BERI).
Cain, Maureen and Hunt, Alan (1979) *Marx and Engels on Law* (London: Academic Press).
Caldwell, Malcolm (1979) *Lee Kuan Yew: The Man, His Mayoralty and His Mafia* (London: Federation of United Kingdom and Eire Malaysian and Singaporean Student Organisations).
Callinicos, Alex (1976) *Althusser's Marxism* (London: Pluto Press).
Castells, Manuel (1989) *The Informational City: Information Technology, Economic Restructuring, and the Urban–Regional Process* (Oxford: Basil Blackwell).
Chan, Heng Chee (1970) 'Nation Building in Southeast Asia: The Singapore Case', in Bernard Grossman (ed.) *Southeast Asia in the Modern World* (Wiesbaden: Otto Harrassowitz) 33/IV, pp. 165–79.
Chan, Heng Chee (1971) *Singapore: The Politics of Survival 1965–1967* (Singapore: Oxford University Press).
Chan, Heng Chee (1975) 'The Role of Intellectuals in Singapore Politics', *South East Asian Journal of Social Science*, 3/2, pp. 59–64.
Chan, Heng Chee (1976) *The Dynamics of One Party Dominance* (Singapore: Singapore University Press).
Chan, Heng Chee (1984) *A Sensation of Independence: A Political Biography of David Marshall* (Singapore: Oxford University Press).
Chan, Heng Chee (1985) 'Political Parties', in Quah, Jon S. T., Chan, Heng Chee and Seah, Chee Meow (eds) *Government and Politics of Singapore* (Singapore: Oxford University Press) pp. 146–72.
Chan, Heng Chee (1989) 'The PAP and the Structuring of the Political System', in Sandhu, K. S. and Wheatley, Paul (eds) *Management of Success: The Moulding of Modern Singapore* (Singapore: Institute of Southeast Asian Studies) pp. 70–89.
Chang, Chen-Tung (1976) 'The Changing Socio-demographic Profile', in Hassan, Riaz (ed.) *Singapore: Society in Transition* (Kuala Lumpur: Oxford University Press) pp. 271–89.
Cheah, Boon Kheng (1979) *The Masked Comrades – A Study of the Communist United Front in Malaya 1945–48* (Singapore: Times Books International).
Chee, Heng Leng and Chan, Chee Khoon (eds) (1984) *Designer Genes: IQ, Ideology and Biology* (Kuala Lumpur: Institute for Social Analysis).
Chen, Peter S. J. (1975) 'Elites and National Development in Singapore', *South East Asian Journal of Social Science*, 3/1, pp. 17–25.
Chen, Peter S. J. (ed.) (1983) *Singapore Development Policies and Trends* (Singapore: Oxford University Press).
Chew, Ernest C. T. (1991) 'The Foundation of British Settlement', in Chew, Ernest C. T. and Lee, Edwin (eds) (1991) *A History of Singapore* (Singapore: Oxford University Press) pp. 36–40.

References

Chew MacDougall, Sock Foon (1982) *Ethnicity and Nationality in Singapore* (Ann Arbor, Mich.: University Microfilms International).
Chia, Siow Yue (1972) 'Export Performance of the Manufacturing Sector and of Foreign Investment', in Wong, Kum Poh and Tan, Maureen (eds) *Singapore in the International Economy* (Singapore: Singapore University Press) pp. 33–47.
Chia, Siow Yue (1989) 'The Character and Progress of Industrialization', in Sandhu, K. S. and Wheatley, Paul (eds) *Management of Success: The Moulding of Modern Singapore* (Singapore: Institute of Southeast Asian Studies) pp. 250–79.
Chiew, Seen Kong (1983) 'Singapore in 1982: Economic Slowdown and Normative Change', *Southeast Asian Affairs 1983* (Singapore: Institute of Southeast Asian Studies) pp. 249–74.
Chin, Kin Wah (1983) *The Defence of Malaysia and Singapore: The Transformation of a Security System 1957–71* (Cambridge: Cambridge University Press).
Chomsky, Noam (1972) 'I.Q. Tests: Building Blocks for the New Class System', *Ramparts*, July 1972, pp. 24–30.
Choo, Hakchung (1989) 'The Asian Newly Industrializing Economies (NIEs): Are "Economic Miracles" Equally Miraculous?', *The Singapore Economic Review*, XXXIV/1, pp. 2–12.
Chua, Beng Huat (1989) 'The Business of Living in Singapore', in Sandhu, K. S. and Wheatley, Paul (eds) *Management of Success: The Moulding of Modern Singapore* (Singapore: Institute of Southeast Asian Studies) pp. 1003–21.
Chui, Kwei-Chiang (1991) 'Political Attitudes and Organisations, c.1900–1941', in Chew, Ernest C. T. and Lee, Edwin (eds) *A History of Singapore* (Singapore: Oxford University Press) pp. 66–91.
Clad, James (1989) *Behind the Myth: Business, Money and Power in Southeast Asia* (London: Grafton).
Clammer, John (1985) *Singapore: Ideology, Society, Culture* (Singapore: Chopmen Publishers).
Clammer, John (1987) *Beyond the New Economic Anthropology* (New York: St Martin's Press).
Clarke, Simon (1977) 'Marxism, Sociology and Poulantzas' Theory of the State', *Capital and Class*, 2, pp. 1–31.
Clarke, Simon (1988) 'Overaccumulation, Class Struggle and the Regulation Approach', *Capital and Class*, 36, pp. 59–92.
Cleaver, Harry M. (1979) *Reading Capital Politically* (Sussex: Harvester Press).
Clutterbuck, Richard (1973) *Riot and Revolution in Singapore and Malaysia 1945–1963* (London: Faber and Faber).
Cohen, S. and Scull, A. (1986) (eds) *Social Control and the State* (Oxford: Basil Blackwell).
Colony of Singapore (1955–9) *Singapore Legislative Assembly Debates* (Singapore: Government Printing Office) pp. 1–10.
Connolly, William (ed.) (1984) *Legitimacy and the State* (London: Basil Blackwell).
Daw, Rowena (1972) 'Preventive Detention in Singapore – A Comment on the Case of Lee Mau Seng', *Malaya Law Review*, 14/2, pp. 276–93.
Deyo, Frederic C. (1981) *Dependent Development and Industrial Order: An Asian Case Study* (New York: Praeger).
Deyo, Frederic C. (ed.) (1987) *The Political Economy of the New Asian Industrialism* (Ithaca, NY: Cornell University Press).
Dhanabalan, S. (1989) 'Social Integration Must Be Maintained', *Speeches '89* (Singapore: Ministry of Communication and Information) 13/1, pp. 3–7.
Dow Jones and Company Inc. (1990) *Lee Kuan Yew vs. The News: A History* (dossier by Dow Jones Corporate Relations, New York).
Drysdale, John (1984) *Singapore: Struggle for Success* (Sydney: George Allen and Unwin).

Economist Intelligence Unit (1987) *Country Profile 1987–88: Singapore* (London: The Economist).
Edelman, Murray (1971) *Politics as Symbolic Action – Mass Arousal and Quiescence* (Chicago: Markham).
Eisenstein, Zillah (1980) 'The State, the Patriarchal Family and Working Mothers', *Kapitalistate*, 8, pp. 43–66.
Elegant, Simon (1989) 'Singaporeans Say Government Exaggerates Brain-drain Problem', *Asian Wall Street Journal Weekly*, 16 October.
Emergency Committee for Human Rights in Singapore (1987) *A Report on the Detentions in Singapore May and June 1987: A Statement of Facts* (Christchurch: ECHRIS).
Emergency Committee for Human Rights in Singapore (1987–9) *Singapore Human Rights Alert: Updates* (Christchurch: ECHRIS) issues 1–28.
European Committee for Human Rights in Malaysia and Singapore (1990) *The Rule of Law and Human Rights in Malaysia and Singapore* (Utrecht: KEHMA-S/GRAEL).
Evans, Keith R. and Fordham, Margaret (1985) 'Singapore Appeals to the Judicial Committee of the Privy Council – An Endangered Species?', *Malaya Law Review*, pp. 27, 284–309.
Evans, Peter (1987) 'Class, State, and Dependence in East Asia: Lessons for Latin Americanists', in Deyo, Frederic C. (ed.) *The Political Economy of the New Asian Industrialism* (Ithaca, NY: Cornell University Press) pp. 203–26.
Fine, Ben (1980) *Economic Theory and Ideology* (London: Edward Arnold).
Foucault, Michel (1979) *Discipline and Punish* (New York: Vintage).
Frank, Andre Gunder (1978) *Dependent Accumulation and Under-development* (London: Macmillan).
Frank, Beatrice S., Markowitz, Joseph C., McKay, Robert B. and Roth, Kenneth (1991) 'The Decline of the Rule of Law in Malaysia and Singapore: Part II – Singapore', a Report of the Committee on International Human Rights, The Association of the Bar of the City of New York, *The Record*, 46/1.
Gamer, Robert E. (1972) *The Politics of Urban Development in Singapore* (Ithaca, NY: Cornell University Press).
Gayle, Dennis John (1986) *The Small Developing State* (Hampshire: Gower Publishing Company).
Geiger, Theodore and Geiger, Frances M. (1973) *Tales of Two City-states: The Development Progress of Hongkong and Singapore* (Washington, DC: National Planning Association).
George, T. J. S. (1984) *Lee Kuan Yew's Singapore* (Singapore: Eastern Universities Press).
Godelier, Maurice (1978) 'Infrastructures, Societies and History', *New Left Review*, 112, pp. 84–96.
Goh, Keng Swee (1972) *The Economics of Modernization* (Singapore: Asia Pacific Press).
Goh, Keng Swee (1977) *The Practice of Economic Growth* (Singapore: Federal Publications).
Goldring, John (1988) 'The Legal Profession and Government in Singapore and Malaysia', *The Australian Quarterly*, 60/4, pp. 488–98.
Gopinathan, S. (1976) 'Towards a National Education System', in Hassan, Riaz (ed,) *Singapore: Society in Transition* (Kuala Lumpur: Oxford University Press) pp. 67–83.
Gopinathan, Saravanan (1979) 'Singapore's Language Policies: Strategies for a Plural Society', *Southeast Asian Affairs 1979* (Singapore: Heinemann) pp. 280–98.
Government of Singapore (1966) *Separation* (Singapore: Ministry of Culture).
Government of Singapore (1969) *Singapore's New Labour Laws: Towards Greater Productivity and Economic Growth* (Singapore: Ministry of Labour).
Government of Singapore (1973) *Towards Tomorrow* (Singapore: National Trades Union Congress).

Government of Singapore (1979) *Report on the Ministry of Education 1978* (Singapore: Ministry of Education).

Government of Singapore Economic Committee (1986) *The Singapore Economy: New Directions*, report and executive summary (Singapore: Ministry of Trade and Industry).

Government of Singapore (1988a) *Economic Survey of Singapore 1987* (Singapore: Ministry of Trade and Industry).

Government of Singapore (1988b) *Green Paper on Agenda for Action: Goals and Challenges* (presented to Singapore Parliament 15 February 1988).

Government of Singapore (1988c) *White Paper on Constitutional Amendments to Safeguard Financial Assets and the Integrity of the Public Services* (presented to Singapore Parliament 29 July 1988).

Government of Singapore (1989a) *Singapore 1989* (Singapore: Ministry of Communications and Information).

Government of Singapore (1989b) *Parliamentary Debates Singapore – Official Report 30 May 1989*, 54/3.

Government of Singapore (1990a) 'Safeguarding Financial Assets and the Integrity of the Public Services',The Constitution of the Republic of Singapore (Amendment no. 3) Bill, tabled 27 August 1990.

Government of Singapore (1990b) *Maintenance of Religious Harmony Bill*, Bill No. 1/90.

Government of Singapore (1991) *The Next Lap* (Singapore: Times Editions).

Government of Singapore (1994) *Religion, Childcare and Leisure Activities* Singapore Census of Population 1990, Statistical Release 6 (Singapore: Department of Statistics).

Gurr, Ted Robert (1988) 'War, Revolution, and the Growth of the Coercive State', *Comparative Political Studies*, 21/1, pp. 45–65.

Gwee, Yee Hean (1975) 'The Changing Educational Scene', in Seah, Chee Meow (ed.) *Trends in Singapore* (Singapore University Press) pp. 87–98.

Haas, Michael (1988) 'Dissent and the Demand for Democracy in Singapore', *Far Eastern Economic Review*, 10 March 1988, pp. 24–6.

Haas, Michael (1989) 'The Politics of Singapore in the 1980s', *Journal of Contemporary Asia*, 19/1, pp. 48–77.

Haggard, Stephan and Cheng, Tun-jen (1989)'State and Foreign Capital in the East Asian NICs', in Deyo, Frederic C. (ed.) *The Political Economy of the New Asian Industrialism* (Ithaca, NY: Cornell University Press) pp. 84–135.

Hakchung, C. (1989) 'The Asian Newly Industrialising Economies (NIEs): Are Economic Miracles Equally Miraculous?', *The Singapore Economic Review*, XXXIV/1, pp. 2–12.

Hall, Stuart (1980) 'Popular-Democratic vs Authoritarian Populism: Two Ways of "Taking Democracy Seriously"', in Alan Hunt (ed.) *Marxism and Democracy* (London: Lawrence and Wishart).

Hall, Stuart, Critcher, Chas, Jefferson, Tony, Clarke, John and Roberts, Brian (1978) (eds) *Policing the Crisis* (London: Macmillan).

Hamill, Ian (1981) *The Strategic Illusion – the Singapore Strategy and the Defence of Australia and New Zealand* (Singapore: Singapore University Press).

Hamilton, Clive (1983) 'Capitalist Industrialisation in East Asia's Four Little Tigers', *Journal of Contemporary Asia*, 13/1, pp. 35–73.

Harding, A. J. (1981) 'Natural Justice and the Constitution', *Malaya Law Review*, 23, pp. 226–36.

Harding, A. J. (1983) 'Parliament and the Grundnorm in Singapore', *Malaya Law Review*, 25, pp. 351–67.

Harper, R. W. E. and Miller, Henry (1984) *Singapore Mutiny* (Singapore: Oxford University Press).

Harvey, David (1982) *The Limits to Capital* (Chicago: University of Chicago Press).

Harvey, David (1985) *The Urbanization of Capital* (Oxford: Basil Blackwell).

Hassan, Riaz (ed.) (1976) *Singapore: Society in Transition* (Kuala Lumpur: Oxford University Press).

Hassan, Riaz (1977) *Families in Flats: A Study of Low Income Families in Public Housing* (Singapore: Singapore University Press).

Hassan, Riaz (1983) *A Way of Dying: Suicide in Singapore* (Kuala Lumpur: Oxford University Press).

Hay, Douglas (1975) 'Property, Authority and the Criminal Law', in Hay, D., Linebaugh, P. and Thompson, E. P. (eds) *Albion's Fatal Tree – Crime and Society in Eighteenth Century England* (London: Allen Lane) pp. 17–64.

Herrnstein, Richard (1971) *IQ in the Meritocracy* (Boston: Little, Brown).

Heyzer, Noeleen (1978) *Economic Dependency, Foreign Technology and Social Change: A Study of the Formation, Organisation, and Maintenance of Peripheral Capitalism in Singapore*, doctoral dissertation, University of Cambridge.

Hill, R. M. (1979) *Women, Capitalist Crisis and the Reserve Army of Labour*, MA thesis, University of Canterbury.

Hirsch, J. (1978) 'The State Apparatus and Social Reproduction: Elements of a Theory of the Bourgeois State', in Holloway, J. and Picciotto S. (eds) *State and Capital* (London: Edward Arnold). pp. 57–107.

Hitler, Adolf (1942) *Mein Kampf*, translated and annotated by James Murphy (London: Hurst and Blackett).

Ho, Kwon Ping (1980) 'The Implications of Export-oriented Industrialisation for South East Asia', paper presented at conference on *Trade – To Whose Advantage?* Burgman College, Australian National University, pp. 20–2 February.

Ho, Wing Meng (1989) 'Value Premises Underlying the Transformation of Singapore', in Sandhu, K. S. and Wheatley, Paul (eds) *Management of Success: The Moulding of Modern Singapore* (Singapore: Institute of Southeast Asian Studies) pp. 671–91.

Holloway, John (1988) 'The Great Bear, Post-Fordism and Class Struggle: A Comment on Bonefield and Jessop', *Capital and Class*, 36, pp. 93–104.

Holloway, John and Picciotto, Sol (1977) 'Capital, Crisis and the State', *Capital and Class*, 2, pp. 76–101.

Hua, Wu Yin (1983) *Class and Communalism in Malaya – Politics in a Dependent Capitalist State* (London: Zed/Marram).

Hughes, Helen and You, Poh Seng (eds) (1969) *Foreign Investment and Industrialisation in Singapore* (Canberra: Australian National University Press).

Humphrey, John W. (1985) *Geographic Analysis of Singapore's Population* (Singapore: Department of Statistics).

Husin Ali, S. (ed.) (1984) *Ethnicity, Class and Development* (Kuala Lumpur: Persatuan Sains Sosial Malaysia).

Ibrahim, Ahmad (1989) 'Chng Suan Tze v The Minister of Home Affairs & Ors and Other Appeals', *Malayan Law Journal*, 1, pp. 69–90.

International Mission of Jurists (1987) *Report of the International Mission of Jurists to Singapore, July 1987* (Hong Kong: Asian Human Rights Commission).

Islam, Iyanatul and Kirkpatrick, Colin (1986) 'Export-Led Development, Labour Market Conditions, and the Distribution of Income: The Case of Singapore', *Cambridge Journal of Economics*, 10.

Iyer, T. K. K. (1987) 'Kidney Donations – Singapore's Legislative Proposals', *The Malayan Law Journal*, July, pp. liii–lxi.

Jayakumar, S. (1978) 'Emergency Powers in Malaysia: Development of the Law 1957–77', *The Malayan Law Journal*, January 1978, pp. ix–xxv.

Jenkins, Rhys (1984) 'Divisions over the International Division of Labour', *Capital and Class*, 22, pp. 28–57.

Jessop, Bob (1988) 'Regulation Theory, Post Fordism and the State: More than a Reply to Werner Bonefield', *Capital and Class*, 34, pp. 147–68.

Jessop, Bob (1990) *State Theory* (Cambridge: Polity Press).

References

Jomo, K. S. (1988) 'Race Religion and Repression: "National Security" and the Insecurity of the Regime', in *Tangled Web – Dissent, Deterrence and the 27 October Crackdown in Malaysia* (Haymarket, Sydney: Committee Against Repression in the Pacific and Asian) pp. 1–27.

Josey, Alex (1968a) *Lee Kuan Yew in London* (Singapore: Donald Moore).

Josey, Alex (1968b) *The Crucial Years Ahead: Republic of Singapore General Election 1968* (Singapore: Donald Moore).

Josey, Alex (1968c) *Lee Kuan Yew* (Singapore: Donald Moore).

Josey, Alex (1972) *The Singapore General Elections 1972* (Singapore: Eastern Universities Press).

Josey, Alex (1980) *Singapore: Its Past, Present and Future*, (London: André Deutsch).

Kaye, Lincoln and Buruma, Ian (1984) 'Twenty-five Years On', *Far Eastern Economic Review*, 18 October, pp. 45–51.

Khong, Kim Hoong (1984) *Merdeka! British Rule and the Struggle for Independence in Malaya, 1945–1957* (Kuala Lumpur: Institute for Social Analysis).

Khoo, Ee Hong (1990) '*Economic Development and Democracy in Singapore: State and Civil Society Relationship in the Context of International Capital – Searching for Alternatives*', research paper for MA degree, Institute of Social Studies, The Hague, Netherlands.

Koh, Ai Tee (1989) 'Diversification of Trade', in Sandhu, K. S. and Wheatley, Paul (eds) *Management of Success: The Moulding of Modern Singapore* (Singapore: Institute of Southeast Asian Studies) pp. 227–49.

Krause, Lawrence B. (1989) 'Government as Entrepreneur', in Sandhu, K. S. and Wheatley, Paul (eds) *Management of Success: The Moulding of Modern Singapore* (Singapore: Institute of Southeast Asian Studies) pp. 436–54.

Krause, Lawrence B., Koh, Ai Tee and Lee, (Tsao) Yuan (1987) *The Singapore Economy Reconsidered* (Singapore: Institute of Southeast Asian Studies).

Kuo, Eddie C. Y., Quah, Jon S. T. and Tong, Chee Kiong (1988) *Religion and Religious Revivalism in Singapore* (Singapore: Ministry of Community Development).

Lau, Albert (1991) *The Malayan Union Controversy 1942–48* (Oxford: Oxford University Press).

Lee, Edwin (1989) 'The Colonial Legacy', in Sandhu, K. S. and Wheatley, Paul (eds) *Management of Success: The Moulding of Modern Singapore* (Singapore: Institute of Southeast Asian Studies) pp. 53–69.

Lee, Hsien Loong (1989) 'The National Identity – A Direction and Identity for Singapore', *Speeches '89* (Singapore: Ministry of Communication and Information) 13/1, pp. 26–38.

Lee, Kuan Yew (1961) *The Battle for Merger* (Singapore: Ministry of Culture).

Lee, Kuan Yew (1967) *New Bearings in Our Education System* (Singapore: Ministry of Culture).

Lee, Kuan Yew (1983) 'The Education of Women and Patterns of Procreation' (National Day Speech 14 August 1983) Regional Institute of Higher Education and Development (RIHED) Bulletin 10/3, pp. 1–7.

Lee, Soo Ann (1973) *Industrialisation in Singapore* (Melbourne: Longman).

Lee, Soo Ann (1974) *Economic Growth and the Public Sector in Malaya and Singapore 1948–1960* (Singapore: Oxford University Press).

Lee, Soo Ann (1989) 'Expansion of the Services Sector', in Sandhu, K. S. and Wheatley, Paul (eds) *Management of Success: The Moulding of Modern Singapore* (Singapore: Institute of Southeast Asian Studies) pp. 280–99.

Leong, Choon Cheong (1978) *Youth in the Army* (Singapore: Federal Publications).

Leong, Victor Wai Meng and Samosir, Roland (1986) 'Forever Immune? Abdul Wahab b. Sulaiman v. Commandant Tanglin Detention Barracks', *Malaya Law Review*, 28, pp. 303–22.

Lerner, Gerda (1986) *The Creation of Patriarchy* (Oxford: Oxford University Press).
Li, Dun Jen (1982) *British Malaya – An Economic Analysis* (Kuala Lumpur: Institut Analisa Sosial).
Lim, Chong Yah (1983) 'Singapore's Economic Development: Retrospect and Prospect', in Chen, Peter S. J. (ed) *Singapore Development Policies and Trends* (Singapore: Oxford University Press) pp. 89–104.
Lim, Chong Yah (1989) 'From High Growth Rates to Recession', in Sandhu, K. S. and Wheatley, Paul (eds) *Management of Success: The Moulding of Modern Singapore* (Singapore: Institute of Southeast Asian Studies) pp. 201–17.
Lim, Chong Yah and You, Poh Seng (eds) (1984) *Singapore: Twenty-five Years of Development* (Singapore: Nan Yang Xing Zhou Lianhe Zaobao).
Lim, Linda Yuen-Ching (1983) 'Singapore's Success: The Myth of the Free Market Economy', *Asian Survey*, XXIII/6, pp. 752–64.
Lim, Linda Yuen-Ching (1989) 'Social Welfare' in Sandhu, K. S. and Wheatley, Paul (eds) *Management of Success: The Moulding of Modern Singapore* (Singapore: Institute of Southeast Asian Studies) pp. 171–97.
Lim, Linda Yuen-Ching and Pang, Eng Fong (1986) *Trade, Employment and Industrialisation in Singapore* (Geneva: International Labour Organisation).
Lim, Mah Hui and Teoh, Kit Fong (1986) 'Singapore Corporations Go Transnational', *Journal of Southeast Asian Studies*, XVII/2, pp. 336–65.
Lim, Paul Huat Chye (1989) *The Authoritarian State in Singapore*, PhD thesis, Catholic University of Louvain.
Ling, Trevor (1989) 'Religion', in Sandhu, K. S. and Wheatley, Paul (eds) *Management of Success: The Moulding of Modern Singapore* (Singapore: Institute of Southeast Asian Studies) pp. 692–709.
Locksley, Gareth (1986) 'Information Technology and Capitalist Development', *Capital and Class*, 27, 81–105.
Low, Linda and Toh, Mun Heng (1989) *The Elected Presidency as a Safeguard for Official Reserves: What is at Stake?* (Singapore: Institute of Policy Studies).
Luther, Hans U. (1975) 'The Example of Singapore – The Function of Elites and Westernised Systems in the Dependent Reproduction of Developing Countries', in Bernhard Dahm, and Werner Draguhn (eds), *Politics, Society and Economy in the ASEAN States* (Hamburg: Institute of Asian Affairs) pp. 115–63.
Luther, Hans U. (1978) 'Strikes and the Institutionalization of Labour Protest: The Case of Singapore', *Journal of Contemporary Asia*, 8/2, pp. 219–30.
Macfarlane, Leslie (1974) *Violence and the State* (London: Nelson).
Macpherson, C. B. (1965) *The Real World of Democracy* (Montreal: CBC Enterprises).
Macpherson, C. B. (1977) *The Life and Times of Liberal Democracy* (Oxford: Oxford University Press).
Macpherson, C. B. (1989) 'Do We Need a Theory of the State?', in Graeme Duncan (ed.), *Democracy and the Capitalist State* (Cambridge: Cambridge University Press) pp. 15–32.
Mahathir bin Mohamad (1970) *The Malay Dilemma* (Singapore: Donald Moore Press).
Margolin, Jean-Louis (1989) *Singapour 1959–1987* (Paris: L'Harmattan).
Mathiesen, T. (1980) *Law, Society and Political Action: Towards a Strategy under Late Capitalism* (London: Academic Press).
Mayer, John A. (1986) 'Notes towards a Working Definition of Social Control in Historical Analysis', in Cohen, Stanley and Scull, Andrew (eds) *Social Control and the State* (Oxford: Basil Blackwell) pp. 17–38.
Meiksins-Wood, Ellen (1981) 'The Separation of the Economic and the Political in Capitalism', *New Left Review*, 127, pp. 66–95.

Mepham, John (1979) 'The Theory of Ideology in Capital', in Mepham, John and Ruben, D.-H. (eds) *Issues in Marxist Philosophy*, vol. III: *Epistemology, Science, Ideology* (Sussex: Harvester Press) pp. 141–69.
Milne, Robert S. and Mauzy, Diane K. (1990) *Singapore: The Legacy of Lee Kuan Yew* (Boulder: Westview Press).
Minchin, James (1986) *No Man is an Island* (Sydney: Allen & Unwin).
Mirza, Hafiz (1986) *Multinationals and the Growth of the Singapore Economy* (London: Croom Helm).
Nasir, Hashim and Chee, Heng Leng (1984) 'Mahathir's Genetic Dilemma', in Chee Heng Leng and Chan Chee Khoon (eds) *Designer Genes: IQ, Ideology and Biology* (Kuala Lumpur: Institute for Social Analysis) pp. 14–20.
O'Grady, Ron (1990) *Banished: The Expulsion of the Christian Conference of Asia from Singapore* (Hong Kong: Christian Conference of Asia International Affairs).
Ong, Jin Hui (1989) 'Community Security' in Sandhu, K. S. and Wheatley, Paul (eds) *Management of Success: The Moulding of Modern Singapore* (Singapore: Institute of Southeast Asian Studies) pp. 928–48.
Oshima, Harry T. (1986) 'East Asia's High Growth', *The Singapore Economic Review*, XXXI/2, 1–22.
Pang, Cheng Lian (1971) *Singapore's People's Action Party* (Singapore: Oxford University Press).
Pang, Eng Fong and Lim, Linda (1982) 'Foreign Labour and Economic Development in Singapore', *International Migration Review*, 16/3.
Parliament of Singapore (1986) *Report of the Select Committee on the Legal Profession (Amendment) Bill (Bill No. 20/86)*.
Pateman, Carole (1970) *Participation and Democratic Theory* (Cambridge: Cambridge University Press).
Pateman, Carole (1979) *The Problem of Political Obligation: A Critical Analysis of Liberal Theory* (Chichester: John Wiley and Sons).
Phang, Andrew, Boon Leong (1983) 'Jury Trial in Singapore and Malaysia: The Unmaking of a Legal Institution', *Malaya Law Review*, 25, pp. 50–86.
Phillips, Paul (1980) *Marx and Engels on Law and Laws* (Oxford: Martin Robertson).
Pillai, Philip N. and Tan, Kevin Yew Lee (1989) 'Constitutional Development', in Sandhu, K. S. and Wheatley, Paul (eds) *Management of Success: The Moulding of Modern Singapore* (Singapore: Institute of Southeast Asian Studies) pp. 647–68.
Poulantzas, Nicos (1969) 'The Problem of the Capitalist State', *New Left Review*, 58, pp. 67–78.
Poulantzas, Nicos (1973a) *Political Power and Social Classes* (London: New Left Books).
Poulantzas, Nicos (1973b) 'On Social Classes', *New Left Review*, 78, pp. 27–54.
Poulantzas, Nicos (1974) *Classes in Contemporary Capitalism* (London: New Left Books).
Poulantzas, Nicos (1976) 'The Capitalist State: A Reply to Miliband and Laclau', *New Left Review 95*, pp. 63–83.
Poulantzas, Nicos (1978) *State, Power, Socialism* (London: New Left Books).
Pritt, D. N. (1970) *Law, Class and Society: Employers, Workers and Trade Unions* (London: Lawrence and Wishart).
Pritt, D. N. (1971) *Law, Class and Society: The Apparatus of the Law* (London: Lawrence and Wishart).
Privy Council (1988) *Joshua Benjamin Jeyaretnam v The Law Society of Singapore from the High Court of Singapore* (Reasons for Decision of the Lords of the Judicial Committee of the Privy Council of 25th October 1988, delivered 21st November 1988 in London).

Pugh, Cedric (1989) 'The Political Economy of Public Housing', in Sandhu, K. S. and Wheatley, Paul (eds), *Management of Success: The Moulding of Modern Singapore* (Singapore: Institute of Southeast Asian Studies) pp. 833–59.
Quah, Jon S. T. (1983) 'Public Bureaucracy, Social Change and National Development', in Chen, Peter S. J. (ed.) *Singapore Development Policies and Trends* (Singapore: Oxford University Press) pp. 197–223.
Quah, Jon S. T. (1985) 'Public Housing', in Quah, Jon S. T., Chan, Heng Chee and Seah, Chee Meow (eds) *Government and Politics of Singapore* (Singapore: Oxford University Press) pp. 233–59.
Quah, Jon S. T. (1989) 'Singapore in 1988: Safeguarding the Future', in *Singapore 1989* (Singapore: Ministry of Communications and Information) pp. 1–24.
Quah, Jon S. T. (ed) (1990) *In Search of Singapore's National Values* (Singapore: Times Academic Press).
Quah, Jon S. T. and Quah, Stella R. (1989) 'The Limits of Government Intervention', in Sandhu, K. S. and Wheatley, Paul (eds) *Management of Success: The Moulding of Modern Singapore* (Singapore: Institute of Southeast Asian Studies) pp. 102–27.
Quah, Jon S. T., Chan, Heng Chee and Seah, Chee Meow (eds) (1985) *Government and Politics of Singapore* (Singapore: Oxford University Press).
Rao, V. V. Bhanoji and Ramakrishnan, M. (1980) *Income Inequality in Singapore* (Singapore: Singapore University Press).
Rawlings, H. F. (1983) 'Habeas Corpus and Preventive Detention in Singapore and Malaysia', *Malaya Law Review*, 25, pp. 324–50.
Regnier, Philippe (1991) *Singapore: City-state in South-East Asia* (London: Hurst).
Robison, Richard, Higgott, Richard and Hewison, Kevin (eds)(1987) *Southeast Asia in the 1980s* (Sydney: Allen and Unwin).
Rodan, Garry (1985) 'Industrialisation and the Singapore State in the Context of the New International Division of Labour', in Higgott, Richard and Robison, Richard (eds) *Southeast Asia: Essays in the Political Economy of Structural Change* (Melbourne: Routledge and Kegan Paul) pp. 172–94.
Rodan, Garry (1987) 'The Rise and Fall of Singapore's "Second Industrial Revolution"', in Robison, Richard, Higgott, Richard and Hewison, Kevin (eds) *Southeast Asia in the 1980s* (Sydney: Allen and Unwin) pp. 149–76.
Rodan, Garry (1989) *The Political Economy of Singapore's Industrialisation: National State and International Capital* (London: Macmillan).
Salaff, Janet W. (1988) *State and Family in Singapore* (Ithaca, NY: Cornell University Press).
Sandhu, K. S. and Wheatley, Paul (eds) (1989) *Management of Success: The Moulding of Modern Singapore* (Singapore: Institute of Southeast Asian Studies).
Sartori, Giovani (1976) *Parties and Party Systems* (Cambridge: Cambridge University Press).
Saw, Swee-Hock (1980) *Population Control for Zero Growth in Singapore* (Singapore: Oxford University Press).
Saw, Swee-Hock (1983) *Population Projections for Singapore 1980–2070* (Singapore: Institute of Southeast Asian Studies).
Saw, Swee-Hock and Bathal R. S. (1981) *Singapore Towards the Year 2000* (Singapore: Singapore University Press).
Sayer, Derek (1979) *Marx's Method: Ideology, Science and Critique in Capital* (Hassocks, Sussex: Harvester Press).
Schmitter, Philippe C. (1979) 'Still the Century of Corporatism?', in Schmitter, P. C. and Lehmbruch, G. (eds) *Trends Towards Corporatist Intermediation* (Beverly Hills: Sage Publications) pp. 7–52.

Seah, Chee Meow (ed.) (1975) *Trends in Singapore* (Singapore: Singapore University Press).
Seah, Chee Meow (1985) 'Parapolitical Institutions', in Quah, Jon S. T., Chan, Heng Chee and Seah, Chee Meow (eds) *Government and Politics of Singapore* (Singapore: Oxford University Press) pp. 173–94.
Seah, Chee Meow (1989) 'National Security', in Sandhu, K. S. and Wheatley, Paul (eds) *Management of Success: The Moulding of Modern Singapore* (Singapore: Institute of Southeast Asian Studies) pp. 949–62.
Seah, Chee Meow and Seah, Linda (1983) 'Education Reform and National Integration', in Chen, Peter S. J. (ed) *Singapore Development Policies and Trends* (Singapore: Oxford University Press) pp. 240–67.
Selvan, T. S. (1990) *Singapore: The Ultimate Island* (Clifton Hill: Freeway Books).
Seow, Francis T. (1990) 'The Tyranny of the Majority: Some Recent Pointers to the Erosion of Fundamental Rights in Singapore', paper delivered at the Singapore Forum, London School of Economics, 14 October 1989, reprinted in *Index on Censorship*, 19/3, 3–8.
Seow, Greg F.-H. (1980) *The Service Sector in Singapore's Economy: Performance and Structure* (Singapore: University of Singapore).
Shotam, Nirmala Puru (1989) 'Language and Linguistic Policies', in Sandhu, K. S. and Wheatley, Paul (eds) *Management of Success: The Moulding of Modern Singapore* (Singapore: Institute of Southeast Asian Studies) pp. 503–22.
Singapore Association of Women Lawyers (1989) *You and the Law* (Singapore: SAWL).
Singh, Bilveer (1992) *Whither PAP's Dominance?* (Singapore: Pelanduk).
Spitzer, Steven (1986) 'The Rationalization of Crime Control in Capitalist Society', in Cohen, S. and Scull, A. (eds) *Social Control and the State* (Oxford: Basil Blackwell) pp. 312–33.
Stenson, M. R. (1971) *The 1948 Communist Revolt in Malaya: A Note on Historical Sources and Interpretation* (Singapore: Institute of Southeast Asian Studies).
Steven, Rob (1983) *Classes in Contemporary Japan* (Cambridge: Cambridge University Press).
Steven, Rob (1990) *Japan's New Imperialism* (London: Macmillan).
Sugarman, D. (ed.) (1983) *Legality, Ideology and the State* (London: Academic Press).
Sumner, Colin (1979) *Reading Ideologies: An Investigation into the Theory of Ideology and Law* (London: Academic Press).
Szymanski, A. (1983) *The Logic of Imperialism* (New York: Praeger Publishers).
Tan, Wah Piow (1984) 'Ten Years Later: Reflections on the Singapore Student Movement', in *Imperialism, No! Democracy, Yes! – Student Movements in the ASEAN Region* (Institute for Social Analysis: Kuala Lumpur) pp. 61–71.
Tan, Wah Piow (1987a) *Let the People Judge: Confessions of the Most Wanted Person in Singapore* (Institute for Social Analysis: Kuala Lumpur).
Tan, Wah Piow (1987b) *Frame-Up: A Singapore Court on Trial* (Oxford: TWP Publishing).
Tan, Yock Lin (1987) 'Some Aspects of Executive Detention in Malaysia and Singapore', *Malaya Law Review* 29, pp. 237–253.
Tang, Fong Har (1989) '*Question of Human Rights of Persons Subjected to any Form of Detention and Imprisonment*', Intervention on behalf of Pax Romana at the 41st Session of the UN Sub-commission on Prevention of Discrimination and Protection of Minorities (Geneva: Pax Romana).
Tang, Sok-Chun (1973) *International Investments in Singapore – Techniques in Industrialization* (Singapore: Malayan Law Journal).
Tay, Kheng Soon (1989) 'The Architecture of Rapid Transformation', in Sandhu, K. S. and Wheatley, Paul (eds) *Management of Success: The Moulding of Modern Singapore* (Singapore: Institute of Southeast Asian Studies) pp. 860–78.

Tham, Seong Chee (ed.) (1972) *Modernization in Singapore: Impact on the Individual* (Singapore: University Education Press).

Tham, Seong Chee (1989) 'The Perception and Practice of Education', in Sandhu, K. S. and Wheatley, Paul (eds) *Management of Success: The Moulding of Modern Singapore* (Singapore: Institute of Souteast Asian Studies) pp. 477–502.

Thompson, E. P. (1975) *Whigs and Hunters – The Origin of the Black Act* (London: Allen Lane).

Turnbull, C. M. (1989) *A History of Singapore 1819–1975* (Singapore: Oxford University Press).

Vasil, Raj K. (1984) *Governing Singapore: Interviews with the New Leaders* (Singapore: Times Books International).

Vasil, Raj K. (1989) 'Trade Unions', in Sandhu, K. S. and Wheatley, Paul (eds) *Management of Success: The Moulding of Modern Singapore* (Singapore: Institute of Southeast Asian Studies) pp. 144–70.

Wallerstein, Immanuel (1979) *The Capitalist World Economy* (Cambridge: Cambridge University Press).

Wee, Chong Jin CJ (1989) 'Chng Suan Tze v The Minister of Home Affairs & Ors and Other Appeals', *Malayan Law Journal*, 1, pp. 69–90.

Wilkinson, Barry (1988) 'Social Engineering in Singapore', *Journal of Contemporary Asia*, 18/2, pp. 165–88.

Willmott, W. E. (1989) 'The Emergence of Nationalism', in Sandhu, K. S. and Wheatley, Paul (eds) *Management of Success: The Moulding of Modern Singapore* (Singapore: Institute of Southeast Asian Studies) pp. 578–98.

Wilson, Dick (1972) *The Future Role of Singapore* (London: Oxford University Press).

Wilson, H. E. (1978) *Social Engineering in Singapore* (Singapore: Singapore University Press).

Wong, Aline K. and Ooi, Giok Ling (1989) 'Spatial Reorganisation', in Sandhu, K. S. and Wheatley, Paul (eds) *Management of Success: The Moulding of Modern Singapore* (Singapore: Institute of Southeast Asian Studies) pp. 788–812.

Wong, Aline K. and Yeh, Stephen H. K. (eds) (1985) *Housing A Nation: Twenty-Five Years of Public Housing in Singapore* (Singapore: Maruzen Asia/Housing and Development Board).

Wong, Evelyn S. (1983) 'Industrial Relations in Singapore: Challenge for the 1980s', *Southeast Asian Affairs 1983* (Singapore: Institute of Southeast Asian Studies) pp. 263–74.

Wong, Kum Poh and Tan, Maureen (eds) (1972) *Singapore in the International Economy* (Singapore: Singapore University Press).

Wong, Lin Ken (1991) 'Commercial Growth before the Second World War', in Chew, Ernest C. T. and Lee, Edwin (eds) *A History of Singapore* (Singapore: Oxford University Press), pp. 41–65.

Wright, Shelley (1987) *Detention Under the Internal Security Act: A Preliminary Legal Brief* (Christchurch: Emergency Committee for Human Rights in Singapore).

Wu, Teh-yao (ed.) (1975) *Political and Social Change in Singapore* (Singapore: Institute of Southeast Asian Studies).

Wurfel, David and Burton, Bruce (eds) (1990) *The Political Economy of Foreign Policy in Southeast Asia* (London: Macmillan).

Yap, Mui Teng (1989) 'The Demographic Base', in Sandhu, K. S. and Wheatley, Paul (eds) *Management of Success: The Moulding of Modern Singapore* (Singapore: Institute of Southeast Asian Studies) pp. 455–76.

Yeh, Stephen H. K. (ed.) (1975) *Public Housing in Singapore: A Multi-disciplinary Study* (Singapore: Singapore University Press for Housing and Development Board).

Yeh, Stephen H. K. (1989) 'The Idea of the Garden City', in Sandhu, K. S. and Wheatley, Paul (eds) *Management of Success: The Moulding of Modern Singapore* (Singapore: Institute of Southeast Asian Studies) pp. 813–32.

Yeh, Stephen H. K. and Pang, Eng Fong (1973) 'Housing, Employment and National Development: The Singapore Experience', *Asia*, 31.
Yeo, Stanley, Meng Heong (1981) 'Unrepresented Defendants in the Subordinate Criminal Courts of Singapore (1979–1980)', *Malaya Law Review*, 23, pp. 41–51.
Yeo, Stanley, Meng Heong (1985) 'Mandatory Minimum Sentences: A Tying of Judicial Hands', *The Malayan Law Journal*, November 1985, pp. cixxxvi–cxcii.
Yeung, Yue-man (1973) *National Development Policy and Urban Transformation in Singapore: A Study of Public Housing and the Marketing System* (Chicago: University of Chicago).
Yoshihara, Kunio (1976) *Foreign Investment and Domestic Response: A Study of Singapore's Industrialisation* (Singapore: Eastern Universities Press).
Yoshihara, Kunio (1988) *The Rise of Ersatz Capitalism in Southeast Asia* (Singapore: Oxford University Press)

Index

abortion and sterilisation, 103, 115, 116
Academy of Law, 198
administrative law, 188, 190–211
alternative subsistence, denial of, 46, 49, 51, 61
Anglo-Dutch Treaty (1824), 6
anti-communism, 14–16, 26, 27, 45, 179
Association of Women for Action and Research (AWARE), 61

banishment and deprivation of citizenship
　by deportation, 13, 15, 29, 209–10
　by legislation, 26, 210
Barisan Sosialis (Socialist Front), 26–7, 28, 46, 47, 48, 81, 82, 84, 154, 155, 170, 185, 192, 204
breeding programme of PAP-state, 103, 109, 113–17, 121, 123–7, 128–35, 147, 149, 230
　see also ideology of eugenics
British Military Administration (BMA), 12, 13
Burma, 135

caning, 134, 211, 213–15, 219–20, 231
capital punishment
　see hanging
Catholic Church, 118, 124, 144–5, 148, 196, 198–9, 205
Central Provident Fund, 53–8, 61, 116, 134, 138, 174, 225
Cheng, Vincent, 205
Chiam See Tong, 64, 162, 163, 164, 169
Chia Thye Poh, 203, 204
Citizens' Consultative Committees (CCCs), 48, 164
communalism, 76–7, 81–6, 107, 138–44, 146–7
　see also racism
Community Centres, 47, 48, 164, 184
Confucian ethics
　see moral education
corporal punishment
　see caning
criminal law, 188–91, 211–21
Criminal Law (Temporary Provisions) Act, 200

Democratic Socialist Club, 93
Dhanabalan, 165, 166
domestic capitalist class
　and construction industry, 49, 56, 61
　emergence of, 6–10
　weakness of, 10, 17, 25, 29, 31, 32, 33–4, 37, 75–6, 178, 229

East India Company (EIC), 6, 7, 8
Economic Committee, Ministry of Trade and Industry, 36–7, 41–2, 127
Edusave scheme, 137–8
elected presidency, 171, 172, 173–6, 179
elections
　Anson by-election (1981), 57, 61, 157
　manipulation of, 28, 33, 153–4, 163–4, 169–70
　see also Tables
Emergency, 14–16, 45
emigration, 122–3
Employment Act (1968), 33, 95
eugenics
　see graduate mothers scheme; ideology
export-oriented industrialisation (EOI), 33–8, 40, 42, 43, 49, 52, 86, 88, 103, 155, 196, 211, 227, 228

Federation of Malaya, 13
Feedback Unit, 161
forced resettlement, 45–7, 49
foreign capital
　alliance with PAP-state, 4, 20, 24, 29, 33, 34, 35–8, 41, 43, 71, 74, 80, 86, 94, 108, 178–9, 205, 227, 228, 233–4
　scale of investment in Singapore, 33–4
　transnational finance capital, 39
foreign reserves, 55, 173–4

248

foreign workers, 69–70, 113–14, 126, 134–5, 149, 219–20, 234

Gifted Education Programme (GEP), 111
Goh Chok Tong, 36, 38–9, 64, 139, 142, 150–1, 158, 160, 161, 162, 169, 171, 172, 174
Goh Keng Swee, 18, 107, 110–11, 117–19, 185
Goode, Sir William, 20–1
Government Parliamentary Committees (GPCs), 162–3, 172
graduate mother scheme, 114–17, 122, 128–9, 135, 149
    see also breeding programme of PAP-state
Group Representation Constituencies (GRCs), 63, 167–9, 170, 171
Growth Triangle (Singapore–Johor–Batam), 42–3, 143
    see also Singapore's role in Southeast Asia

hanging, 189, 211, 213, 215, 220–1, 231
home ownership, 57–8
Hong Kong immigrants, 133–4
Housing and Development Board (HDB), ix, 46, 47, 49, 50–3, 55, 56–73, 116, 126, 127, 147, 218, 230

ideology
    and religious education, 117–19, 144–8
    and the law, 188–9
    of eugenics, 103–4, 115, 122, 130–2
    of meritocracy and choice, 79, 95–8, 123
    of meritocracy and class, 100–2
    of meritocracy and equal opportunity, 98–9, 122, 136, 149
    of multi-racialism, 104–6, 126
    of survival of PAP-state, 106
    of total defence, 223–4
    of voting and choice, 180–3
    see also national ideology; patriarchal social relations
immigration of Chinese, 6, 7, 8, 9, 128, 133–4
import-substitution industrialisation (ISI), 31–3, 43, 77

independent schools, 136
Indians in Singapore, ix, 15, 74, 78, 79, 81, 82, 84, 86, 88, 115, 125, 140–1, 150, 168
Indonesia, 3, 27, 42–3, 107, 135, 143, 185, 225–7, 232
    see also Singapore's role in Southeast Asia
inequality, 3, 51–2, 58–9, 99, 120–1
Internal Security Act, 21, 138, 154, 169, 193, 199, 201–5, 206, 209, 210
    see also Preservation of Public Security Ordinance; Operation Coldstore; Operation Spectrum
Internal Security Council, 22
Internal Security Department, 2, 20, 69, 92, 132, 143, 164, 196, 202–3, 225
    see also surveillance of civilians
Israel, 107, 108, 142

Japan, 10–11, 12, 36, 37, 39, 44, 117
Jayakumar, 190, 197, 198, 214
Jeyaretnam, Joshua Benjamin, 57, 157, 158, 159, 162, 163, 164–6, 167, 170, 193–4, 197, 206–9, 218, 225
Johor
    British acquisition, 6
    see also Growth Triangle
judiciary, 164–5, 173, 188, 193–4, 207, 211
jury system, 212–13

Labour Front, 17, 21, 23
labour movement, 10, 13, 14, 15, 26, 32, 155
    see also trade unions
Land Acquisition Act (1966), 53
Law Society, 61, 138, 169, 196, 197–8
Lee faction of People's Action Party (PAP)
    control of Central Executive Committee (CEC), 20, 22–3, 183
    formation of, 18–19
    links with British internal security, 20–1, 22, 23–4, 26
    parliamentary strategy, 21
    power base, 29
    victory over the left, 26–9

Lee Hsien Loong, Brigadier-General, 41, 161, 171, 172, 182, 201, 220, 222–3, 225, 226–7
Lee Kuan Yew
  assessment of, 232–3
  at University of Singapore, 93
  on abortion and sterilisation, 103
  on adopting Israeli defence strategy, 108
  on arbitrary executive powers, 210
  on arrest without trial, 21, 203
  on a split in the PAP, 172
  on breeding bright children, 114–15, 129, 130, 131
  on Chinese unity, 85
  on civil liberties, 2, 190, 191, 203
  on class right to govern, 101
  on class strategy for attaining power, 17
  on communists, 19, 26
  on deficiencies of universal franchise, 101, 159
  on elected presidency, 173
  on electoral success, 181
  on emigration, 123
  on equality, 98–9
  on identifying governing class, 100–2
  on government community organisations, 67, 164
  on graduate mothers, 129
  on fighting Indonesia, 107
  on his continuing influence, 184
  on interrogation of political prisoners, 203
  on importing foreign workers, 135
  on J. B. Jeyaretnam, 163, 165, 166
  on jury system, 212
  on language policy, 80
  on preventing Malay party, 142–3
  on Malay loyalty, 142
  on Malay underachievement, 141
  on marriage, 130, 131
  on marriage to white men, 131
  on mistresses, 131
  on rewards of loyalty, 65
  on targeting educational investment, 130
  on the Law Society, 197–8
  on the poor, 102
  on racial *status quo*, 133–4
  on racial superiority, 104, 133–4
  on serving foreign capital, 39
  on voting for the opposition, 63
  on women, child-care and domestic help, 60
Lee Siew Choh, 170
Lester, Anthony, 204
liberal democracy, 177–86
Lim Chin Siong, 22, 28
Lim Yew Hock, 23–4

Mahathir bin Mohamad, 104
Maintenance of Religious Harmony Act, 145, 175, 194, 198–9
Malayan/Malaysian Chinese Association, 28, 31, 85
Malayan Communist Party (MCP), 10, 12, 13, 14, 15, 16, 17,18, 25
Malayan Democratic Union (MDU), 19
Malayan Forum, 17
Malayan National Liberation Army (MNLA), 15
Malayan Peoples' Anti-Japanese Army (MPAJA), 12
Malayan Union, 11, 13
Malays in Singapore
  discrimination against, ix, 47, 65–6, 71, 72, 91, 97, 104–6, 112, 115, 125–6, 133–4, 136, 139–44, 145, 146, 147, 149–51, 167–8
  loss of sovereignty, 6
  numbers of, 6, 7, 74
Malaysia, 3, 27, 28, 35, 42–3, 49, 80, 82, 85, 86, 87, 100, 106, 107, 113–14, 126, 128, 134, 135, 143, 145, 153, 185, 225–7, 223
  see also Singapore's role in Southeast Asia
mandatory sentences, 213–16
Marshall, David, 21, 23
Marxist conspiracy (1987)
  see Operation Spectrum
merger with Malaya, 11, 18, 27–9, 31, 85, 86, 106
militarisation of civilian life, 15, 92, 221
military bases, 25, 46, 69, 227
military service, 69, 92, 93

Ministry of Education, 79, 91, 95, 96, 110, 128, 135
Miscellaneous Offences (Public Order and Nuisance) Act, 218
moral education, 91, 117–19, 121–2, 139, 144–8

Nair, Devan, 157
Nanyang University, 83, 89
national ideology, 146–8, 150
National Service (NS)
    see military service
National University of Singapore, 89, 111, 127, 128, 212
    see also University of Singapore
Neighbourhood Police Posts (NPPs), 67–8
Newspaper and Printing Presses (Amendment) Act, 197
Ngee Ann College, 84, 89
Non-constituency Member of Parliament (NCMP), 159, 160, 170, 171, 172
Non-elected Member of Parliament (NMP), 171–2
nuclear family, 50–2, 121

Operation Coldstore, 28, 32
Operation Spectrum ('Marxist conspiracy', 1987), 132, 138, 143, 169, 190, 198, 200–1, 203–4, 205

Parliament (Privileges, Immunities and Powers) Act, 165, 207
patriarchal social relations, 59–60, 112–13, 119, 121–2, 123–5, 130–2, 147, 149, 233
    see also breeding programme of PAP-state; women
Penal Code, 214–15
People's Action Party (PAP)
    Central Executive Committee, 20, 156, 183, 184, 231; see also Lee faction of PAP
    class origins of leadership, 7
    failure in Malaysia, 28–9
    formation of, 20
People's Association, 47, 164, 184
population
    see racial composition of Singapore

poverty
    see inequality
Preservation of Public Security Ordinance, 21, 22, 23, 204
    see also Internal Security Act
Presidential Elections Act (1991), 174
privatisation, 126, 135–8, 150, 231
Privileges Committee, 165–6, 194, 207–8
Privy Council, 208–9
Progressive Party, 16–17
Public Service Commission, 92

racial composition of Singapore, 6, 7, 74, 133
    see also immigration of Chinese
racial quotas in housing, 65–6, 126, 142
racism, 65–6, 71, 72, 97, 104–6, 113–14, 115, 125–6, 131, 133–4, 140–4, 149–50, 167–8
    see also communalism
Raffles, Sir Stamford, 6
Rajaratnam, S., 18, 121, 155, 158, 185
relative autonomy, 32, 178–9
religious education
    see moral education
Rendel Commission, 16
Rendel Constitution, 23
reserve army of labour, 60, 113–14, 125, 132–5, 141–4, 149, 234
Residents' Committees (RCs), 64, 66–8, 164, 184

Second Industrial Revolution, 35–8, 41, 56, 58, 109–26, 157, 196, 211, 216, 230
secret societies, 7, 8, 9, 200
Seow, Francis, 169–70, 180, 203
shared values
    see national ideology
Singapore Association of Women Lawyers (SAWL), 61
Singapore Democratic Party (SDP), 64, 163, 175
    see also Chiam See Tong
Singapore's role in Southeast Asia, 3–4, 6–10, 15–16, 30–1, 38–43, 65, 70, 83, 100, 107, 143, 221, 225–7, 231–2

Index

Single Member Constituencies (SMCs), 63
Sinnathuray, 193–4, 207
Skills Development Fund, 113
Social Development Unit (SDU), 132, 149
Societies Act, 195–6
Societies Ordinance, 9, 14
surveillance of civilians, 67–9, 92–3, 164, 196

Tan Lark Sye, 83–4
Tan Wah Piow, 210
Teo Soh Lung, 205
Toh Chin Chye, 18, 93, 167
toilet flushing, 217
town councils, 62–5, 127, 167
trade unions
    National Trades Union Congress (NTUC), 32, 33
    Postal Workers' Union, 19
    Singapore Association of Trade Unions (SATU), 28
    Singapore Federation of Trade Unions, 14
    Singapore General Labour Union, 13
    Teachers' Union, 15

United Malay National Organisation (UMNO), 13, 85, 227
United States of America, 11, 12, 15, 32, 34, 35, 36, 37, 39, 40, 44, 86, 90, 127, 226–7
University of Singapore, 89, 91, 92–3
    see also National University of Singapore
University Socialist Club, 15, 93
urine sensor, 217

women
    and education, 103, 111, 112–13, 114, 123–5
    and housing, 52, 59–60, 147
    and non-cooperation, 61, 122–6, 132, 205, 230, 233
    and wage labour, 60, 132–3, 149, 230
    see also breeding programme of PAP-state; patriarchal social relations
Workers' Party, 157, 158, 169–70, 175, 197
    see also J. B. Jeyaretnam

Yong Pung How, 193